CURRICULUM FOR UTOPIA

SUNY Series, Teacher Empowerment and School Reform
Henry A. Giroux and Peter L. McLaren, editors

CURRICULUM FOR UTOPIA

Social Reconstructionism and
Critical Pedagogy in the Postmodern Era

William B. Stanley

STATE UNIVERSITY OF NEW YORK PRESS

Published by
State University of New York Press, Albany

© 1992 State University of New York

Printed in the United States of America

For information, address State University of New York
Press, State University Plaza, Albany, N.Y., 12246

Production by Cathleen Collins
Marketing by Theresa A. Swierzowski

Library of Congress Cataloging in Publication Data

Stanley, William B.
    Curriculum for Utopia : social reconstructionism and critical
pedagogy in the postmodern era / William B. Stanley.
        p.   cm. — (SUNY series, Teacher empowerment and school
reform)
    Includes bibliographical references and index.
    ISBN 0-7914-0971-6 — ISBN 0-7914-0972-4 (pbk.)
    1. Educational sociology—United States.   2. Education—United
States—Philosophy.   3. Curriculum change—United States.
4. Educational change—United States.   I. Title. II. Series:
Teacher empowerment and school reform.
LC191.4.S72   1992
370.19—dc20   91-15152
                                                                  CIP

10 9 8 7 6 5 4 3 2 1

To Lynn,
for everything.

CONTENTS

ACKNOWLEDGMENTS

Like most authors, I owe more intellectual debts than I am aware or could ever repay. But I wish to acknowledge those who have certainly inspired me and influenced my thinking while writing this book. They include: Mark Amsler, Mike Apple, Landon Beyer, Nicholas Burbules, Eric Chappel, Cleo Cherryholmes, Jacques Daignault, Elizabeth Ellsworth, Bill Frawley, Sandra Harding, Jim Gee, Madeline Grumet, Christopher Lasch, Cameron McCarthy, Spencer Maxcy, Jack Nelson, William F. Pinar, Nel Noddings, Joanne Pagano, Jim Shaver and Phil Wexler among others.

Henry Giroux urged me to take on this project and I am most grateful for the editorial advice and support he and Peter McLaren have given throughout. I also wish to thank my coeditor Cathleen Collins for her excellent editorial suggestions and assistance. I owe a special debt to James A. (Tony) Whitson. Tony, more than any person, has helped me rethink and deepen my understanding of curriculum. I also wish to thank the following for their help preparing the manuscript: Dianne Carter, Cindy Leung, Theresa Grant, Stella Bagot and Suzanne Hillman. Finally, I wish to thank Lynn Stanley for all her love, patience, and support. She helped me through the hard times.

INTRODUCTION

The United States appears to be at a historical conjuncture in which the notion of democracy has been eclipsed as both an ideal and precondition for creating a literate public and critical citizens. In fact, the construction of new forms of knowledge, social practices, and critical public cultures linked to a deepening of democracy have declined in proportion to democracy's dissolution and retreat from contemporary social life. Democracy has frequently been perceived as dangerous over the past two decades, and its "excesses" are under attack on a number of fronts. In the arts, Senator Jesse Helms wages a battle for "patriotism" by making censorship a respectable practice. In education, the charge of political correctness is used against any progressive who dares protest against racism, sexism, or any other practices that subjugate and violate. A cold war has decended on the universities and colleges of the United States as those who hold power claim that they are the real victims because they are being asked to be accountable for the social relations they produce, sustain, and legitimate. In the cities, a new underclass is developing that justifies using terms like colonialism to characterize the growing division in wealth and cultural resources between the rich and the poor. It comes as little surprise that this particular historical juncture is witnessing an acute unease surrounding critical educational theorizing.

On the one hand, there are the increasingly predictable calls for educational theorists to retreat into the language of "plainspeak." The call to clarity has overtaken the call for social justice as the importance of producing clear language becomes one of the few defining spaces that critical educators can lay claim to as a worthy theme over which to struggle. Such developments reinforce James Baldwin's claim that mediocrity and commodification are the central features of American culture and intellectual life. Unfortunately, since ideological lines are being refigured, educational criticism appears to emulate a species of antiintellectualism that is transformed into a catch-all radicalism wearing its dissent in a romantic anticapitalism and the activist garb of the grass-roots union organizer. We do not wish to disparage the importance of community activism and political intervention at local, state, and federal levels. In fact, we have always encouraged teachers to make active and critical alliances with existing social movements and to struggle for the creation of new social movements that are better able to construct public spheres that avoid differentiation along Eurocentric, logocentric, and masculinist conceptions of emancipation and citizenship. What we are seeing, however, is a retreat from theory (often in the name of practice and action) and an assault on any educational ideas that do not make simplistic appeals to commonsense, union-style politics, and the supposedly self-evident truths of personal experience.

That this rather simple epistemic separation between theory and practice—not to mention the form of political self-privileging that underwrites it—should be occurring (expecially among the left) in an era that is witnessing some of the most innovative work in critical social theory at any time in our history, is perhaps not so surprising given the primacy and power of the icon and image in today's age of mechanical reproduction and the tyranny of simulated meanings. To enter into an engagement with new theoretical traditions is not an easy task when the investments necessary for intellectual endeavor in contemporary culture hold less currency for the general public, and especially when educational reformers (for whom one would imagine intellectual pursuit to be integral to emancipatory social change) consider such investments to be more or less futile. For these reformers, the notion of "commonsense" has been colonized by an all too simple understanding of the relation among language, power, culture, and critically informed practice. As critical educators, we do not uphold the binary distinction that separates the domain of being-in-the-world from the domain of deliberative, purposeful action.

We suggest that the new forms of sociality that have developed in this era of post-Fordist late capitalism, as well as new forms of domination and exploitation that have followed, should encourage teachers to attempt an engagement with new theoretical descriptions of the social world. We agree with Bill Stanley that the new ideational, conceptual, and evaluative terrains opened up by critical social theory can "give us a better understanding of the human condition" as well as "heighten our sense of humility and the importance of keeping our options open." In arguing for the contingencies of values, we are not suggesting a form of ethical relativism that offers no possibility for referencing how relations between the self and others either enhance or violate human possibilities. On the contrary, what is at issue here is the possibility of recognizing the historical and social limits of the questions raised and the answers given in the name of diverse forms of ethical address. In this case, the discourse of ethics becomes open to dialogue, argumentation, and struggle within specific contexts inhabited by concrete human agents. Hence, we are arguing for forms of ethical practice in which the issues of difference, dialogue, and moral responsibility become the foundation for human judgments and actions. The enemy of ethics is not only a debased relativism, but also the refusal of an ethical discourse to address how it might be complicit with forms of injustice and human suffering.

We want to suggest that teachers not simply take a symbolic stand against leftist antiintellectual vanguardism that fosters unwittingly complicit alliances with the hegemony of the New Right, but that they apprise themselves of the most sophisticated analyses of the social condition that are available. Unlike those critics who assume teachers should stick to their role as clerks and technicians and leave the "intellectual stuff" to university scholars, we support the idea of teachers engaging in transformative intellectual labor for the purpose of not only changing the conditions of their own work, but for struggling towards a larger vision and realization of human freedom.

Few scholars in the field of education have paid as close attention to the current debates within critical social theory as Bill Stanley. Not only has he formulated a perceptive analysis of the evolutionary trends in continental social theory, critical pragmatism, feminist theory, and other perspectives in contemporary critical thought, he has managed to analyze how such perspectives have been challenged, debated, misunderstood, and selectively appropriated by educational theorists. *Curriculum for Utopia* offers readers not only an adept summary of the fundamental characteristics of such seemingly disparate theoretical perspectives as poststructuralism and social reconstructionism, it also reveals some surprising commonalities and affinities.

What is particularly important in Stanley's account is his ability to place radical educational traditions in an illuminating historical context. In doing so, Stanley is able to reveal how some of the social reconstructionists such as Rugg, Counts, and Brameld anticipated many of the views of contemporary cultural theorists. According to Stanley, reconstructionist thought and radical educational theory share the following characteristics: they explore the political nature of schooling and how it often serves dominant social interests, hold to a conception of schools not simply as forms of institutionalized protection for discourses of domination but rather as institutional sites that contain the promise of counterhegemonic struggle, refigure the role of teachers from that of technicians and clerks to transformative intellectuals working towards social change and the common good, hold that all forms of knowledge are ideologically constituted, stress the importance of ethical imperatives guiding transformative practice and the rejection of the idea that schooling is a neutral or radically relativistic social practice, and appropriate from both theoretical variants of American pragmatism and indigenous radicalism.

Stanley acknowledges some of the problems with reconstructionist theory (at times it verged on becoming an authoritarian form of social engineering) and recent critical educational theory but contends that the latter "presents a more complex and useful critique of educational theory and practice having incorporated the insights of the new sociology, critical theory, neo-Marxism, feminism, cultural studies, neopragmatism, and postmodern thought." He concludes that reconstructionist theory "remains relevant to educational reform but only in a reconceptualized form."

While he remains unconstrained by any single discursive or disciplinary system, Stanley's own theoretical location is situated firmly within the critical tradition of revisionary curriculum theorists. Working from a perspective that resists a transhistorical and transpersonal set of first principles, totalizing critiques, or appeals to knowledge on the basis of transcedent values, Stanley's anti-essentialism and antifoundationalism does not prevent him from firmly locating his criticism within an emancipatory politics of social change. He remains convinced that "while radical hermeneutics and deconstruction have revealed our knowledge to be more contingent and problematic it does not follow that projects aimed at human betterment are either irrational or impossible." Nevertheless, he is quick to uncover internal contradictions and logical inconsistencies wherever he finds them, despite the perspective under consideration.

What is particularly important to Stanley in the search for a concrete basis for a radical theory of education is the need for educators to work out of a postaxiological position, that is, from a perspective that is not grounded in the affirmation of any transcendent, objective, or intrinsic values. Consequently, Stanley recognizes the need for critical educators to develop basic human interests and interpretive competence prior to assuming ethical positions. This is crucial to Stanley's emancipatory project. Because the meaning of values (however provisional or radically contingent) and their application must necessarily be interpreted within localized contexts, he is aware that any interpretation is subject to continual reinterpretation as new contexts arise and new knowledge is acquired. For Stanley, it is crucial that educators develop the competence necessary for ethical practice, that is, for the exercise and expansion of *phronesis*. This means formulating and reformulating goals and the social practices necessary to achieve them throughout the flux of changing social conditions. Interpretation and critique is always necessary because knowledge is always incomplete. Consequently, it is important to ask the question: What social effects do you want your evaluations to have?

Social conditions provide the concrete mode in which every intellectual and ethical vision and re-vision presents itself, and educational reforms cannot risk ignoring the creation of new social and economic relations because reform efforts cannot be articulated before the problems within the social formation become concretely specified. In other words, Stanley is not arguing that educational reform be left as a spontaneous or sporadic occurrence. He is taking a stand against forms of domination and exclusion such as racism, sexism, homophobia, political oppression, censorship, and monological approaches to the curriculum because these behaviors limit the development of the critical competence required to realize human interests.

For Stanley, discursive practices not only encode inequalities or asymmetries of power and privilege, they also can serve as forms of advocacy for social change and the betterment of the human condition, even though he acknowledges that debates will always arise over what a better human situation might be. This underscores Stanley's call for nothing less than human competence for judgment in all dimensions of human activity that he identifies as the aesthetic, the linguistic, the political, and the social. Critical educational praxis is, for Stanley, a type of personal *phronesis* in which contingent and provisional values are grounded in a shared culture. The common social good cannot be pre-specified—not even contingently—but must emerge in praxis, which for Stanley sometimes means negotiation and sometimes struggle, but in every case points to the desirability of a truly dialogic educational project.

Curriculum for Utopia is an intellectually honest work. Stanley's aim is not to foster further divisiveness within the field, but rather to build stronger alliances by seizing the vast potential that exists among divergent fields to create what we might call an arch of social dreaming. Fortunately for the reader, Stanley is not a dispassionate critic; he constantly refuses the stance of a mere chronicler of intellectual histories and theoretical trajectories. More than an intellectual commentator on the field of radical educational theory, Stanley is one of its most skillful analysts and exponents. While his grasp of the debates within educational theory and his ability to distinguish the most central and urgent concerns from the more tangential is truly impressive, it is his ability to extend the analysis and situate it in new, dynamic ways that marks the singular importance of this book. When the questions of human empowerment and social justice tend to get lost in the debates among educational theorists, Stanley quickly brings this focus into the foreground. The end result is a book that will advance the theoretical and ethical debate over curriculum reform, illuminate the various and variegated contexts in which curriculum theory must necessarily move in the future, and challenge the binary oppositions that have hampered a serious revitalization of critical educational theory.

Henry A. Giroux and Peter L. McLaren

1

CRITICAL PEDAGOGY AND EDUCATIONAL REFORM: AN INTRODUCTION

THE DISCOURSES OF EDUCATIONAL REFORM

Reform has been a continuing feature of the history of education in the United States. Even a casual analysis of education in this century reveals numerous shifts in the focus of reform including: scientific management, progressive education, "life-adjustment" curriculum, teaching the structure of the disciplines, critical thinking, values education, career education, accountability, the "back-to-basics" movement, and, most recently, education for "excellence." The constant and often conflicting shifts in the focus of educational reform appear to have left the public confused, angry, and somewhat disillusioned (Goodlad 1984). Nevertheless, and despite the perceived failures of public education, there remains a persistent faith in education's potential to improve society and help solve social problems (Adler 1982; Bloom 1987; Giroux 1988c; Hirsch 1987; Lasch 1979; Pinar 1988; Raywid, Tesconi, and Warren 1984).

In the 1980s education again became the focus of an intense national debate that is still in progress. The current debate has been largely dominated by a "mainstream" discourse reflected in various research reports, commission reports, and popular books (e.g., Adler 1982; Bloom 1987; Boyer 1983; Cuban 1984, Goodlad 1984; Hirsch 1987; Presseisen 1985; Ravitch and Finn 1987; Sizer 1984). Many of the current educational concerns raised by mainstream reformers were embedded in the proposals for accountability, career education, "back-to-basics," Competency-based Teacher Education (CBTE), and other reforms of the 1970s (Shor 1986). The reform proposals of the 1980s involve more complex arguments as displayed in the scholarship related to "teacher effectiveness," "education for excellence," and "cultural literacy."

The mainstream reform movement is not monolithic, as any comparison of the work of Adler, Bennett, Berliner, A. Bloom, Boyer, Brophy, Chenney, Cuban, Finn, Good, Goodlad, Hirsch, Ravitch, Sizer, and Shulman,

1

among others, would reveal. Liberal and conservative views are represented, and some of the reform proposals would involve significant social
change and expenditure. Nevertheless, there is a certain underlying
consistency to the discourse of mainstream reform that tends to preclude
the serious consideration of certain approaches to research and educational
change (Apple 1986b; Aronowitz and Cherryholmes 1988; Giroux 1985,
1988c; Grumet 1988; Stanley 1985).

Mainstream educational discourse is, by and large, constructed within
the parameters of our dominant social, economic, cultural, and political
arrangements, including the limits of certain research traditions. These
characteristics of contemporary educational reform are neither surprising
(in a wider historical context) nor intrinsically sinister. However, to the
extent these characteristics are typical, they reflect a concern raised by
Nelson, Carlson, and Linton (1972) who argued that the failure to give
adequate attention to "radical" ideas denies educators a major source of
knowledge and unduly limits the process of social inquiry and change.
In a democratic culture, "[t]he intellectual energy required to reject a radical
idea is more important to. . .social vitality than the passive acceptance of
the status quo" (p. 15). Furthermore, it is often the case that radical ideas
from the past have eventually been incorporated into the mainstream
perspective. One could argue, therefore, that in a democratic society
educators have a fundamental obligation to explore divergent ideas,
including those that are radical.

In addition to the discourse of mainstream educational reform, another
discourse of "critical pedagogy" exists that challenges the basic assumptions of current reform proposals, draws on other research traditions, and
poses a rather different educational reform agenda. During the past two
decades, a substantial body of critical pedagogical scholarship has emerged
(e.g., Apple 1979, 1982, 1986b; Aronowitz and Giroux 1985; Beyer and
Apple 1988; Cherryholmes 1988; Ellsworth 1989; Giroux 1983a, 1988c;
Giroux and McLaren 1989; Grumet 1987; Pinar 1988; Roman, Christian-
Smith and Ellsworth 1988; Wexler, 1987). As we will see, like the mainstream reform discourse, the critical scholarship on educational reform is
far from monolithic and has been characterized by serious internal disputes
over theory, approaches to research, and interpretation of data. Critical
pedagogy is a general term that refers to, among other things, revisionist
education history, the "new sociology" of education, reconceptualist
curriculum theory, cultural studies, feminist scholarship, Critical Theory,
and various forms of postmodern and poststructuralist analysis. This
scholarship now represents a significant knowledge base to orient the
critical analysis and reform of education. Yet this discourse tends to remain
on the periphery of the debate over educational reform, and as mainstream
educators have demonstrated (e.g., Cuban 1984; Goodlad 1984; Sirotnick

1989), there has been a persistent resistance to radical education reform proposals throughout this century.

The resistance to critical pedagogy has deep roots in our national history and the history of education in particular (Kliebard 1986). There are, of course, formidable structural and cultural obstacles to any kind of radical change in our society. In addition, the periodic failure of critical educators to develop a consensus regarding the direction educational reform should take has also been a major problem. Some have argued that radical educators have focused too much on a negative critique without formulating a moral vision or proposal for a preferred society that might motivate widespread opposition to the dominant order (Giroux 1988c).

The analysis of earlier radical educational reform efforts can help provide a rich source of knowledge and examples to inform current attempts to construct a theory of critical pedagogy. Too often, the anti-intellectual, ahistorical, and narcissistic temper of our present culture has tended to undervalue or ignore the past (Lasch 1979, 1984). Such tendencies must be resisted, and it is especially vital that critical educators highlight the history of struggle against domination to counter the oppressive practice of ignoring or distorting the history of radical educational reform. One recent example of such distortion is the reductionist attempt to blame progressive educational theory and the education reforms of the 1960s for the current educational "crisis" as defined by certain conservatives (e.g., Bloom 1987; Hirsch 1987; Ravitch and Finn 1987).

THE RECONSTRUCTIONIST LEGACY

A radical educational reform of potential relevance to today's critical pedagogy is the social reconstructionist movement that began in the 1920s and was most influential in the 1930s. Reconstructionism was an indigenous radical movement that has been defined in several ways. Disagreement remains regarding the nature of reconstructionism and which specific educators should be considered members of the movement (e.g., Bowers 1969, 1970; Cremin 1961; Kliebard 1986; Stanley 1981b, 1981c). Still, there is some agreement as to the general characteristics and goals of the movement. Social reconstruction is particularly interesting, because it anticipated many of the methods, concerns, and theoretical perspectives of the critical pedagogy scholarship that has emerged over the past twenty years. Consequently, a comparative analysis of social reconstructionism and critical pedagogy should enhance our understanding of both movements as well as the more general quest for radical educational reform.

The following definition of social reconstructionism, although oversimplified, does convey some of the major concerns of social reconstructionism during the 1930s.

The concept of reconstructionism evolved from the basic notion that social change is inevitable: (1) The course of social change may result from undirected "drift" or it may be led in more-or-less directed fashion by some group or cooperating groups in the society. (2) It is better that social change be directed. (3) Since the future decrees some sort of collectivism—the choices being authoritarian (Communism, Fascism) or democratic—some groups need to push for democratic collectivism. (4) There are many groups eager to direct social change, most of them in an authoritarian direction; and in the presence of a vacuum in leadership, they will do so. (5) The group most dedicated to democratic values, most knowledgeable about cultural trends, and in the most strategic position to direct social change, is school teachers. (6) School teachers, therefore, should be the architects of the new social order. (Hunt and Metcalf 1968, 278)

The social reconstructionist "movement" emerged in the decade after World War I and reached its peak in the 1930s. Several factors contributed to the rise of reconstructionism. New developments in educational, social, and political theory from 1880 to 1920 were very important, especially the work of Henry George, Edward Bellamy, William Graham Sumner, Albion Small, Lester Frank Ward, Thorstein Veblen, C. S. Peirce, John Dewey, William James, Charles Beard, and Upton Sinclair. These writers questioned the prevailing views of social Darwinism and laissez-faire capitalism. Peirce, Dewey, and James developed the influential philosophy of pragmatism, and the writing of these and other critics often complemented the populist and progressive political movements of the times. The result was the generation of a large body of ideas and literature to stimulate thought about alternative social, political, economic, and educational models. Another factor was the concrete model for radical change provided by the success of the Marxist revolution in Russia in 1917.

Kleibard (1986) argues that social reconstructionism was rooted in the social meliorism that has been one of the major curriculum reform impulses of the twentieth century. An early exposition of this view is found in the work of Albion Small who had been strongly influenced by Lester Frank Ward. Small (1896) was critical of the 1893 *Report of the Committee of Ten* because it lacked any social philosophy and offered instead a "catalog of subjects" to study. The report appeared to seek the individuals' adaptation to the present society and placed too much emphasis on intelligence while neglecting other aspects of the individuals' personality. The school subjects were also presented as distinct bodies of knowledge with little sense of their role as interactive parts of a total reality. For Small (1896), it was this reality and not conventionalized abstractions that was most important to education. Students must come to grasp this whole reality to help them organize their thought and action. In the spirit of Lester Frank Ward, Small endorsed social meliorism and urged educators to be "makers of society" (p. 182). Teachers, he believed, held the leverage for timely and radical social reform (p. 184). Often, however, teachers were too timid and reluctant to take political action. Small believed that teachers need to execute their true role in helping to bring about a better society. George Counts, a leading reconstructionist, studied with Small while getting his doctorate at the University of Chicago.

When the U.S. economy faltered and appeared on the verge of collapse in 1929, many social critics, including some educators, turned to the literature on alternative social, political, and economic systems for possible solutions to the economic crisis. The social reconstructionists emerged as one of the groups who were highly critical of the traditional socioeconomic system in the 1930s, although they were not the most radical critics of the period. In fact, the reconstructionists were bitterly attacked by the American Communist party as apologists for capitalism (Bowers 1970). Still, the reconstructionists were clearly on the left in terms of the U.S. political tradition. Their most unique characteristic was a commitment to education as the vehicle for bringing about the reconstruction of society along the lines of social justice and the extension of democracy.

The reconstructionists were more specifically a very small faction within the much larger and more popular Progressive Education Association (PEA). In terms of the general reform movements of this period their numbers were minuscule. According to C. A. Bowers (1970):

> compared to Upton Sinclair's "End Poverty in California" program, the Minnesota Farmer-Labor Party, and the large following of Huey Long, Father Coughlin, and Francis Townsend, their movement seemed insignificant indeed. Yet, they were taken seriously by political groups on both the Left and Right. This was in marked contrast to the large body of classroom teachers, who remained indifferent to the Promethean role they were being called upon to perform. (p. 221)

The reconstructionists seldom realized any of their goals except on a small scale and for a rather short time. Yet, they did manage to engender a great deal of controversy and to leave a legacy of ideas and questions that have had some impact on curriculum and are worthy of further consideration. The movement all but vanished under the pressure of censorship (e.g., the attacks on Harold Rugg's social studies textbook series in the late 1930s and early 1940s), the needs of a nation at war from 1941–45, the subsequent "Cold War," McCarthyism, and the conservative restoration in educational thought after 1945. For these and other reasons, the ideas of the reconstructionists have received only limited attention by curriculum theorists. Yet, reconstructionist scholarship has continued over the past four decades (especially the work of Theodore Brameld), and, more recently, critical pedagogy has begun to give attention to and extended the analysis of issues raised by the reconstructionists (e.g., Giroux 1988c).

Although there is still controversy regarding the nature of social reconstructionism, few would disagree that among the most prominent reconstructionists were the educators Harold O. Rugg, George S. Counts, and Theordore Brameld. It is primarily their work and the reaction to it that forms the basis of the reconstructionist perspective used in this study. Each was a prolific writer and together they have contributed a substantial body of work over almost six decades. The work of these educators, especially the synthesis provided by Brameld, contains the essence of the reconstructionist philosophy of education and approach to curriculum theory. But, as we shall see, each of these writers held significantly different views regarding curriculum. What they shared was a conviction that education can and should be employed to help solve social problems and reconstruct the sociocultural order to create a more ideal society.

As noted earlier, the social reconstructionist position was not entirely new. The concern over whether the schools should function to reflect or reform society has deep roots in the history of education. In America, progressive educators had long been concerned with the creation of the "good society." According to Lawrence Cremin (1961), "progressive education began as part of a vast humanitarian effort to apply the promise of American life—the ideal of government by, of, and for the people—to the puzzling new urban industrial civilization" that emerged between 1850 and 1900 (p. viii). It was "the educational phase of American Progressivism," that is, a multifaceted attempt "to use the schools to improve the lives of individuals" (p. viii). This effort necessitated a revised and expanded view of the role of the school which included attempts to improve the quality of family and community life, health, and the workplace. Education should also be based on the best available research and adapted to the needs of the new groups and classes entering the schools in the last half of the nineteenth century. And, finally, the progressives assumed that our culture could "be democratized without being vulgarized" (Cremin 1961, vii–ix).

Yet, when one moves from the pedagogic rhetoric of the child-centered progressives to an examination of what the new society would be like, only the vaguest of outlines are to be found. The prevailing assumption was that the kind of individual produced by the child-centered school would be sufficient to create the good life and that its creation should be left to these "new" individuals. Progressive educators tended to focus their attention on the needs of the child and avoided the development of a particular social program. As the president of the PEA explained in 1930:

> Although our association has never promulgated or approved anything like
> a program...we do endorse, by common consent, the obvious hypothesis

that the child rather than what he studies should be the center of all educational effort and that a scientific attitude toward new educational ideas is the best guarantee of progress. (Fowler 1930, 159)

Those progressives who supported a child-centered approach did see themselves as contributing to a new and better society by correcting and reversing more traditional formalistic approaches to education. In their view, these traditional approaches had tended to promote the regimented and normative socialization of our youth. The child-centered progressives, by focusing on the child's interests and the enrichment of his powers of observation, believed they were contributing to the creation of citizens with scientific attitudes capable of handling new problems as they arose. In this sense, they believed they were helping to create a new society of independent, free-thinking individuals.

Most progressives also shared Dewey's commitment to experimentalism and democracy. Those progressives favoring a child-centered approach believed that both of these ends could be served by their approach to curriculum design. Furthermore, since experimentalism and democracy required an open-ended curriculum, no question was ever settled and no course content was ever fixed. Most of all these child-centered educators, reacting again to the formalism of the past, tended to oppose any form of imposition or indoctrination. While they did promote democracy, this was seen as the imposition of a process and not a content of fixed truths to be learned. One sense of this approach to education is captured in Marietta Johnson's (1926) comment that "childhood is for itself and not a preparation for adult life" (p. 349).

The activities and goals of the social reconstructionists posed a direct challenge to the child-centered progressives who tended to dominate the PEA throughout the 1920s. Social reconstructionism, however, was not the first challenge to the child-centered approach. Prior to the reconstructionists, critique of the child-centered progressives led to a split in the PEA. Many who considered themselves progressives were concerned that the emphasis on child centeredness was evidencing a growing disparity between Dewey's educational philosophy and the way it was being applied in child-centered classrooms. Dewey (1928) himself spoke out at the 1928 convention of the PEA and criticized some of his followers for maintaining a pedagogical approach that seemed to regard "the organized presentation of school subjects as antithetical to freedom and the needs of students" (p. 200). Dewey (1962) believed the schools to be an "embryonic community" whose activities and occupations reflected the life of the general society (p. 29). He proposed the study of a wide range of social problems that the child-centered classrooms tended to ignore. Dewey believed that we could neither derive the curriculum from the child's needs nor restrict it to such needs. Teachers not only had the right but also the professional obligation "to suggest lines of activity, and to show that there need not be any fear of adult imposition" (p. 203).

The reconstructionists agreed with Dewey's critique of child-centered progressivism and wanted to go even further in terms of organizing the curriculum to help direct the future course of society. While Dewey would only impose what he called the method of intelligence on students, the reconstructionists were concerned with using schools to challenge directly the dominant social order and to achieve specific changes in our social, cultural, and economic institutions. Since socialization was essential to being human, the reconstructionists believed that we should use education to socialize our young in ways calculated to expand and reinforce a democratic culture (Counts 1930, 1932).

Approximately three decades after the decline of social reconstructionism, a new radical reform movement began to emerge in educational discourse. For the purpose of our discussion, I refer to this movement as critical pedagogy, while recognizing that this terminology will not be acceptable to some of those theorists to whom the label is applied.[1] While critical pedagogy appeared to have much in common with reconstructionist theory, it was also significantly different in several ways. In particular, critical pedagogy has been more strongly influenced by European theoretical perspectives including: the new sociology movement in Great Britain, Critical Theory, neo-Marxism (especially the work of Gramsci and Althusser), structuralism, phenomonology, and more recent developments in postmodernism and poststructuralism. Nevertheless, in the U.S., critical pedagogy also retains a strong neopragmatic orientation mainly rooted in the work of Dewey and it has also forged some direct links to social reconstructionist thought (e.g., Giroux 1988c). A second major difference between reconstructionism and critical pedagogy is the powerful influence of feminist thought on the latter. While some feminists have taken very different positions regarding the status of a feminist pedagogy versus critical pedagogy (e.g., Brennan 1989; Ellsworth 1989), it is clear that what I am calling critical pedagogy has, to a great extent, been influenced and shaped by feminist thought.

Finally, critical pedagogy has developed in what some have called the postmodern era, while the reconstructionist movement was largely part of the earlier modernist discourse. Now there is a great danger in oversimplifying the break between modernism and postmodernism (e.g., see

---

1. Elizabeth Ellsworth (1989), for example, contends that feminist pedagogy is a distinct approach with significantly different theory and aims from those of critical pedagogy. For the purpose of this study, I will include feminist pedagogy within the rather broad category of critical pedagogy. Ellsworth's position will be presented in Chapter 4.

Cherryholmes 1988; Giroux 1988c; Habermas 1987; McLaren 1988a, 1988b; Montag 1988; Poster 1989). Still, while a clear break between modernism and postmodernism is an exaggeration, we can discern a dramatic shift with important implications for pedagogy. Postmodernism has questioned the central assumptions of the Enlightenment legacy, including the possibility of reflexive rationality, the existence of the human subject required for agency, claims for an objective ground for knowledge, any metanarrative or totalizing critique, and the very possibility of human progress via education. These dimensions of postmodernism have caused many to question its political potential and whether or not it undermines any possibility of building an educational theory oriented by the goal of student emancipation. In short, some fear that postmodernism is, or will lead to, a new form of radical relativism, nihilism, and a flight from political possibility (e.g., Dews 1987; Giroux 1988c; Habermas 1987; West 1988 and 1989). On the other hand, postmodernism (more particularly poststructuralism) can be understood as constituting a new critique that gives us a much better sense of the nature of knowledge, modes of domination, the relation between power and knowledge, and the limits of critical inquiry (Culler 1982; Derrida 1988; Norris 1985, 1987; Poster 1989; Wexler 1987). We will explore the distinctions between postmodernism and poststructuralism in more detail in Chapter 6.

The reaction to critical pedagogy has been mixed, including rejection, ambivalence, and strong endorsement. Since social reconstructionism was grounded in the Enlightenment tradition, any assessment of its current relevance must be located within the context of the postmodern challenge to critical pedagogy.

ORGANIZATION OF THE BOOK

In Chapter 2, I present a summary of the major theoretical perspectives and policy recommendations of the social reconstructionist critique. This summary is drawn mainly from an analysis of the work of Harold Rugg, George Counts, and Theodore Brameld. Particular attention is given to Brameld's work as the most radical and developed example of reconstructionist theory. In Chapter 3 I discuss the critical reaction to social reconstructionism and examine some of the traces of reconstructionist thought in mainstream curriculum theory.

In Chapter 4 I present a summary of several major approaches to critical pedagogy over the past two decades and how these approaches relate to reconstructionist curriculum theory. Some of the critical reaction to critical pedagogy as well as a number of major disputes among different approaches to critical pedagogy also are discussed, including the critique by some feminists who understand critical pedagogy as a largely male-dominated approach to critical educational reform.

In Chapter 5 some recent developments in postmodern and poststructuralist theory are examined in terms of their relation to critical pedagogy and social reconstructionism. As noted above, many critical educators are concerned that postmodern theory has undermined the theoretical basis for critical curriculum theory, and this issue is examined in some detail by an analysis of recent work on neopragmatism and the poststructuralist theory of Jacques Derrida as these relate to political criticism and reform. I also examine how a critical pragmatism informed by poststructuralism might contribute to a theory for critical pedagogy.

Finally Chapter 6 presents a summary of the conclusions we might draw from the present study. This summary includes a consideration of the current relevance of reconstructionist theory and some suggestions regarding how critical pedagogy and educational reform should evolve as we move toward the twenty-first century. In brief, the argument presented here holds that reconstructionist theory remains relevant to current efforts to develop an approach to curriculum based on critical pedagogy. However, the relevance of reconstructionism to contemporary approaches to critical pedagogy will require an extensive reconceptualization of reconstructionist theory. Some form of critical pedagogy that incorporates the insights of poststructuralism and critical pragmatism appears to offer the most promise. But to say this is only to offer a brief sketch of an argument to come. I leave it to the reader to consider the relevance of this argument over the next five chapters.

2

THE RECONSTRUCTIONIST PROGRAM

UNITED STATES SOCIETY AND CULTURE

The historical and current importance of reconstructionism lies in its insistence on confronting directly the political, social, economic, and moral dimensions of schooling. The reconstructionists recognized that education could not (and should not) be reformed without a clear sense of existing sociocultural conditions. They also believed that education neither could nor should be a neutral institution. By its very nature, education is part of the total process of socialization into a culture. As George Counts (1932) observed, no culture can be maintained or improved without socialization. Thus, educators have a professional obligation to assist in the progressive socialization of their students. Indeed, to be human is to be socialized in some way, since one is not human apart from a social environment. The question posed by reconstructionists was how to best do this in a democratic culture and society.

The following summary of the reconstructionist position on society, culture, and education is mainly derived from the work of Harold Rugg, George Counts, and Theodore Brameld. These three authors represent a wide range of reconstructionist thought from the more moderate position of Rugg to Brameld's more radical, Marxist-oriented version of reconstructionism. Certainly the work of other writers might have been considered (e.g., John Childs), but these three authors provide a representative sample of reconstructionist thought.

The reconstructionists frequently used the term "crisis" to describe what they perceived to be the condition of our society and culture. This was not a particularly remarkable position to take in the 1930s, since critics representing all points on the political spectrum believed we faced a crisis during the depression. But the roots of the reconstructionist position had developed prior to the 1929 stock market crash, and the reconstructionist critique persisted into the affluent decades following World War II. Thus, while the depression did serve to bring out the more radical implications of reconstructionism, economic decline does not explain the persistence of the reconstructionist position (that is, a focus on the centrality of crisis) during periods of affluence. An overview of the reconstructionist critique will shed some light on this issue.

For the reconstructionists, a fundamental problem was that our social philosophies, theories, and institutions lagged behind the reality of social change. The evidence for this was the failure of our social, political, and economic institutions to serve the legitimate interests of significant numbers of people. The reconstructionists argued that certain groups (e.g., the poor, blacks) suffered relatively greater exploitation, while certain "dominant" groups exercised controlling power over major social institutions and used an outmoded ideology to help maintain their control. This arrangement posed a threat to the very survival of our democratic system.

Harold Rugg

In the 1930s, the most obvious gap between social theory and the reality of change was in the area of economics. Social reconstructionists joined the wider chorus of critics who questioned the continued social value of laissez-faire economics and the emphasis on individualism. As Rugg (1932–1933) argued, our highly interdependent economic system requires "a coordinated scheme of control, laissez-faire is done!" (p. 300). Indeed "such concepts as...laissez-faire and private ownership and control of basic industries and utilities constitutes the vocabulary of a foreign and useless language" (Rugg 1935, 13). While the people of the United States faced a wide range of social problems in the 1930s, the root cause of those problems was economic (Rugg 1936a, 399). A central assumption held by Rugg and other reconstructionists was that we now had the productive capacity to provide all of our people with an adequate standard of living (e.g., Rugg 1933, 401–8). In other words, poverty could no longer be rationalized as an inevitable phenomenon but must be understood instead as a direct consequence of current social and economic arrangements that we had the power to change.

Rugg (1932–1933) contended that a careful analysis of our economic system revealed that the laissez-faire approach to economics "has produced enormous inequalities in wealth and social income" (p. 13). In fact, our nation's history "has been largely the story of the conflict between struggling economic classes" (p. 13). It is vital that people come to understand that the economic arrangements that have emerged from this conflict are, at best, experimental. There is tentative validity in various socioeconomic systems each of which "must be regarded frankly as an experiment" (p. 13). What is evident is that the lack of central control over our economy has contributed to the cycles of recession and unemployment as well as the unfair and unequal distribution of income and wealth. Rugg believed that these consequences could be avoided if we followed a policy of "scientific control and operation of economic activities in the interest of all the people" (p. 13). He also supported the eventual move toward a "central world economic government."

Such economic changes could only be brought about via the careful construction of popular support for "permanent social reconstruction" (Rugg 1932–1933). The new social order posited by Rugg would be based on a scientific design developed by "experts" but approved by democratic consent and administered by elected and appointed officials (p. 172). In Rugg's proposed system, "basic industries must be taken from the sphere of political manipulation and carried on purely as a scientific and technological enterprise" (p. 175). Rugg was never entirely clear as to how the "scientific" management of industry would eliminate or control political motivations or manipulation.

Rugg (1933) believed that, to a great extent, those groups who controlled our economic system also controlled our government policy. Nevertheless, this undesirable situation could be remedied without resorting to the socialistic solution of collective ownership of the means of production (p. 180). While necessary reforms would not be accomplished easily, it was most probable that economic change in the United States will feature "private ownership, collective control, and restrictions on industrial investment and profits consistent with the public interest" (p. 180).

Like most domestic liberal critics of our economic system in the 1930s, Rugg (1936a, 1936b) did not accept the basic arguments of orthodox Marxism. Instead, he favored a pluralistic interpretation of our economic problems wherein certain "interest groups" had gained unfair power and economic advantage. Rugg realized that his rejection of class analysis and revolutionary solutions would be labeled gradualism by some. Nevertheless, he believed it was a "gradualism which would be dynamic to succeed in our current crisis" (1936b, 224). The alternative to gradual change was the "violent imposition of dictatorship," and this was not acceptable within a democratic culture. It should be clear that Rugg's views were relatively moderate in the context of the 1930s. Nevertheless, he did demand significant reform and advocated using the schools to help reconstruct society. We will return to this last point in the next section.

George Counts

George Counts (1932) helped push reconstructionist thought in a more radical direction. He had been a student of Albion Small, an early advocate of the social meliorist position in curriculum theory (Kliebard 1986). Like Rugg and other reconstructionists, Counts believed our society was in a state of crisis. He argued for the creation of a new social order based on a fundamental redistribution of economic power. In 1932, such power was largely held by a relatively small class or group. Until this was changed, "the survival or development of a society that could in any sense be called democratic is unthinkable" (Counts 1932, 46). Consequently, Counts argued, "natural resources and all important forms of capital will have to be collectively owned" (pp. 44–45). This was a far more radical economic view than any ever expressed by Rugg. Over time, Counts' economic views became more moderate, but in 1932 he claimed that the capitalist economy of the United States would either have to be eliminated "or changed so radically in form and spirit that its identity will be completely lost" (p. 47). Still, this permitted the retention of capitalism in *some* form and left room for an accommodation with various "liberal" reform proposals. In any case, Counts believed there existed ample evidence to indict capitalism on moral grounds, and the depression of 1929 provided evidence of the profound failure of capitalism in economic terms.

Counts' identification with some form of socialism was perceived as radical by many American educators who feared that socialism represented a loss of democratic freedoms. Counts, however, insisted that he only meant to restrict the opportunity for economic exploitation by individuals seeking to serve their own interests (pp. 49–50). In his view, these kinds of restrictions would actually help preserve and expand democratic freedoms. But Counts also realized that to accomplish such changes would not be easy and the possibility of violent change could not be ruled out. History indicated that the process of persuading powerful classes to give up their privileged position "has commonly been attended by bitter struggle and even bloodshed. Ruling classes never surrender their privileges voluntarily" (p. 51).

There was one important advantage for dealing with this problem during the 1930s. Like Rugg, Counts believed we had progressed to an industrial stage which was historically unique in that we were "able to produce all the goods and services our people can consume" (p. 52). This assumption regarding the diminished significance of economic scarcity is also found in Theodore Brameld's work, as we will discuss later. It was a somewhat ironic assumption to assert in the depths of our nation's worst depression, but Counts was thinking in terms of the great industrial potential to be released once we made the necessary changes in our economic system. Recent economic developments during the 1980s have reasserted the concern with scarcity and raised serious questions about our industrial potential. But we must recall that Counts was speaking at a time when we *did* appear to have the economic capacity (but not the will or a working system) to provide a "good" life for all. This helped create a sense of moral urgency and provided an important issue for reconstructionists to present and examine in schools.

The way our society was organized and maintained was dependent, to a large extent, on public support or at least acquiescence. Such support was facilitated by social theories that made the current institutional arrangements appear natural and necessary. Yet in a period of rapid social change, our social theories could soon become outmoded and even dysfunctional. In Counts' estimation, the ideologies of laissez-faire economics and rugged individualism were good examples of obsolete social theories. During the depression decade, these theories helped to rationalize the disproportionate power of certain groups that dominated key social institutions (Counts 1934b, 519–20). In this way, powerful groups used these ideologies to help block the emergence of some form of democratic socialism and maintain their effective control over the economy. Counts (1938), like Rugg, was also aware that economic problems were no longer limited to a national setting but were global in nature and required global solutions (pp. 210–14).

Counts believed that the transformation of society entailed the assertion of democratic control over our industrial society so that it could be used to promote the general welfare (1934a, 5). Although he had considered seriously the possible need for a violent solution to the major social and economic problems of the depression (Counts 1932, 51), Counts gradually moved to a more moderate position. He agreed with scholars such as Berle and Means, Ferdinand Lundberg, Lewis Carey, and T. M. Sogge who demonstrated that American society in the decade of the 1930s had produced a propertied class that constituted less than twenty percent of the population and yet owned more than half of all the nation's wealth. As a result of this development, more than eighty percent of the population labored for the dominant class (Counts 1938, 52–54). While this was an undesirable condition and cause for grave concern, Counts believed that certain unique features in our society helped to prevent this situation from developing in a revolutionary direction.

For example, our society might be stratified along class lines, but families and groups were not (Counts 1938, 254–55). The hereditary nature of class had been broken down in the United States, and there was little chance of genuine class conflict happening here (p. 255). In addition, the power of the economic aristocracy had been "weakened by insecure moral foundations, . . . [and] divided by interest, outlook, loyalties, and jealousies" (p. 300). Thus, Counts' earlier fear that dominant groups might have to be physically forced to redistribute power and wealth seemed to diminish over time. He never expected that the necessary social changes would come about easily, but he came to believe that an effective educational program could help accomplish the required reforms democratically and without violence.

While Counts (1938) seemed far more comfortable with some variant of democratic socialism than Rugg, the two held much in common. For Counts,

> the best outlook for individual freedom and economic efficiency in the long run would seem to lie in the recognition of the great divisions of the economy and placing of the responsibilities of operations on their respective laboring, technical, and managerial personnel. The integration of the economy could presumably be achieved through some kind of parliament, commission, or even economic state composed of representatives from the several branches or divisions.
>
> * * *
>
> The civil liberties of the masses. . .can be preserved and developed, not by making the democratic political state responsible for the entire conduct of the economy, but rather by breaking the hold of property ownership and introducing the democratic principle into the economic system. (pp. 96–97)

Counts seemed more skeptical than Rugg regarding the desirability of having a technocratic elite run the economy, but both men agreed that we needed to exert collective control over the economic system. This democratic form of control did not, however, require either violent revolution or collective ownership of the means of production. Counts and Rugg, like Dewey, were far more strongly influenced by variants of the social meliorist and democratic socialist tradition in this nation than the orthodox Marxism originating in Europe.

Theodore Brameld

Theodore Brameld was the most "radical" of those reconstructionists whose work first appeared in the decades between the two world wars. Brameld was younger than Rugg and Counts, and his earliest contributions to the reconstructionist discourse appeared in 1935. Despite producing a number of relevant publications, Brameld appears to have been a relatively marginal figure in the early debates over reconstructionism. This changed following World War II when Brameld emerged as the leading advocate of reconstructionism as an educational philosophy. By that point, however, reconstructionism was already in decline.

Brameld was also the reconstructionist most influenced by orthodox Marxism. He completed his dissertation, *A Philosophic Approach to Communism*, at the University of Chicago in 1931. His first publication of direct significance to the reconstructionist debate was "Karl Marx and the American Teacher" which appeared in the *Social Frontier* in 1935. Like Counts, Brameld (1935) emphasized the difficulties faced by those who sought to create a collective society in the United States. In fact, he was often critical of more "liberal" advocates of reform (including Rugg and

Counts) who too often underestimated the means required for significant social change. Initially, Brameld, like Counts, did not rule out the use of violence and pointed out that violence cannot categorically be considered immoral in all circumstances. He also speculated on the possible need for a dictatorship of the proletariat until the general citizenry developed an understanding of the superiority of collectivism as opposed to capitalism (pp. 53–56). Not surprisingly, Brameld's early views provoked a strong critical response, and this will be discussed in the next chapter as we examine the wider critical reaction to reconstructionism.

For Brameld (1936a), class struggle should be understood as one important component of the educational reform process. Furthermore, he did not see the Marxist methodology as fundamentally incompatible with the pragmatic method of Dewey and other progressives (p. 8). In other words, class struggle could be viewed as an hypothesis that seemed to best characterize the crisis of our capitalist society during the 1930s. It did not explain all circumstances and conditions, but that is true of any hypothesis regarding human behavior. Still, the class-struggle hypothesis served as a strong argument for the superiority of a collectivist solution to the crisis of capitalism. Brameld acknowledged that violence (or any undemocratic means) should only be accepted as a last resort in the effort to achieve necessary reforms (p. 15).

As Brameld's (1938) ideas developed, he further qualified his Marxist assumptions and realized that we must look beyond Marxism to construct an adequate model for social change. He recommended contemporary naturalism as one possible source of new methods to critique social, political, and economic structures (p. 258). Like Rugg and Counts, Brameld believed that rapid social change had rendered obsolete and dysfunctional many of our current philosophies and social theories. Unfortunately, those most exploited by the present society and economy were often unaware of the historically conditioned and socially constructed nature of our institutions and the ideologies used to support them.

A case in point was the way theories of individualism functioned in our society. Our cultural emphasis on individual rights and the value of acting to realize our individual interest often led us to use individualism as an argument against collective intervention by government or groups in the society. But Brameld held that individuals are both a "cause and effect of a complex environment" (Brameld 1941a, 284). Mass association in society requires that we revise our view of individuals as merely *ends* worthwhile in themselves. Individuals must also be seen as *"means* to the development and welfare of other individuals" (p. 284). This implied a revival of the ancient Christian values of brotherhood and comradeship. Beyond individual efforts, democratic society requires group loyalty and action.

Social reconstruction also required future planning, and this entailed a move away from the ideology of laissez-faire capitalism wherein it was assumed that an economic system motivated by individual interests was self-correcting, that is, guided by an "invisible hand" (Brameld 1940, 112, 126–7). At least since the depression of 1929, it had become obvious that some democratic social planning was essential. For Brameld, such planning was probably the best antidote to the threat of fascism during the depression.

Long after the depression had ended, Brameld (1950) still held that our society and culture were in a state of crisis (pp. 62–70). Brameld saw crisis in a more complex sense than economic conflict and decline. Crisis also involved cultural contradictions or bifurcations over human values. These contradictions tended to create a critical imbalance in one or more of the basic aspects of the social structure thereby resulting in confusion, loss of purpose, and the gradual disintegration of the social system. A major problem, in this regard, was our cultural tradition of progress and optimism that tended to conceal the abnormalities of our schizophrenic age (pp. 23–4). What we required was a new philosophical orientation to provide an accurate critique of the current crisis and recommendations for necessary reforms.

Brameld (1971, 24–33) identified six major cultural contradictions that characterized the current crisis and required immediate attention:

(1) *Self-interest versus social interest.* This is manifest in our national commitment to the philosophy of competitive enterprise and our system of rewards and reinforcement of those who succeed in this environment. Yet, we also display some strong tendencies toward philanthropy, group affiliations, and various programs of government aid funded by taxes drawn from the society at large.

(2) *Equality versus inequality.* This conflict is reflected in our national commitment to the belief in equal treatment of all people as opposed to the reality of discriminatory practices and outcomes in our society. Such discrimination is most obvious in terms of sex, race, and religious and ethnic discrimination, but it does not stop there. Our cultural emphasis on self interest frequently leads to economic discrimination; that is, those who fail to achieve success in our economic system are often blamed for their failure. This form of class discrimination was based on the assumption that lower classes were inferior in the first place. Of course, the reverse implication was frequently applied to those who succeed.

(3) *Planlessness versus planning.* There is an apparent ideological antipathy in our culture to the idea of planning that somehow seems communistic or un-American. It is partly rooted in our laissez-faire economic and political traditions, yet this contrasts sharply with the obvious need to plan on all levels of society. Indeed, our giant national or multinational

corporations are prominent examples of planning in action. Still the belief persists, despite successful examples of planning on various levels and the obvious need for national planning to meet certain issues, that somehow national planning will not work and is a threat to our economic and democratic way of life.

(4) *Nationalism versus internationalism.* The tenacity with which we cling to parochial national goals conflicts with the obvious need, and at times inclination, to develop a global approach to problems including population, growth, hunger, pollution, and war. The negative consequences that could result from this contradiction have increased dramatically with the advent and spread of nuclear technology.

(5) *Absolutism versus experimentalism.* Our cultural commitment to traditional forms and outlooks permeates all the conflicts described above. Free enterprise or nationalism, for example, are at times described as if they were outgrowths of natural and inviolable laws. Yet, there is also an experimental attitude in our nation that is indicated by our creative approach to solving various technological and scientific problems. Even in the social field we have a tradition of experimentalism that is evident in the many new social programs established over the years. Unfortunately, these programs are frequently limited and undermined by our absolutist cultural perspectives.

(6) *Man-against-himself versus man-for-himself* [sic]. This conflict incorporates a summary of the previous five conflicts in the sense that inequality, self-interest, planlessness, nationalism, and absolutism are dehumanizing and degrading of the human character, thereby turning humans against themselves. Conversely, the opposite values such as equality and social interest represent the best in human thinking. Thus, we are involved in a struggle to establish those values best suited to improve the human condition.

The conflicts described by Brameld tend to be more manifest during periods of cultural revolution. Brameld (1971) defined cultural revolution as "the shifting of cultural patterns at such accelerated rates that patterns hitherto dominant begin rapidly to collapse, looking toward replacement, by others that have never before been tried" (p. 33). The current cultural revolutions to which Brameld referred were in the areas of technology, economics, politics (especially the advent of state ownership and management), and the revolution of abundance by which adequate resources could be provided for mankind (pp. 33–37). Brameld believed, like Rugg and Counts, that we had developed the technological and industrial capacity to deal with the vast majority of human physical needs. There was, therefore, no economic excuse for the continuance of poverty and extreme inequality.

In the light of the recent energy, resource, and pollution crises that have emerged over the past two decades, one might be cautious about conceding that the age of abundance has arrived. Still, it could be conceded that basic needs are far more capable of being satisfied at present than they have ever been throughout human history. Furthermore, and this is critical to Brameld's view, we also possess the economic and political understanding to begin to devise the systems necessary to provide both physical and cultural needs. However, he believed that we have clearly lagged in this area of inquiry, mainly because we lack the necessary philosophical orientation to transform our culture in a more egalitarian direction.

In his analysis, Brameld (1971) employed the term "culturology" which referred to "a philosophy of mankind that is primarily governed by, and exerts profound influence upon, the life of members of culture" (p. 5). This is a sort of anthropological philosophy in which "culture is regarded as the fulcrum of an effort to interpret" human meaning, existence, and actions (p. 14). The reconstructionist task was to examine our culture and find the extent to which current social institutions were unequal to our crisis situation so that we can work to realize the changes required to achieve a complete cultural transformation. The notion of cultural transformation requires further clarification.

Every culture contains deeply ingrained patterns of belief that "exert subtle but persistent influence upon even the most casual events and attitudes," and any careful examination of beliefs about reality will reveal a cultural context (Brameld 1971, 360). The conflicts that exist among beliefs are generally manifested in group conflict, and an understanding of the role of the group and its influence on the individual is a central concern of reconstructionism. This is especially true in terms of prejudicial attitudes, such as racism, sexism, and forms of class oppression. In our society, certain powerful groups tend to corrupt the thinking and awareness of the masses on these issues (p. 370).

Brameld (1971) believed we had the power to shape our destiny and were not subject to any deterministic historical laws, although history did exert a strong influence on human action. Specifically, the reconstructionist holds that humans become what they are largely because of the characteristics of the historic period in which they live. Every historical period emerges from preceding ones and leads into later ones. In this way, each historical period is influenced by earlier ones and in turn influences those which follow, but no metaphysical design determines the course of history. Instead, we help construct our own history, however awkwardly and blindly. Put another way, history has no "ingrained purpose" or "preordained goal." The course it takes and the goals achieved depend upon human choices and the effects of such choices (p. 372).

If we accept that humankind can shape history, it is logical to ask, what direction are we taking? Brameld (1971) believed that we lived in an age of struggle between two major coalitions of groups. One coalition sought to maintain the inherited social structure and included: (1) investors for profit, (2) the managerial class, (3) military castes, (4) agencies that mold public opinion and, (5) other miscellaneous groups, for example, small businessmen, who, at times, are opposed to the views of one or more of the other groups. This coalition's power had been reinforced by the advent of monopoly and state capitalism in this century (p. 374).

In opposition to these groups was a coalition of: (1) factory and farm workers, (2) some rank and file military, (3) some professional workers, (4) some small businessmen and students, and (5) the poor both in the United States and in underdeveloped nations (pp. 375–76). This coalition was less cohesive, coordinated, and powerful than the other. Although it represented more people, it also lacked the same level of resources as the other coalition. But these groups did represent the forces that sought to alter the current social structure in such a way as to insure a more full realization of human potential for all mankind. Educational policy is one way to stimulate these oppositional groups to form an effective base for social reconstruction.

ROLE OF THE SCHOOL IN SOCIETY

Reconstructionists believed that we can and should use the public schools to help reconstruct society is such a way as to resolve our social and cultural crises. At times, they displayed a naive faith in the potential of education to change society. Taking their work as a whole, however, the reconstructionists were well aware that education could not accomplish much without wide public support and the cooperation of other major institutions. But these constraints should not obscure the critical role of education as a major site of resistance to the dominant social order. Furthermore, the reconstructionists believed that teachers, despite their limited power, had the opportunity to be in the vanguard of social reform.

Harold Rugg

Early in his career, Rugg (1923b) held that education was an agency that could be used effectively to "coordinate the power of individual teachers to remake the world" (pp. 261–62). After the onset of the depression, Rugg (1932–1933) believed that a "thorough going social reconstruction" was demanded, and "there is no social institution known to the mind of man that can compass that problem except education" (p. 41). But he added that for the school to be "used as an agent for social regeneration, it must undergo thorough reconstruction" (p. 11).

Rugg very quickly entered the debate between the child-centered and society-centered curriculum theorists during the 1920s and 1930s. Although he tried to achieve a balanced view, Rugg's approach to curriculum favored a strong social orientation for the schools. More importantly, Rugg did not accept the inevitability of the child-centered/society-centered split that divided progressives. Like Dewey, Counts, and Brameld, Rugg held that both groups seemed to share important goals, and the schools could (and should) respond to the needs of both individual students and society (Rugg 1926). The key point was that education required a planned program with planned experiences. Therefore, a curriculum must be developed prior to the expressed interests of the child, and the guidelines for this planning would require a clear view of a desirable or preferred society.

While Rugg acknowledged that the content and goals of the curriculum will be derived, in part, from rigorous analysis of society, he believed the process of curriculum development was far more complex.

> Social analysis merely gives us the techniques and knowledge we should have on tap. For the basic insights and attitudes we must rely, as we do for the statements of the goals of education, upon human judgment. It is imperative, however, that we make use of only the most valid judgments. The forecasting of trends and social movements, and perception of the focal problems and issues, and the connections underlying them, demand erudition and maturity of reflection that eventuates only from prolonged and scientific study of society. To the frontier of creative thought and of deepest feeling we go for guidance as to what to teach. (Rugg 1926, 82)

The frontier of creative thought referred to the work of those Rugg called "frontier thinkers" (Rugg 1921, 1926, 260–73). These were intellectual leaders in various areas including history, the social sciences, the humanities, journalism, and the fine arts. As the quote above indicates, Rugg had come to see that "facts" do not speak for themselves; they must be interpreted in the light of social values and an informed view of the social order. This required the insight of those engaged in "prolonged scientific study of society" coupled with the capacity for "creative thought." Finally, this process involved an affective dimension, that is, the "deepest feelings" of the frontier thinkers regarding what should be done.

Rugg can be criticized for an overreliance on "experts" as a source of curriculum knowledge, but to stop there would ignore much of value in his position. For example, Rugg focused on the work of "frontier thinkers" and not merely disciplinary experts. He wanted students to have an interdisciplinary orientation and access to the best available knowledge regarding social problems. Furthermore, it is apparent that the important knowledge Rugg would use to build the curriculum could not be determined by a rule-governed, decisionistic process. He argued that there was no empiricist, scientific process by which we could conclude what "ought" to be taught or even how to "best" teach it in all situations.

Rugg spent a great deal of time analyzing the history of curriculum. While past curriculum studies had been valuable, too often they recommend a curriculum that sought "to fit children to take part in life as it is today" (Rugg 1926, 261). This orientation ignored the problem of rapid social and cultural change. While we must prepare our children to take an active part in our current society, "we need also to prepare them to improve the situation in which they will find themselves as adults. We must equip them to be constructively critical of contemporary social, economic, and political organization" (Ibid.).

Rugg (1941), in his autobiography, discussed his belief in the power of ideas to change human behavior and improve society (p. 261). If properly executed, education had a unique capacity and potential to use ideas to alter and deepen students' understanding. As part of this task we must work to reduce the lag between the curriculum content and the realities of social conditions and change. The curriculum he proposed would include the critical study of contemporary economic, social, and political problems (Rugg 1923a, 22). As noted earlier, the choice of specific problems for study should be influenced by the views of the frontier thinkers noted earlier (Rugg 1926, 260–73). He believed that this approach to curriculum would help develop citizens who would continue to be "constructively critical" as adults (pp. 261–62).

Although Rugg wanted to expose students to the most thoughtful analysis of social issues and problems, he was reluctant to suggest solutions and did not expect students to provide solutions to these problems. More important was the "unpartisan, open-minded review of the evidence on both sides" of the issues studied (Rugg 1926, 261). Despite this rather neutral approach, Rugg believed that "the school *is our most important agency for the improvement of society*" (p. 262). Consequently, we would fail in our professional responsibility if we only had students study problems without helping to equip them with the understanding and skills to deal with such problems as adults.

It is evident that Rugg was struggling with some conflicting ideas. The schools were to be used to affect social change, but he also wanted to preserve the objectivity of the curriculum and avoid an ideological position. The practical impossibility of this strategy should become clear as we proceed, and Rugg was forced to struggle with this dilemma for much of his professional life. For example, Rugg wanted to change the school curriculum so that students would focus on the study of current social problems, all of which he believed to be essentially economic (Rugg 1936a, 399). In addition, students should be made aware of our economic capacity to eliminate poverty and provide an adequate standard of living for all citizens. If this knowledge could be communicated to students, perhaps the prevailing cultural emphasis on individual competitiveness and self-aggrandizement could be reduced (Rugg 1933a, 401–8).

In my view, Rugg was not denying that goods and services are not scarce in some absolute sense, but the relevant question was "scarce for what?" The answer to this question depends on one's conception of a desirable social order. Put another way, how scarce things are is, at least in part, a function of the cultural significance attached to such things, and education has the potential to change our cultural conceptions. In brief, Rugg wanted to teach students the tentative and experimental nature of all economic systems and their related sociocultural assumptions. Rugg (1932–1933) would also have students learn specifically about the inadequacies of laissez-faire economics and traditional approaches to individualism. A careful analysis of economic problems would include an appraisal of the possible advantages of a democratic, collective regulation of the economy informed by scientific management. While he might have sought to remain open-minded and objective, it is clear that Rugg's program was not neutral.

Schwartz (1979) makes the case that the attempt to reduce personal and social alienation was also a major influence on Rugg's approach to curriculum. Rugg believed that using the schools to give students "an honest and intelligible" understanding of our social order would help address the problem of alienation (p. 151). Rugg realized that the students initial confrontation with controversial issues might even increase alienation. This is a possibility that still concerns some social educators (e.g., Newmann 1981a). But, for Rugg, the potential long-term effects were worth the risks. His position was linked to his conception of the political. Rugg (1941) argued that true consent can only be given when one understands the issue under discussion. Therefore, the mere right to vote or participate in the political process was necessary but insufficient. One also needs both to grasp the importance of exercising consent and to have a clear view of how they are using it. Because these needs were neglected by the schools, education tended to function as another source of social alienation. Consequently, this was a form of alienation the schools had the potential to reduce significantly.

Another way the schools could reduce alienation was to help students deal with the effects of stereotypes. According to Schwartz (1979), Rugg came to see stereotypes as "necessary psychological reactions" to the complex stimuli presented by modern societies filled with a great variety of different groups representing many interests. As Schwartz summarizes Rugg's position,

An individual simply cannot react to all stimuli at once. So individuals react only partially to certain aspects; e.g., conspicuous phrases of a certain

type, certain gestures, or selected features of events. This is the manner in
which the infant gradually learns to adjust to the world. (p. 152)

People in communities tend to classify others according to features such
as race, class, gender, religion, ethnicity, political ideology, occupation,
lifestyle, and so forth. This human propensity certainly had the potential
to increase alienation, and the poor school curriculum intensified this
alienation by perpetuating negative stereotypes. For Rugg (1941), the task
of the curriculum was obvious, that is, to *"Build better stereotypes!"* (p. 230).
Since Rugg saw the school as the prime agency of socialization charged
with the role of building community, better (i.e., more objective) stereotypes could help in this task. Of course, Rugg's emphasis on using schools
to build "better" stereotypes was an ideological position and in conflict
with some of his rhetoric on objectivity.

As Schwartz (1979) makes clear, Rugg's conception of objective knowledge was not something that could be reduced to an unproblematic
statistical or other "scientific" description. For Rugg, "facts" about social
phenomena did not lend themselves to such obvious truths; they needed
to be interpreted. In my view, Rugg was seeking better interpretations or,
at the very least, to present alternative interpretations to undermine the
"taken for grantedness" of negative stereotypes. Schwartz (1979) illustrates
how Rugg applied this same analysis to stereotypical viewpoints of
historical and social science knowledge as well as the more conventional
conception of stereotypes that represented distorted views of various social
groups.

Another concern expressed by Rugg and other reconstructionists was
the impact of a philosophical instrumentalism on curriculum development
and educational practice (Rugg 1931).

> The instrumental theory has pointed the experimental ways to everlasting
> salvation. Its ruthless scientific analysis has shown us that the old loyalties
> have disappeared. Yet, it has put no new "objects of allegiance" in their place.
> (p. 141)

Rugg pointed to four shortcomings of instrumentalism (pp. 226–29). First,
it places too great an emphasis on "preparatory" as opposed to
"consummatory" acts, that is, more emphasis on "becoming" rather than
"being." Second, it tended to deemphasize the emotional aspect of
behavior. Thus, the creative and artistic side of education was neglected.
Third, instrumentalism stressed adaptation to the social group. This could
serve "to deepen the rut of conformity in which most of us move" (p. 228).
Fourth, the concern with problem solving had underemphasized the need
to develop "happy" individual personalities. Rugg maintained that
education must have goals which were beyond the scope of instrumentalism alone.

George Counts

Although they shared many assumptions and objectives, many of Counts' recommendations regarding the role of public education were more radical than those posed by Rugg. His speech before the Progressive Education Association (PEA) in 1932, "Dare Progressive Educators be Progressive?," caused immediate controversy and was a comprehensive summary of his educational views to that time. The speech was subsequently published in *Dare the Schools Build A New Social Order* (Counts 1932).

Counts maintained that the focus of the PEA had become too narrow, placing undue emphasis on the individual in education. Furthermore, and despite the progressive's often naive faith in the power of education to solve all social problems, the effects of the depression of 1929 seemed to "suggest that our schools, instead of directing the course of change, are themselves driven by the very forces that are transforming the rest of the social order" (p. 3). Counts believed that "under certain conditions" our educational system might be as effective as we suppose. But no educational program yet existed to accomplish this task.

Counts admitted that progressive educators had accomplished much in the first decades of the twentieth century. They were right to place more emphasis on the interests of the child than did those who advocated a subject-centered curriculum, and they were correct when they argued that "activity lies at the root of all true education" (pp. 5–6). Learning should, as the progressives argued, be related to "life situations" and character development. But, while this was an excellent beginning, it was not a sufficient program for education. For an educational movement to be truly progressive, "it must have orientation; it must possess direction" (p. 6). The very term "progress" implies moving forward and this "can have little meaning in the absence of clearly defined purpose" (p. 6). Thus, the chief weakness of progressive education was its failure to develop a theory of social welfare, "unless it be that of anarchy or extreme individualism" (p. 7). Counts believed that the overemphasis on individualism in our culture reflected the view of the upper middle class, many of whom sent their children to progressive schools. The members of this class seemed "entirely incapable of dealing with any of the great crises of our time" (p. 8). They had become too fond of their material possessions and, in a crisis, would likely "follow the lead of the most powerful and respectable forces in society and at the same time find good reasons for doing so" (p. 6).

It was necessary, therefore, for progressive educators to free themselves from the undesirable influences of the upper middle class. Such freedom would permit the development of "a realistic and comprehensive theory of social welfare" and "a compelling and challenging vision of human destiny" (pp. 9–10). The construction of an educational program oriented by such a vision and theory of social welfare would also entail freeing progressive education from its apparent fear of imposition and indoctrination. Put another way, progressive educators must come to accept

> that all education contains a large element of imposition, that in the very nature of the case this is inevitable, that the existence and evolution of society depend upon it, that it is consequently eminently desirable, and that the frank acceptance of this fact by the educator is a major professional obligation. (p. 12)

Over the years, progressive educators had developed a strong opposition to imposition or indoctrination in education. This was an understandable reaction given the imposed, rigid, formalistic, and subject-centered curriculum that was dominant in most schools at the start of this century. Yet, Counts believed that there were a number of fallacies that underlay the progressive's theoretical opposition to indoctrination.

First, the progressive educator assumed that people were "born free"; when in fact, we enter the world in a helpless state. We achieved freedom "through the medium of culture. . . .The individual is at once imposed upon and liberated" (Counts 1932, 13). Counts realized that this argument might be regarded as a non sequitur by some progressives, but this was a result of their failure to understand the nature of the socialization process. This misunderstanding is related to a second fallacy, that is, "that the child is good by nature" (p. 15). In fact, as the anthropological evidence indicates, the newborn "is merely a bundle of potentialities which may be developed in manifold directions" (p. 15).

Another serious fallacy is the belief that "school should be impartial in its emphases" without any bias in instruction. But Counts insisted that "complete impartiality is utterly impossible, that school must share attitudes, develop tastes, and even impose ideas" (p. 19). There is no sense in which education can "be completely divorced from politics, . . . and pursue ends peculiar to itself" and to believe otherwise "is one of the most dangerous fallacies" (p. 18). Consequently, even though Dewey speaks in *Democracy and Education* of the need for education to provide a "purified" environment for learning, Counts was certain "that this means stacking the cards in favor of the particular systems of value which we may happen to possess" (Counts 1932, 20).

While many of the progressive fallacies were derived from their overemphasis on the needs of the child, the need for neutrality could, in Counts' estimation, be linked to the instrumentalist philosophy of Dewey and his followers. This philosophical orientation "adopts an agnostic orientation towards every important social issue," wherein one "sees all sides to every question without making a commitment or taking action until all the facts are in..." (pp. 20–21). Except it is already understood that we will never have all the facts. Thus, judgement is held "in a state of indefinite suspension" (pp. 21). As Counts explains

> For any complex social problem...there are probably tens, even scores, if not hundreds of solutions, depending upon the premises from which one works. The meeting of a social situation involves the making of decisions and the working out of adjustments. Also, it involves the selection and rejection of values. (p. 21)

But most progressive educators lacked any clear social vision or sense of direction. In short, they failed to realize that a "genuinely free" person does not spend the day contemplating his or her navel but is one who is involved in "a great cause or glorious adventure". (p. 23).

Although Counts (1932) urged educators to join forces to help solve social problems, he was realistic concerning the power of public education, acknowledging that "[t]he school is but one formative agency among many, and certainly not the strongest at that" (pp. 23–24). Still, we must use education to its best advantage. As Counts pointed out, even when other progressive educators agree (as did Dewey) "that imposition of some kind is inevitable" in education, they fail to draw the correct conclusion. Rather, they are guided by the fallacy "that there is something essentially profane in any effort to understand, plan, and control the process" of imposition (p. 24). This is a case of "laissez-faire, driven from the field of social and political theory, seeking refuge in the domain of pedagogy" (p. 24).

This line of thinking is related to a final fallacy regarding the primary importance of preparing students for social change. It is true that rapid and continuous change has been typical of this century. Students must be made aware of this phenomenon and helped to cope with it. But, according to Counts, the focus of this approach to education had taken a perverse turn. The "ideal" individual would need "an agile mind, be bound by no deep loyalties, hold all conclusions and values tentatively, and be ready at a moments notice to make even fundamental shifts in outlook and philosophy..." (p. 27). This is an anarchistic outlook which

> exalts the irrational above the rational forces of society, makes of security an individual rather than a social goal, drives every one of us into an insane competition with his neighbors...and assumes that man [sic] is incapable of controlling in the common interest the creatures of his [sic] brain. Here we have imposition with a vengeance, but not the imposition of the teaching of the school...it is the imposition of the chaos and cruelty and ugliness produced by the brutish struggle for existence and advantage. (p. 27)

Teachers should expose all these fallacies, not remain neutral in the face of social and economic crises, and seek political power in the interest of the masses (p. 29). Given their unique position as intellectual leaders, teachers could contribute significantly to achieving these goals.

Nevertheless, Counts was not insensitive to problems posed by social change. He argued that every generation must reconstruct its own educational philosophy. If this did not happen, the extant educational philosophies would become outmoded in the wake of social change. Social values and institutions did not remain static, thus educational philosophies too must be reconstructed to maintain their relevance (Chapman and Counts 1924, 81). This position was especially true during a period of rapid social change, such as the 1920s and 1930s. Counts (1932) also believed that education, because of the central role it played in the transmission of the culture, was uniquely suited to help promote the necessary reconstruction of the larger society (pp. 9–12).

As mentioned earlier, schools do not perform their normative and residual functions as autonomous institutions within society. Rather, they interact with a wide variety of other institutions that shape school policy and curricula. But even in a pluralistic society, dominant social groups tend to set this policy. Unless the schools could develop their own programs, coupled with more autonomy, these conditions of group domination were unlikely to change (Counts 1926, 310–13). According to Counts, the social groups that dominated the schools throughout most of recent American history were an elite economic aristocracy. He urged that the schools be used to help dislodge these groups from power and to help enable the common people to assume direction of their social and political institutions.

Among the more powerful dominant groups were those linked to corporate interests. The domination of the schools by certain business groups has deep roots in American history. Indeed, business alliance with education was promoted by prominent educational leaders such as Barnard and Harris (Rippa 1971, 117, 185–88). The growth of industrialization infused the schools with new revenue, and the schools in turn helped produce a docile labor force. Furthermore, the schools tended to promote the ideology of rugged individualism and laissez-faire. For example, much of the school curricula emphasized competition among individuals for admission to a privileged class with access to wealth, power, and status (Counts 1934b, 519–20). In the depression decade, this entrenched business ideology blocked the development of democratic collectivism. Capitalism, Counts maintained, also paradoxically isolated the schools from community life by using them to sustain an outmoded social philosophy that ran counter to the trends of social development.

Counts (1927) had studied the composition and influence of local school boards. He found them to be staffed, in the main, by a privileged social class who benefited from the socioeconomic status quo and seemed to be rigidly opposed to social change. While one might hope that such a privileged group would rise above narrow self-interest, there was little evidence that this ever happened. As Counts noted, the "best of us are warped and biased by the very process of living" (p. 51). Counts' study of the composition of school boards further confirmed his belief that schools were dominated by and run in the interests of a business elite and other elements of the upper middle class who shared their views.

The ability of these special interest groups to control education was greatly facilitated by the dominance of certain "controlling ideas" in our educational philosophy. Among these ideas were individualism, local control of schools, nationalism, social conformity, efficiency, utility, and philosophic uncertainty (Counts 1930, 10). Counts documented the influence of these ideas not so much by examining the writing of our great educational theorists but from a study of "the educational institutions which have. . .evolved in the United States" (pp. 4–5). By a studying of the actual practices of education one might better understand the principles underlying them.

The negative impact of individualism has been suggested above, especially in reference to laissez-faire capitalism, and the progressive, child-centered approach to education. Counts (1930) believed that the desire for local control of schools also had a negative effect. For one thing, it tended to limit the role of the federal government and the ability of educators to plan and implement programs to deal with national problems (pp. 44–45). The emphasis on local control also contributed to the great disparities that existed in the quality of education among the various states (p. 45). Furthermore, "low standards of scholarship. . .which have commonly characterized educational practice in the United States, may be traced to the fact that ordinary men and women have controlled the schools" (p. 50). Local control also tended to subject education to "those gusts of passion which sweep through the masses" (p. 51). Thus, local control often functions to restrict freedom rather than to expand it. This appeared to be a somewhat contradictory assertion, given Counts' commitment to democracy and his critique of the control of education by elite groups representing the interests of the powerful in society. Certainly, Counts did not oppose returning control of schools to the masses. But, his studies of school boards indicated local control was no guarantee that the "real" interests of the masses would be served.

In the case of higher education, its relative institutional autonomy seems to be a great source of academic freedom, but Counts feared:

> . . .that the control of higher education seems to be passing increasingly into
> the hands of business men and the further fact that the same individuals,
> men of great financial power and influence, may serve on the board of

trustees of several different institutions tends to bring the universities more completely under the domination of a particular class—and a class which is peculiarly interested in maintaining the existing social order. (Counts 1930, 191–92)

Our cultural emphasis on social conformity also helped to promote the status quo. When our nation was first formed, our culture put a premium on originality, but more recent developments in the areas of politics, economics, morals, and religion seemed "to discourage bold speculation and radical experimentation of every kind" (p. 119). This problem was carried into the school in the process of curriculum construction in conjunction with the new emphasis on scientific education. A "cult" of scientism in education had resulted in the emphasis "on objective and even mechanical methods of analysis and measurement" (pp. 124–25). This amounted to a conservative approach to curriculum in that it tended to begin with the study of the present social order and thereby functioned to reify the status quo.

Counts (1930) did not take a simplistic position against science, as his commitment to free inquiry and experimentalism attest. What he specifically objected to (much like Rugg) was the subordination of the scientific method to the mere quantitative study of the learning process. Counts believed that scientifically derived data must be harmonized with theory to be socially significant (p. 170). However, the strong influence of our prevailing cultural beliefs regarding the desirability of efficiency and utility tended to shape the school along the contours of industrial institutions (Counts 1926, 138–39, 156–62). Thus, schools had become preoccupied with measuring output and developing hierarchial administrative organization, vocational training, and scientific management. The goals of efficiency and utility, therefore, tended to thwart attempts to reconstruct educational theory to meet current social needs.

Another problem noted by Counts was the pervasive influence of a philosophic uncertainty that functioned to block the development of a theory of social reconstructionism by promoting relativism under the guise of objectivity and academic freedom (pp. 185–92). Counts believed that philosophic uncertainty, combined with the instrumentalism of most progressives and the narrow scientific approach of other educators, had resulted in the general tendency to avoid resolving pressing social problems.

Finally, Counts claimed that the influence of strong nationalistic tendencies had promoted the biased presentation of much of our social studies curriculum (pp. 114–16). The emphasis given to patriotism in our schools frequently served the interests of dominant groups, while expressing intolerance for racial and cultural minorities (pp. 104–7). Even when motivated by high interests, the teaching of patriotism tended to dwell primarily on the nation's history, thus largely ignoring the need for radical changes in the present (p. 117).

Counts (1938) was also aware that the major problems of this century were no longer simply national in scope. It was becoming more evident that many economic and social issues were global in nature and, thus, could not be resolved by any nation acting alone (pp. 210–14). This theme would become increasingly significant in the latter writing of the reconstructionists, especially the work of Theodore Brameld.

Theodore Brameld

Like Rugg and Counts, Brameld maintained that our society faced serious economic and cultural crises and that the schools could use a reconstructionist curriculum to help bring about the social change necessary to create a better social order. As discussed earlier, Brameld's early views on education were strongly influenced by Marxism, and he thought Marxist theory held great utility for educators in the United States (Brameld 1935, 1936a). But he was more supportive of Marxist methodology and critique than its worldview which he believed contained dogmatic elements. Brameld viewed teachers as members of the working class whose task was to enable students to understand capitalism's weaknesses and the potential superiority of democratic collectivism. He also believed that the Marxist hypothesis of the class struggle was, in reality, a particular application of the scientific method espoused by Dewey, Raup, Bode, and other progressives (Brameld 1936a, 8). He did not see Marx's commitment to a socially relevant hypothesis (class struggle) not yet proven false as incompatible with Dewey's scientific, instrumentalist approach to education (Ibid.).

Brameld (1936a) acknowledged that evidence is not always clearly supportive of the class-conflict hypothesis as a guide to establishing a collectivist society. However, the evidence generally supported a move toward some form of collectivism, and Brameld was critical of liberals who, seeking to learn *all* the relevant facts, tended "to shift their objectives in accordance with their welter of interests" and are unlikely to commit to any significant hypothesis for reform (p. 11). The danger of such an "objectivist" orientation is that important decisions are seldom made or are made too late. To those like Raup (1936) and Dewey (1936) who accused Brameld of advocating the indoctrination of students, he (1936a) replied that indoctrination should be understood as

the effort to establish the truth of a theory which one regards with a tentative though already enthusiastic respect. The question which should be asked is whether the right of any expert in the natural sciences to gather evidence, to set up hypotheses on the basis of it, and to demonstrate their validity as far as possible, is a right which should be extended also the expert in social science. (pp. 15–16)

Over time, Brameld's views on the relevance of Marxism to education moderated considerably. He noted three major failings in the Marxist position. First, it presented an oversimplified analysis of culture by "reducing it to economic class alignments without sufficient regard for other relationships and structures" (Brameld 1971, 352). Second, Marxism suffered from an ontology of natural historic laws that was at least partly absolutist. Finally, the most serious problem was the Marxist advocacy of a proletarian dictatorship "as an interim political-economic order under which democratic rights and processes are to be abridged indefinitely" (p. 352). Nevertheless, Brameld never abandoned his conviction that Marxism provided a valuable source of ideas for a reconstructionist philosophy of education.

Much of Brameld's reconstructionist program involved the elaboration of an improved educational philosophy. He argued that a critique of the existing culture and the construction of new theories required a toughmindedness that liberal progressives seemed to lack (1936b). The narrow scientific attitude of many progressives, their apparent openness to consider all points of view, often resulted in a refusal to accept any position as sufficiently worth fighting for or against. The irony was that the same scientific method that glorifies action can become a rationalization for inaction or even "a devotee of reaction when. . .the evils of the status quo threaten to engulf the scientist himself [sic]" (p. 131). A new philosophy of social change must use aggressive techniques for social critique and retain a collective democratic commonwealth as an ideal. Brameld (1938) believed his approach differed from pragmatism; for while both philosophies held that human intelligence is basically derived from interaction with the environment, the reconstructionist position contends that human intelligence is restricted by environmental forces (e.g., political, cultural, and economic institutions) that are far more powerful than most pragmatic educators realize (p. 22).

Brameld (1941a) also urged that the school curriculum be changed to give more attention to the interests of those students who will not go on to college and the professions. Generally, vocational education programs do not emphasize the skills and knowledge future workers need to be competent citizens. The college-bound students tend to receive a relatively better education in this regard, but they also tended to go into business and the professions and, therefore, to be more conservative than the general population. Consequently, the college students' virtual monopoly on citizenship competencies often served to block the necessary democratization of society.

The reconstructionist faith in the power of education to help transform society amounted to a rejection of other reactionary and radical views of education. The reactionaries were either elitist and saw no point in trying to educate the lower classes, or, in an extreme expression of individualism, argued that anyone with intellectual potential and initiative could become economically successful without the benefit of educational programs (Brameld 1941a, 282). Conversely, orthodox Marxism maintained that education had little or no potential to effect social change, because it was a social institution dominated by and functioning in the interest of the capitalist class. Thus, orthodox Marxists held that schooling could not be reformed until society was reconstructed. For Brameld, this was a defeatist philosophy that would ultimately postpone needed social change. He agreed that education *was* used by those in power to help rationalize and maintain the status quo. But this process was never total, and education, by its very nature and organization, provided numerous opportunities to challenge the dominant social order.

A different position was held by Dewey and others who supported educational reform and believed pragmatism provided the necessary philosophic orientation. While Brameld (1941b) agreed with much of the pragmatist's position, he also believed it was too present-oriented to support an adequate critique or social theory. One essential aspect of a new educational philosophy was future planning, and reconstructionism was superior to pragmatism in this regard (pp. 5–10). In addition, reconstructionists, unlike pragmatists, would take the necessary steps to politicize the curriculum. Students would be required to analyze major social problems, would be taught the impact of economic conditions on our thinking, would be shown the tentative nature of and limitations of current institutions, and would learn the potential inherent in alternative institutional arrangements (e.g., democratic collectivism and world government). Brameld et al. (1942) also believed that the schools should be used to help provide basic social services (including food, clothing, shelter, and health care) to those unable to afford them (Brameld 1942, 363–64).

Brameld's reconstructionist recommendations were implemented to some degree in a special project he helped conduct in 1944–45 at the Floodwood High School in Minnesota. The basic goal of the project was to decide on a society that would best satisfy our human wants. Eleven human wants were identified by the project including food, shelter, clothing, health, education, religion, family life, work, recreation, participation, and recognition (Brameld 1945, 22). Democracy was settled upon as the best system for satisfying such wants, and the degree to which they were satisfied was to be the basic test of the system's success (p. 21).

The Floodwood project placed the greatest emphasis on political and economic questions, because Brameld (1945) believed that unless we solve the recurrent evil of depression "there is very little practicality to other areas of reconstruction which depend upon economic security and stability" (p. 39). Indeed, all the other content of the project including science, humanities, and the arts was explored in terms of its political and economic dimensions (pp. 59–60, 62–69).

One of Brameld's central concerns (similar to Rugg's views noted earlier) was that people could only achieve and maintain their freedom in direct proportion to their competence to understand and act in their own interests, which included an adequate knowledge of the structure and functions of the society in which they live. This essential knowledge is often blocked or distorted by our major social, political, and economic institutions, including education. Our understanding can also be blocked or distorted by the rapid development of new technologies. As a result, there is a constant gap between the subjective political knowledge of the masses and the objective reality of social development (Brameld 1948, 329–30). As early as 1948, Brameld suspected the developing technology of mass communication was shaping public opinion in detrimental ways and might be a more powerful influence than "the whole of formal education" (p. 330). This result was not inevitable, but the great potential of mass communications seems to incite those in power to use it for their own self interest (p. 331). Generally, public education also served the interests of those in power, because teachers and administrators tended to act as the "naive or timid servants of those forces...which spread confusion and distortion" about basic social meanings (p. 331).

The full development of Brameld's reconstructionist educational philosophy occurred in the decades following World War II. The depression had ended, but he continued to view the United States as a culture and society in crisis. Brameld believed there were four basic ways educational philosophers could respond to the continuing crisis: (1) a transmissive or *essentialist* orientation that confirmed most existing beliefs and practices, (2) a moderative or *progressive* orientation that supports liberal reforms, (3) a restorative or *perennialist* orientation that seeks a restoration of the views and practices of an earlier age, and (4) a transformative or *reconstructionist* orientation that is critical of the present culture and calls for the development of a new social order (Brameld 1971, 62–63). Brameld believed that only reconstructionism was adequate to deal with the existing cultural crises.

Progressivism, with its roots in pragmatism, had the most in common with reconstructionism, but its educational potential was limited. In essence Brameld (1971) was elaborating and expanding on his earlier criticisms of liberal progressive thought. One difficulty was the progressive's emphasis on a problem-solving methodology which, while necessary, tended to become so central that it might provide a "philosophic justification for lack of strong commitment to anything so much as the process itself" (p. 162). Brameld acknowledged that certain progressives, especially Dewey, recognized the importance of "positive, far sighted conclusions." Our experience can become "an intrinsically valued end" and "provide an ontological basis for the view that intelligence mediates. . . such experiences" (p. 162). Since the test of truth is tied to the "consequences of thinking" it would be a grave distortion to not recognize the importance of means as well as ends (p. 162). Still, a problem remains when attained ends "become subject to such further modification that often they seem to slip from our grasp" (p. 162). The progressive, however, is inclined to back away from commitment to any "end" in an effort to retain flexibility and oppose dogmatism.

The progressive's emphasis on process was especially important because it was in harmony with twentieth-century American culture. In other words, in a culture oriented toward movement, development, action, and change, a problem-solving process was very important (p. 163). But, of equal importance was "the need for commitment to solutions that should result from problem solving" (p. 163). Yet, Brameld warned against oversimplification of the issue.

> We reiterate that the choice—strictly speaking—is never between mutually exclusive alternatives, and. . .artificial issues are raised by critics who attempt to dichotomize ends and means. What is not artificial is the point of stress. The stress of the progressivist is upon "how" rather than "what," upon process rather than product, upon hypothesis rather than commitment. (p. 163)

Finally, and despite the objections of Dewey and others, Brameld believed there remained an overemphasis on child-centered individualism in progressive thought. This individualist orientation is most congenial to the middle class, and this powerful group is unlikely to challenge seriously an orientation that helps rationalize their controlling position in the status quo (p. 169). Here, Brameld echoed Counts' concerns discussed earlier.

The problem of individual orientation was exacerbated further by the general "reluctance of liberal-progressivists to assess sufficiently the stubborn, illogically maintained obstacles that impede their own pleas for intelligent action" (p. 169). For example, progressives like Bode and Kilpatrick "largely bypassed psychoanalytic aspects of human behavior, and hence the hidden, unrational springs of the learning experience. . ." (p. 169). Brameld felt that this tendency to avoid or be uncertain in making a "sharp negative analysis of psychocultural obstacles" raised serious doubts about the likelihood of developing adequate strategies for effective social change (p. 170).

Another problem inherent in the progressivist view was an overly narrow analysis of Marxism. Dewey, for one, did correctly reject dialectic materialism for its absolutistic and metaphysical aspects, but he failed to ask "whether other aspects of this theory might not have strengthened his own methodology in dealing with...economic conflict" (Brameld 1971, 170). Like Dewey, most progressives have rejected a neo-Marxist orientation, resorting instead to a more congenial approach based on "multiple means and social compromise." The progressive analysis of class conflict was especially revealing in this regard. Their orientation toward this issue was operational, and consequently, progressives refused to believe that classes had any fixed structure or were locked in a dialectic struggle (Brameld 1965, 133). Instead, classes were viewed as pluralistic entities that must be understood in relation to the given cultural environment. Thus, many types of classes might exist, for example, political and social as well as economic. This conception of class was desirable, in the progressives' view, since it helped maximize social diversity and options (pp. 132–34). The progressivist approach to dealing with class conflict was to "learn how to practice *creative bargaining* between conflicting groups through reflective analysis of the motivations that lie behind their behavior" (p. 134). Progressives assumed that this tends to reduce the gaps between classes, keep them fluid, and provide no rigid grounds for class superiority.

Brameld (1971) admits that progressives have made a positive contribution by calling attention to the fact that "social science lags behind natural science, and that we have not as yet approached most economic, national, and similar issues in an experimental manner..." (p. 170). Still, it was not clear that they had developed an effective model to deal with such issues. The prime characteristic of progressivism seemed to be caution, and this approach to education begged the question as to whether or not our greatest failure was the progressive educators "reluctance to assess the unreasonableness of his [sic] enemies...ruthless political and national power" (p. 170).

Reconstructionism, on the other hand, has the potential to fulfill a great historical function of philosophy by envisaging radical, innovative projections (Brameld 1971, 346). This philosophy attempts to design actual cultural patterns for the future based on a solid understanding of human nature and the means of realizing human potential. Brameld drew on the work of utopian writers, while admitting to a distinction between those utopian ideas that are escapist and those that are reconstructive. The latter referred to "any construction of the imagination that extends beyond the here-and-now toward realizable human, especially cultural, goals" (p. 347). Brameld objected to those who viewed utopianism only in a negative way, that is, as a flight from reality. In its best sense, utopianism is "a vision of what can be and should be attainable in order that man [sic] may be happier, more rational, more humane than he [sic] has ever been" (p. 347). Our task is to develop a new educational philosophy that both provides a critique of the current crisis and draws on utopian thought to develop specific goals and means for reconstructing society.

This task requires some dramatic changes in our present ways of thinking. For one thing we need a new orientation toward the future. Brameld conceived of both the past and future as real entities that influence the present. The present, in fact, is the least real of the three, for it is too fleeting to grasp and once focused on becomes part of the past. In our day-to-day existence, "we constantly embrace the future even when we believe that we are concerned with the present" (p. 381). Consequently, one must develop some understanding of the future to truly know the present and past (p. 381). Brameld illustrated this point by noting that any construction or coherent plan (e.g., a musical composition) "is one in which each step is so arranged that those at the conclusion are supported by, but also contribute to, the steps taken toward the beginning" (p. 381). The construction of a building illustrates the same point as the initial foundation's design is determined in part by its future requirements which are assumed to be real. Therefore, while the overall building design is influenced by history and present cultural and physical factors, it is also in part determined by beliefs about the future or "future meanings." It is possible that "future meanings" may equal the influence of past and present meanings (p. 381).

The analogy is extended by Brameld to economic, political, educational, and social affairs. These are affairs, as Brameld noted, "in which what we *have* done, and what we will do, affect at every moment what we *do*" (p. 381). In short, the careful analysis of the future is essential in dealing with the "choice between contraction or expansion of freedom, between wholesale destruction or planetary peace" (Brameld 1971, 382). The reconstructionist does not claim to know humankind's inevitable destiny nor does he or she accept that "the groove of the future is already mysteriously cut" (p. 382). But, the reconstructionist orientation "does hold that to know what the future should be like is essential to knowing what it could be like, and that, if we implement our choices with sufficient determination, we can determine what it will be like" (p. 382).

Brameld's views regarding the reality of the future are closely related to his beliefs about knowledge and goal seeking, and he took the position that every human is a "goal-seeking animal" (p. 384). Here again he criticized the progressivist approach to psychology that recognizes the reality of ends and means "but at no time does it allow either—especially ends—to crystallize or absolutize so as to become a criterion of the other"

(p. 385). Instead, the emphasis is placed on the process of goal selection and an experimental approach which tends to reject an activist position during times of social crisis. As a result, the orientation of progressive educational philosophy tends to induce complacency by encouraging satisfaction with short-range, vague goals rather than with the specific goals required for a revolutionary culture (Brameld 1971, 385). Brameld rejected the progressive constraints on goal seeking and argued that we must focus instead on some key questions. First, where does our society want to go? Second, how do we define "goals"? Finally, what is meant by goal seeking?

Brameld accepted, in part, the behavioral psychologist's view of humans as conditioned animals and rejected any notion of fixed goals reflecting human nature. Brameld also agreed that humans were motivated by drives, but he believed that attempts to distinguish between primary drives such as survival, and secondary drives such as appreciation of music are, by and large, artificial. Brameld reasoned that the so-called secondary drives may well have a dominant influence on human behavior. In this sense, culture may determine needs as strongly as needs determine culture (p. 386). Taboos are perhaps a good example of cultural determination of needs. Still, the assertion that no goals are fixed does not prevent us from ascertaining the most important human *wants* for a given period of time or developing goals oriented in that direction. In short, we can attempt "to specify the ends of human nature" for a given cultural period (p. 387).

Brameld assumed further that "most people in most contemporary cultures so passionately seek to achieve their own goals as expressed in their own ways that their lives are devoted to this effort whether or not clearly and consciously they recognize what they are doing" (p. 388). Thus, utopians have perceived a significant fact, that is, that "human beings must have goals in which to believe and for which to struggle, if they are to be fully human beings" (p. 388).

Our ability to determine our goals or interests is facilitated by our ability to prehend, a term Brameld borrowed from Alfred North Whitehead. Prehension is described by Brameld as

> the unity, the organic wholeness, of natural events that constitute experience. It is a unified kind of awareness that precedes and succeeds "apprehension"—that is, the analyzed awareness of an event by which we recognize its component parts. (p. 389)

One's perception of time, therefore, is prehended both "before and after it is being apprehended" (p. 389). In the final analysis, prehension

> is a duration or specious present. Only secondarily do we become aware that it can be divided into distinct . . . instants that succeed one another like

ticks of a clock. Its prehended meaning is just as real to us, if not more so, than its apprehended meaning; indeed the former is indispensable to the latter. (p. 389)

We have all experienced both prehension and apprehension, the former when attending a concert the latter when waiting for a train or an appointment with our dentist. Brameld notes that prehension and apprehension are somewhat similar to Dewey's concepts of "immediate experience" and "consummatory experience" (p. 390). There is also a similarity to certain ideas in Gestalt psychology. Goals, too, may be prehended, not to the exclusion of reflective analysis, but simply as another form of knowledge as when one prehends the essential *being* of humanness (p. 391).

Though humans may have the ability to prehend and delineate goals that represent their most important wants at a given time, they are frequently diverted from this task. Among the main factors that interfere with the human goal-seeking process is ideology. Brameld defines ideology as "the complex of attitudes, beliefs, ideas, purposes, and customs that expresses, more or less systematically and more or less accurately, the programs and practices of a culture" (p. 395). Defined in the most sinister way, ideology functions to rationalize cultural practices. In essence, "it is the effort in everyday symbols of every age to depict itself to itself" (p. 395). In its final form, it becomes a "verbal and sometimes pictorial or auditory superstructure that sanctions the supporting substructures of real institutions and practices" (p. 395).

Ideologies are historical in the sense that they are products of the past. This frequently creates serious problems because "they do not always mirror the structures and practices of their cultures with equal accuracy" (p. 395). Thus, ideologies often represent a cultural lag as they "tend to move more slowly than the cultures they symbolize" (p. 395). From a neo-Marxian viewpoint, the ideology of any culture may become "a device by which its institutions are preserved even when their effectiveness has declined" (p. 395). Brameld (1971) claimed that in our present sociocultural context, the major institutions that shape our public organization tend to be ideological in a negative sense, because they are manipulated by those seeking to maintain the status quo. For instance, there was a frequent tendency in our culture to glorify the economic slogans of "free enterprise," "individual initiative," "private property," and so on. The unreflective glorification of such slogans could encourage "self-righteousness in those who benefit most from the preservation of inherited patterns, just as it may encourage complacency in those they dominate" (p. 396).

Even more disturbing was the strong possibility that "the institutions that assist in rationalization—newspapers, churches, schools—may be totally unaware of the disparity between their ideological descriptions and cultural actualities" (p. 396). An understanding of the role ideology plays in society is crucial to education and requires a "culturology of knowledge that is contributive to maximum understanding of any given cultural order, . . . its process, or its goals" (p. 396).

It should be clear that Brameld's understanding of ideology was never limited to false consciousness. He described ideology as an attempt to portray the values and practices of a culture and noted that this could be done more or less accurately. Thus, ideology was not an intrinsically negative element of culture. On the contrary, ideology was a necessary component of those attempts to describe what the future ought to be. In this sense, ideology had a utopian potential and was always linked to utopian thought. This utopian potential remained even when ideology had assumed a degenerate form which no longer accurately represented the current society and culture. We will explore this issue further in Chapters 4 and 6 where the connections between reconstructionism and critical pedagogy are examined in some detail.

We must look again at the idea of utopia introduced earlier. When related to ideology, utopian thinking may be viewed in a new light. Utopias may be described as "any world picture of attitudes, practices, ideas, and institutions that supports a conception of culture admittedly different from the prevailing one" (p. 396). A utopian may look backwards and forwards for cultural designs. Generally speaking most ideologies contain some utopian elements, either past or future oriented. Furthermore, utopias of one historical period may become ideologies in the next. The lines between ideology and utopia may be blurred in some historical periods or very sharp as in our current crisis culture (p. 397). When the latter situation develops, there can emerge a demand for "new goals and new institutional arrangements under which we can resolve problems that old arrangements have generated and failed to resolve" (p. 397).

The problem facing our age is that we have yet to design a new utopia. As Brameld (1971) argued,

> the obligation before us is twofold. On the one hand, we need to analyze and interpret the use of ideology as a device for retarding democratic change and blocking utopian propensities. On the other hand, we need to intensify such propensities by fostering future-looking attitudes and defining cultural objectives while developing effective strategies for reading them. (p. 398)

The new utopia in its broadest outlines would feature the expansion of freedom. It would be earthwide and "geared to the satisfaction of the maximum number of wants of the maximum number of people" (p. 398). To accomplish this design requires a careful analysis of our current ideologies as well as those economic and political forces that operate on individuals and groups. Ultimately we must develop a process to validate our new knowledge and apply it to the task of cultural transformation.

To facilitate these goals, Brameld developed the concept of "consensual validation" in the process of truth seeking. He explained the need for this process as follows:

> The truths of vital experiences in group life within any culture are determined, not merely by the needful satisfactions they produce, but also by the extent to which their import is agreed upon and then acted upon by the largest possible number of the group concerned. Without this agreement, followed by actions that test the agreement, the experience simply is not validated as "true." (p. 400)

Brameld (1971) viewed consensual validation as perhaps "the most important single process within the subdiscipline of epistemology" (p. 400). By this process knowledge may be "both safeguarded against false consensuses and guided to truer ones." By the process of sharing and agreement, "consensual validation becomes the expressed consent of one (or many) that the testimony another has offered makes sense in that it articulates an experience that both recognize" (p. 401). Brameld does not consider consensual validation a strange or unusual idea inasmuch as "the sciences, too, presuppose agreement about and, hence, the ability to communicate evidence germane to a given field of research" (p. 401).

The consensual validation process has several implications. First, no matter how scientific our methods, "a point arrives at which...we must either agree or disagree upon the testimony that has been offered as to the nature of our goals" (p. 401). It may take some time before we arrive at such a "moment of validation," yet at some point we must conclude that "our goal seeking interests can be sharpened no further" (p. 402). If we have proceeded carefully and considered the best available evidence, some conclusions must be drawn.

One might note the severe limitations on any person's ability to ever become fully aware of another's experience, and take the position that no standards exist by which the similarity of experiences can be proven. This is similar to the anarchist argument in political philosophy which "denies the existence of any sound criterion of social order other than the judgment of the individual" (p. 402). All this should give us just reason to proceed carefully, but it does not excuse us from the need to reach agreement on goal setting. Brameld agrees with the progressivist view that "the workability of an agreement still remains the final test of its truth," but he argues that reconstructionism places more emphasis on group action and interaction.

Brameld (1971) believes that there is much evidence to suggest that consensual validation could work in practice. "Even non-literate people do, after all, reach group decisions in the more or less explicitly expressed belief that they understand one another's interests" (p. 405). The problem is that this has too often been done hastily and uncritically. In our culture the jury system, democratic government, collective bargaining, and the scientific community all represent approximations of consensual validity. Although these are far from perfect examples, they do represent our current best attempts at decision making consistent with human wants and rights. Consensual validation is also a self-correcting process which is experimental in nature.

Finally, consensual validation is a practical necessity with applicability to the construction of local and worldwide cultural designs. Basically the process is meant to help groups "achieve effectiveness, direction, and clear-cut commitment" (p. 408). The primary aim of consensual validation is to overcome the negative effects of the relativism encouraged by progressive education with its traditional and moderate orientation (p. 408). The reconstructionist philosophy, while stressing the modifiability of consensual validation, goes further than progressivism and emphasizes the possibility and necessity of constructing new cultural designs.

If consensual validation were successfully implemented, the result, in part, would be what Brameld (1971) refers to as "group mind." This term is both descriptive and normative and refers to the goals of a group. Group mind also functions as both an end and means to new goals, and Brameld believed that the social structure exerted a powerful influence on group mind (p. 409). In other words, group mind may be viewed at times as part of the current ideology or alternately as a device for cultural transformation. In the latter sense, it would be the outcome of consensual validation (p. 410).

The issue of ends and means is a complex one as it relates to group mind. "If ends are crucial determinants of the 'group mind,' the means are the strategies by which groups attain their ends" (p. 411). Means, therefore, are powerfully influenced by the same conditions that shape goals. This situation creates a dilemma because action must be taken to realize goals. If action is taken too late, the goals may not be achieved; if action is taken too soon, it could engender a backlash of forces that might be stronger than those seeking change (p. 411). There is no formula to determine precisely the right time for action, but Brameld did advocate certain guidelines when dealing with the attempt to achieve group mind on ends and means. The means chosen must be completely democratic. The ultimate aim was to build a group mind that confirms the maximum consensus of a majority whose views are continuously strengthened and revised, if necessary, by the critical scrutiny of minority critical reaction. In this sense, a normative conception of group mind as ends and means is a reflection of the most inclusive cultural conception possible (p. 411).

A consideration of the reconstructionist view of the distinction between truth and knowledge is helpful for understanding the application of group mind. Brameld (1971) accepted the progressive's position that knowledge is the product of tested experience, while "truth is the particular consequence that emerges in the solution of a present problem through the application of intelligence" (pp. 411–12). But he believed the reconstructionist position to be broader. Knowledge designates those "agreed-upon experiences utilized by past and present cultures" and is equivalent to the ideological meaning of group mind (p. 412). Knowledge is also a valuable resource for developing utopian content. But, the value of such knowledge tended to degenerate over time as it lagged behind cultural change. Therefore, "truths" established via consensual validation "can be distinguished, relatively speaking, from knowledge" (p. 412). These truths become the "utopian content" of the group mind and reflect the active determination of cultural goals and means. Such truths are not merely ideas but actions as well, that is, they include the application of group mind to the reconstruction of institutions, values, and practices. To sum up, reconstructionists seek truths that are achievements of the group mind. These truths may be viewed in two ways: As *means* to assist in the achievement of desired utopian goals, and secondly as *ends*, that is, utopian goals or new cultural designs (p. 412).

SUMMARY

This relatively simplified review of the work of Rugg, Counts, and Brameld reveals the rich complexity of the reconstructionist views on educational reform. The reconstructionist legacy has changed in significant ways over time. It also reflects numerous conflicts between the positions of its leading proponents as well as internal conflicts within each proponent's work. The most important tension in reconstructionism was the conflict between pragmatism and the attempt to construct a radical program for sociocultural transformation. This was a tension the reconstructionists never resolved. Perhaps it is an aporia at the heart of any project for radical change. In any event, we shall observe that a similar tension continues to permeate the discourse of radical educational reform.

The reconstructionists have always represented a marginal, or at least minority, view on education and sociocultural criticism. Still, traces of their theoretical position can be found in the discourse on educational reform over the past forty years. In the next chapter, we turn to an examination of the critical response to social reconstructionism and the traces of reconstructionist thought evident in mainstream approaches to educational theory.

3

RECONSTRUCTIONISM: CRITICAL REACTION AND INFLUENCE ON MAINSTREAM CURRICULUM THEORY

CURRICULUM THEORY AND PRACTICE

Social reconstructionism has provoked a good deal of critical reaction, but more often it has been ignored. As noted in Chapter 1, there is reason to believe that reconstructionism has had relatively little impact on mainstream curriculum reform since 1945. But the issue of the impact and relevance of reconstructionism is complex, and social reconstructionism remains as an important component of the social meliorist tradition in curriculum history (Kliebard 1986). In this chapter we examine this issue from two vantage points: the critical reaction to reconstructionism and the traces of reconstructionist thought in mainstream curriculum theory. This is not meant to be an exhaustive account of either area but an attempt to gain a general sense of how reconstructionism has been perceived since its emergence.

Reconstructionism is the sort of educational theory that has tended to provoke critical reaction from all segments of the political spectrum. Conservatives see reconstructionism as far too radical. For many liberals it appears as a threat to bourgeoisie values, and it seems naive or insufficiently radical for some on the far left, orthodox Marxists in particular. Given such reactions, one might wonder why reconstructionism would ever have had much appeal. On the other hand, reconstructionism is one of the approaches to a critical theory of education that ultimately refuses to accept simple answers, whether conservative, liberal, or radical. In particular, the reconstructionists attempted to construct a critical approach to education that did not abandon pragmatism but focused on its more radical implications. This attempt to reconcile liberal values, pragmatic inquiry, and the need for a social orientation motivated by utopian thought was problematic from the start. Nevertheless, it can be argued that some variant of a critical pragmatism similar to reconstructionism remains an important basis for developing a theory of critical pedagogy to orient educational reform (see Cherryholmes 1988 and the discussion in Chapters 5 and 6 in this text). We turn now to the critique of reconstructionism and some example of reconstructionist thought in curriculum over the past several decades.

THE CRITICAL REACTION TO RECONSTRUCTIONISM

It is not surprising that Brameld's work has prompted some of the sharpest critical reaction to reconstructionism. His first article published in the *Social Frontier* in 1935 emphasized the strong Marxist influence on his thinking and provoked a swift negative response. When Brameld (1935) stated that while we should "never resort to [violence] indiscriminately. Let us not characterize violence as categorically immoral under all circumstances" (p. 56), he questioned the efficacy of the democratic method as sufficient for achieving necessary social reforms. This view and an apparent willingness to entertain the need for a "period of oppression" before the collectivist society is established were especially disturbing to William H. Kilpatrick. Kilpatrick was a highly regarded educator who some have labeled as a reconstructionist (e.g., Bowers 1969, 1970; Giroux 1988c). He criticized Brameld's application of Marxism to education because it "rejects democracy, rejects education as a process of social change, and rejects (at least during its revolutionary program) the ethical regard for the personality of others" (Kilpatrick 1936, 274).

Brameld (1936a) objected to Kilpatrick's criticism for several reasons. First, he suggested that Kilpatrick simply did not understand Marxism. Marx was deeply concerned with democracy in its most meaningful form, that is, the more equitable distribution of income and wealth or economic democracy. This, in Brameld's view, was superior to the liberal conception of democracy associated with a capitalist system wherein the actual exercise of democracy was limited to a powerful minority. In essence, the capitalistic form of democracy was oligarchic and, therefore, not a true democratic system (p. 4).

Brameld argued that Marx had a high regard for education, but for education to play a role in social change, educators must try to persuade their students of the superiority of a collectivist state (p. 3). Of course, the true impact of education would not be achieved until the capitalist class lost its control of the state and society.

Finally, contrary to Kilpatrick's assertion, Marxism does hold a high ethical regard for the personality of the individual. As Brameld explained,

> ...it is possible to argue that Marxism as a humanitarian and democratic philosophy is motivated by the deepest regard for others. Not only is release of the values of personality its supreme aim, but even "during its revolu-

tionary program" it strongly disapproved of more coercion than absolutely necessary to achieve or maintain authority. (p. 5)

R. Bruce Raup (1936) and John Dewey (1936) also voiced objections to Brameld's arguments supporting the relevance of Marxism to education. Raup (1936) was especially critical of the Marxist analysis of the class dynamic, and summarized the Marxian conception of classes as follows. For Marxists, classes were

> ...distinctly separable in economic interest and culture; the members of opposed classes are stereotyped into one-motive brutes to be hated and unseated from their power; culture is economically determined throughout and economics is, therefore, the key area in which to take hold for purposes of control. (p. 107)

Raup considered these Marxist principles to be "dangerous oversimplifications" and insisted that:

> we break the spell of such undiscriminating power words as class struggle and choose the dynamics of our cause in the actual purposive relations where our differences can be seen for what they are humanly worth [and] by means other than coercion, intolerance, and exclusion. (p. 109)

Dewey (1936) was happy to associate himself with Raup's position. Dewey rejected the Marxist absolutism in which "class struggle determines of itself the course of events and their issue" (p. 241). He preferred a social to a class viewpoint and identified democracy "as our basic frame of reference and the origin of the directive ideas of educational action" (p. 242).

Responding to these concerns, Brameld (1936a) first noted that there were two basic aspects to the Marxian doctrine. "It is both a world-view, a system of philosophy, on the one hand, and a social methodology, a planned program of action, on the other" (p. 7). Marx had not always drawn a clear distinction between these two aspects, and furthermore, "in the last analysis the two aspects synthesize into a methodological system or a systematic method..." (p. 7). Nevertheless, the distinction was important and sufficiently clear so that "it is quite possible to select one or the other for special consideration" (p. 7).

Brameld had originally discussed his conception of the two basic aspects of Marxism in his first book *A Philosophic Approach to Communism* (1933).

> Communism is primarily a political doctrine; yet, seldom in the history of great movements has there been one where philosophy is admitted to play such an important role.(p. 8)

Brameld quoted Marx's comment "Philosophy cannot realize itself without the abolition of the proletariat. The proletariat cannot abolish itself without realizing philosophy" (p. 8). Also, according to Lenin, "we must understand that without a solid philosophic foundation no natural science...and no materialism...can stand in the battle against the storm of bourgeois ideas" (p. 9). This emphasis on the interaction and duality of philosophy and method in Marxism is apparent throughout Brameld's book.

Raup and Dewey's criticism of Brameld focused mainly on the philosophic or worldview of Marxism. But in his article, Brameld (1935) had focused on the relevance of Marxian methodology. Although Brameld (1936a) felt that Raup's criticisms were extreme, he did concede that

> ...the marxian world view, like all world views, frequently approaches and at times crosses the border of an absolutism which one trained in the functional, pragmatic point of view finds trouble in accepting. (p. 8)

Thus, Dewey's rejection of the Marxian position that "the class concept is a strictly realistic apprehension of the existing social reality and of that which exists," was, according to Brameld, "an expression of loyalty to the premises of his entire operational philosophy" (p. 8). But, Brameld was not concerned with the soundness of the Marxian system or worldview. Rather, his concern was directed at "the significance of the Marxian concept of class struggle as a method...for effecting basic changes which so many liberals agree should be made" (p. 8).

As explained in Chapter 2, a unique aspect of Brameld's (1936a) theoretical position was his attempt to demonstrate that the Marxian class concept was "simply an application in particular of what these educators (Kilpatrick, Dewey, and Raup) may very well mean by the scientific method in general" (p. 8). Since our present view of problems affects the kinds of hypotheses we select as solutions, and since the problem, application, and solution always interact, "the more deep-rooted the social problem..., the more thorough-going the suggested solution, and the more vigorous the means of correction" (p. 8). Therefore, Brameld did not see Marx's total commitment to the class-struggle hypothesis (not yet proven false) as incompatible with Dewey's scientific, instrumentalist approach to education. We have seen in Chapter 2 that Brameld gradually modified and softened his position regarding the relevance of Marxism to education. However, he always retained a neo-Marxist dimension to his thinking, because he saw in Marxism many valuable insights relevant to curriculum and social reform.

Perhaps the most influential critic of reconstructionism was John Dewey. That conservatives and liberals reacted negatively to Brameld's "Marxist" orientation was not surprising. However, left-progressives like Dewey (and even Kilpatrick) might have been thought to be more sympathetic toward the reconstructionist project. Dewey did believe that the schools should assist in the reconstruction of society, but his view of this process differed from those of Rugg, Counts, and Brameld. Dewey wanted the schools to participate in the intellectualization of society. In other words, the "method of intelligence" should serve as the best vehicle for transforming society. If we fail to develop our student's critical skills of inquiry and reflective thought, they might leave school "without power of critical discrimination, at the mercy of special propaganda, and drifting from one plan and scheme to another according to the loudest clamor of the moment" (Dewey 1935b, 334).

Dewey also agreed with the reconstructionist position that the school should have a definite social orientation. In his words, "It is not whether the schools shall or shall not influence the course of future social life, but in what direction they shall do so and how" (Dewey 1937, 236). The way the schools actually "*share* in the building of the social order of the future depends on the particular social forces and movements with which they ally" (Dewey 1934, 11). Teachers cannot escape the responsibility for assisting in the task of social change (or maintenance), and this requires a particular social orientation. Considering such sentiments, it is not surprising that some have regarded Dewey as a social reconstructionist (e.g., Bowers 1969; Giroux 1988c).

Richard Rorty (1986) has called our attention to Dewey's seeming ambivalence on this issue. Dewey and John Childs coauthored two chapters in the *Educational Frontier* (1933b). Their collaboration prompted an interesting exchange concerning the role of the school in the process of social reconstruction (Dennis 1989). In an exchange of correspondence, Childs questioned how far the schools should go to educate "for a cooperative community life when the actual life of the community is still controlled by the policy of individual initiative and private competition" (Childs, as cited in Dennis 1989, 2). Childs wished to conserve essential democratic values but also wanted to use education to help students adjust to cultural and social changes. Dewey, in contrast, urged Childs not to be overly concerned with the "apparent *immediate* situation" (Ibid.). For Dewey, the central aim of education was "to prepare individuals to take part intelligently in the management of conditions under which they will live, to bring them to an understanding of the forces which are moving to equip them with the intellectual and practiced tools by which they can themselves enter into direction of these forces" (Dewey and Childs 1933a, 71). But as Dennis (1989) illustrates, Dewey also appeared to embrace the reconstructionist sentiment when he stated "Education must itself assume an increasing responsibility for participation in projecting ideas of social change and taking part in their execution in order to be educative" (Dewey and Childs 1933b, 319, quoted in Dennis 1989, 2). The changes to which Dewey and Childs refer included "a better, more just, a more open and straight forward, a more public society" (p. 318). Dennis (1989) believes that this flirtation with reconstruction was as far as Dewey ever went (p. 2). On the other hand, Giroux (1988c) reads Dewey as a central figure in the reconstructionist movement.

It is probably a mistake (or at least an oversimplification) to indiscriminately lump Dewey's ideas with those of reconstructionism. Indeed, this is a point Dewey himself took great pains to make clear. Dewey's insistence on a commitment to the method of intelligence was posed as just that—a commitment to a method and not to any specific social outcome as a result of employing that method. He never suggested that the schools should seek to indoctrinate students to a particular social view, although he realized that schools could not help transmitting some social values. The problem, as Dewey saw it, was that no single system of social values existed in our complex modern society. To attempt to indiscriminately follow all the values of the current society would be to abandon the method of intelligence (Dewey 1937, 235).

Dewey thought that educators had three basic choices. First, they might accept the present state of social confusion and conflict and drift in an aimless fashion. Second, "they may select the new scientific, theological, and cultural forces that are producing change in the older order; may estimate the direction in which they are moving and their outcome if they are given freer play, and what can be done to make the schools their ally" (Ibid.). The third choice was the conservative option which strives to use the schools to help maintain the old social order against forces of change. In this case, a choice was made to support the values of the status quo that function to secure special privileges for certain dominant groups. Dewey, of course, rejected the first and third choice and opted for the second. One might argue that since Dewey appeared to reject reconstructionism, it is logical to conclude that a fourth choice was available. Nevertheless, Dewey argued for the method of intelligence by which the schools seek to help students acquire the understanding and insights to enable them "to take part in the great work of construction and organization that will have to be done, and to equip them with the attitudes and habits of action that will make their understanding and insight practically effective" (p. 236).

Dewey understood intelligence as a process to help clarify and achieve desirable social ends but, of itself, it recommended no social end save the necessary social conditions under which the method might survive and be applied. Thus, Dewey would only recommend that teachers hold to an orientation that emphasized the application of intelligence to social problems. This commitment to intelligence could be conceived as instrumental, empirically grounded, and designed to draw tentative conclusions. To go beyond that point would be indoctrination which Dewey rejected.

Dewey was quite specific in his response to reconstructionist critics who attacked his instrumental approach as neutral. He did not believe it was neutral, mechanical, aloof, or "purely intellectual" in analyzing social conflict. Those who had concluded that modern advances in science and technology "were creating a new type of social conflict" did so not via inculcation but by the "intelligent study of historical and existing forces and conditions. . ." (Dewey 1935a, 9). Furthermore, Dewey believed that his method "cannot fail. . .to support a new general social orientation" (p. 9). Consequently, inculcation or indoctrination was unnecessary. In due time, the application of the method of intelligences would reveal ways to improve the social order.

> The upholders of indoctrination rest their adherence to the theory, in part, upon the fact that there is a great deal of indoctrination now going on in the schools, especially with reference to narrow nationalism under the name of patriotism, and with reference to the dominant economic regime. These facts unfortunately *are* facts. But they do not prove that the right course is to seize upon the method of indoctrination and reverse its object. (Dewey 1937, 238)

Dewey defined indoctrination as the "systematic use of every possible means to impress upon [students] a particular set of. . .views to the exclusion of every other" (p. 238). This is a more extreme view than the interpretations of indoctrination or imposition expressed by the reconstructionists. Rugg, Counts, and Brameld insisted on the open access to information, even though it might contradict their views of the "good society." Thus, the deliberate suppression or distortion of information was ruled out as a valid means of inculcation by the leading reconstructionists.

But such qualifications were not enough for Dewey. The only form of indoctrination he entertained was the assertion that the method of intelligence was the preferred approach to education. "If the method we have recommended leads teachers and students to better conclusions than those which we have reached—as it surely will if widely and honestly adopted—so much the better" (Dewey and Childs 1933a, 72). It would appear that Dewey believed that any attempt to inculcate preconceived conclusions could block the method of intelligence, even if the open access to alternative views were maintained. Any such risk was not worth the effort, given Dewey's optimism regarding the potential efficacy of his method if fully applied.

The Social Frontier was a journal published to provide a major forum for reconstructionist and other progressive ideas. Its first editor was George Counts, and many of the journal's editorials promoted reconstructionism. But frequently, contributions by Dewey, Kilpatrick, Boyde Bode, H. Bruce Raup, Goodwin Watson, Kenneth Benne, and William O. Stanley served to diffuse, neutralize, and undercut the more radical orientation of the reconstructionist discourse. These were educators of great status among progressives, and their collective opposition to reconstructionism was apparently too difficult to overcome (Bowers 1969, 190–99).

Since 1945, Brameld has received the bulk of the criticism directed towards reconstructionism. To a great extent, this can be explained by the moderation of Rugg and Counts' views and Brameld's (1971) identification of himself as *the* true proponent of reconstructionism. Brameld tended to view Rugg and Counts as progressives, although he retained a respect for their ideas. Among the most significant critiques of Brameld's work in the postwar period were those by George Kneller.

Kneller is especially critical of Brameld's faith in the potential of teachers, who are essentially conservative, to implement a reconstructionist program. Since the school functions as an agency of the state, and given "the realities of contemporary politics,...no government will allow its schools to be used to promote a point of view that it opposes" (Kneller 1965, 88). The process of change in any society is constrained by deeply entrenched cultural ideas and practices which shape how people conceive of change, what is necessary, and how to achieve it. By "inviting the student to accept a program of social reform that society has not yet approved, reconstructionism can only alienate him [sic] from his [sic] culture" and community (p. 89).

Kneller (1971) argued that Brameld built his case on the assumption that the behavioral sciences have revealed universal values preferred by most humans. But this was only one possible interpretation of recent research. It is more accurate to state that "the established empirical conclusions of the behavioral sciences are scant indeed, and they carry no certain implications for education" (p. 65). Indeed, the conflicts among behavioral scientists appear at least as numerous as those among educators. Consequently, reconstruction cannot claim to be based on reliable scientific knowledge of human behavior.

Kneller (1971) wondered if the "permissive indoctrination" espoused by Brameld is not really a contradiction in terms. In practice, it would be impossible for a reconstructionist teacher to be both ideologically committed and scientifically detached. Yet both goals seem required by reconstructionism. Given the thoroughly pluralistic nature of our society, how could it even reach consensus on a reconstructionist program without turning to some totalitarian form of organization? This would entail a radical change in our political system, "and individual enterprise would be severely enfeebled" (p. 66). Kneller concluded that "reconstructionism seems to lead to a collectivist society, in which men [sic] would believe anything to be true provided it was attained by scientific methods and achieved through informed social consensus when persuasively presented" (p. 66).

Now it is interesting to note that Kneller does not seem to be opposed to an individual teacher acting as if he or she were a reconstructionist. But he cannot conceive of a widespread, successful reconstructionist movement in our culture for all the reasons mentioned earlier. Like Brameld, Counts, and Rugg, Kneller accepted that good teaching included indoctrination. Education "is essentially a normative affair," and teachers will teach what they think "students ought to learn" (Kneller 1971, 106). Nor did Kneller believe indoctrination in a democracy to be a contradiction in terms. He cites Jefferson's view that "the qualifications for self-government are not innate. They are the result of habit and long training." We have every reason and need, therefore, to teach the fundamental principles of democracy "in short to inculcate a belief in them" (p. 106). This does not preclude a critique of these beliefs since the very right to do so is an essential element of democracy.

Thus, Kneller understood that teaching is not a neutral enterprise. Rather it involves "a method inducing acceptable belief" (p. 107). This is quite different from inculcation by threatening, coercion, propagandizing, and so forth. Unlike these methods, teaching "involves rationality, judgment, critical dialogue, and defensibility" (p. 107). Taking a position similar to Brameld's "defensible partiality," Kneller speaks of a teacher giving students reasons for the views he or she would like to transmit. Thus, the teacher's views are also submitted to critical analysis by the students. As Brameld (1966–67) has argued, "without such inquiry any kind of normative position becomes itself indefensible" (p. 100). Kneller (1971) also agrees with Brameld's view that "rational teaching has its own limitations" (p. 107). Teachers must use other than rational means to accomplish learning, especially in the early grades. In short, good teaching involves relating methods to the desired learning outcome, and this often requires inculcation. In the final analysis, it would seem that Kneller accepted much of Brameld's argument, yet rejected a general movement for curriculum reform based on reconstructionist principles.

Herbert Kohl (1980) has reconsidered Counts' question "Dare the Schools Build a New Social Order." He agreed with Counts' support for social and economic democracy, which Kohl characterized as a humane and "community-oriented" variant of socialism. But he cautioned that socialism remains a highly negative concept in our society. In fact, educators who advocate socialism still risk being fired in certain circumstances. These circumstances placed a significant restriction on a teacher's ability to support this political orientation in classrooms. Although Kohl preferred democratic socialism to capitalism and its ethic of selfishness, he was not unduly disturbed by such limitations. A teacher retained the ability to promote political values via example rather than direct instruction (pp. 58–59).

Furthermore, Kohl (1980) did not believe that schools could build a new social order. "We cannot give our children the responsibility for redeeming the world we either messed up or at least witnessed being destroyed" (p. 60). Our public school systems simply will not tolerate teachers who try to use their work to promote a social movement. In addition, as a group, teachers tend to be conservative, and this political orientation is reflected by the major teacher organizations. Finally, the actual influence teachers have on students is both limited and unpredictable. In practice, most teaching seems to promote capitalism, and this outcome is unlikely to change (p. 62). So schools are clearly not neutral but biased toward the status quo. Like Kneller, Kohl agreed with much of the reconstructionist critique but not its proposed solution.

What, if anything, can teachers do? For Kohl (1980), probably the most important thing is to enable students to study schooling itself, for example, textbook bias and the unequal aspects of school structure and financing. To the extent students come to see how schools operate and whose interests they serve, they might be able to conceive of other (perhaps better) ways of doing things (p. 62). While he agreed with the reconstructionists' assessment that schools propagandize for the status quo, this did not justify an educational program based on counterpropaganda. Teachers were entitled to reveal their own views but only following a fair presentation of the issues involved. The key objective is to have students sense that the issues studied have a significant effect on their own lives.

James E. McClellan (1968), another critic of reconstructionism, accepted Brameld's contention that human culture was in a state of crisis with nuclear holocaust as the greatest potential danger. He also agreed that most public education actually miseducates and tends to make things worse. What is more troubling, our educational system appears to function democratically while, in fact, control is largely exercised by "a minority class and...a bureaucratic structure which is quite unresponsive to the real needs of people" (p. 179–80). This dominant minority is best served by status quo institutions in politics, economics, and culture and uses education to maintain its privileged position.

But McClellan believed that despite Brameld's accurate sense of the culture crisis and the role of education, he remained an "architect of confusion." While Brameld dealt with the right issues, he failed to "open any genuinely new perspective on the human condition [or] on the nurture of human values through education" (p. 152). Moreover, his messianic zeal prevented him from developing any effective program to help educators even "do their jobs just a little better" (p. 152). In particular, Brameld demonstrated a naive assessment of social power relations as they shape schools and the very limited influence of classroom teachers. Thus, there were no adequate explanations of how to turn his utopian vision into practice. In the end, Brameld is "a partisan in the very struggle he seeks to define." (p. 262). For some it might be possible to combine the role of "judge and litigant" or "dramatist and protagonist"; however, "Brameld does not succeed" (p. 162).

Far more negative critiques of reconstructionism have been made by Frederic Lilge and D. R. Barnes. Lilge (1952) claimed that Brameld had transformed educational philosophy into ideology to be used on behalf of certain social groups. By defining truth as social consensus, the reconstructionists ask us "to hold as true that which men [sic] like to believe and what they wish to happen" (p. 251). This mode of thought, reconstructionism being an extreme instance, "holds no future for education but leads into the dead end of anti-rationalism" (p. 256).

D. R. Barnes (1971) compiled a list of the major problems with Brameld's educational theory:

1. Brameld's commitment to "defensible partialities," if not indoctrination, is a tendency toward indoctrination and propaganda.
2. His collectivist approach and emphasis on the group neglects the needs of the individual student.
3. His commitment to a global system of world order is utopian, unworkable, and an instance of indoctrination.
4. His philosophical categories are imprecise and inadequate for analysis.
5. Social consensus on social self-realization is a conceptual oversimplification which does not apply in all decision-making situations. For instance, questions involving technological issues might best be settled by informed elites. (p. 158)

Barnes' first criticism is tautological, since the very act of education (as many of Brameld's critics acknowledge) involves an aspect of and tendency toward indoctrination. The second criticism was addressed in Chapter 2 where the individual versus society was rejected as a false dichotomy. Neither the individual nor society should be neglected by educators, and the reconstructionists, as well as Dewey, Raup, Childs, and other progressives, were seeking to redress what they saw as an overemphasis on individualism.

Regarding the charge of utopianism as applied to Brameld's commitment to a system of world order, Brameld would accept this characterization, but not the negative connotations of the critique. For Brameld, it was critical that we applied utopian thinking to the quest for world order. To do otherwise, was to neglect "a central purpose of education" (1965, 6). He constantly argued that the failure to think in utopian terms limits our ability to develop alternative solutions to critical problems like poverty, war, population growth, pollution, and so forth. He further explained his commitment to world order as an instance of a "defensible partiality." Like all such partialities, it must be subjected to the rigorous critique of reflective inquiry and abandoned should it prove to be ill conceived.

In terms of Barnes' fourth criticism, Brameld has acknowledged that his philosophical categories are not definitive but only one way of approaching an analysis of educational philosophy. This particular criticism of Brameld has also been raised by Elizabeth Eames (1966–1967) who held that Brameld's categories did not account for an existentialist position like Kneller's or the analytic approach of Scheffler (p. 90). As such, the categories are not fully inclusive. More seriously, they are not discrete. On many issues, Brameld's categories overlap and often collapse into two major categories—one traditional the other experimental. In addition, Eames claimed that while some major educators did not fit into any of Brameld's categories, others could easily be included in more than one. In the final analysis, these were really not four philosophical categories but merely "different ideas about programs for the schools..." (p. 91).

In fact, Brameld (1971) had been influenced by both existentialism and logical analysis but believed these positions amounted to "subsidiary contributions" not equivalent to his four major philosophical categories. He admitted that his mode of categorization could, at times, place rather different philosophies in a particular group. But more importantly his distinctions were most significant "when they are considered... in terms of their metacultural assumptions and cultural roles" (p. 97). Education is a universal process by which cultures evolve. When viewed in this context, "philosophies of any sort require a significance that they can never acquire so long as they continue to be treated as self-contained systems of thought" (p. 97). In the end, a classification model should be tested not by "a claim to exclusiveness, but its fruitfulness in clarifying and solving the problems of contemporary education" (p. 96).

With reference to Barnes' (1971) criticism of social-self-realization, Brameld (1971) has acknowledged that this process does not apply equally in all situations. Nevertheless, he insisted it was an element in *all* decision making and, thus, must always be taken into account. For example, we must establish some consensus regarding which decisions are to be considered technical. The key point is that social-self-realization is the critical element (or should be) for decision making regarding major social problems. Technical "experts" may be able to provide important information regarding the benefits or efficacy of various technological projects, but this does not address the fundamental normative issues of concern to reconstructionists. Echoing the views of Rugg and Counts, Brameld believed that building a new social order could never be reduced to mere technological expertise.

Barnes (1971) was also critical of Brameld's views concerning social change. He charged that while Brameld rejected the orthodox Marxist analysis of change via revolutionary class conflict, he had not constructed an adequate alternative. Brameld's latter writing includes various attempts to describe the ways by which social change can occur, for example, via diffusion, assimilation, and acculturation, "but Brameld does not describe *how* to initiate such processes nor *when* to do so. [And]...he has not offered an adequate theory on the basis of which change strategies could be devised" (Barnes 1971, 172).

One of the more serious general critiques of reconstructionism has been made by C. A. Bowers (1969). Bowers viewed most progressives, along with the reconstructionists, as "radicals" proposing a program ill suited to our society and culture. He acknowledged that the progressives were divided into various factions, some of whom were critical of reconstructionism. Nevertheless, he argued that the reconstructionists eventually came to dominate the progressive movement. The best evidence for this is, in his view, the success of the "life adjustment" educational movement from 1945 to the early 1950s (Bowers 1969, chap. 6).

Bowers was not persuaded that more moderate progressives like Kilpatrick, Bode, and Dewey were significantly different in their educational philosophy from reconstructionists like Rugg, Counts, and Brameld. He was convinced, for example, that Dewey urged teachers to join in the class struggle and overturn social values in conflict with the goals of a reconstructed educational program (pp. 43, 76, 121).

Bowers identified four major problems with reconstructionism. First, it promoted an "ubiquitous sense of mission" which frequently tended to obscure the need for a more critical analysis of important issues. Second, it was naively utopian in its faith that education could solve all social ills. Third, it uncritically assumed that all men really seek the good life, and fail only out of ignorance or false consciousness. Finally, the reconstructionists lacked a realistic view of the teacher's actual role in our society. According to Bowers, teachers have never had the power or inclination to carry out anything like the reconstructionist program.

Earlier reform movements had accepted the basic values of our culture and focused on correcting individual instances of unfair treatment from within this value framework. In contrast, the reconstructionists tended to reject some important social values while focusing on fundamental institutional and structural reform (p. 51). As Bowers put it, "to claim that the rise of a collectivist order is irrevocable; that the national economy should be put on a production for use basis, and that Roosevelt had failed to fulfill his mandate to make revolutionary changes in American life, seemed both unduly radical and alarmist" (p. 125). Yet Bowers was aware that the radicalism of the reconstructionists tended to be qualified. When their views "are compared with those held by other dissident groups during the latter part of 1934, they appear to fall largely within the mainstream of liberal thought" (p. 125). This is certainly true of much, if not most, of Rugg's and Count's work as discussed in Chapter 2. Brameld's views did present a relatively more radical challenge to mainstream thought, and even Rugg and Counts raised some serious challenges to mainstream liberal theory as applied to education.

Bowers (1969) believed that reconstructionists like Counts and Brameld moved further to the left after 1935 while the majority of progressives rejected Marxism and were more moderate (p. 152). The earlier presentation of Counts' work in Chapter 2 contradicts this view. Even in the case of Brameld, it is a complex question. Brameld's early work reflected a strong Marxist orientation, but he constantly modified and qualified his views of Marxism throughout his career. So while Brameld did bring a more "radical" theoretical orientation to reconstructionism, he also moderated his position significantly after 1935. Bowers acknowledged Counts' strongly anticommunist views and his role in driving the communist element from positions of power in the American Federation of Teachers (p. 166). He also acknowledged the reconstructionist's support of the American war effort from 1940 to 1945 (pp. 188–92).

But such reservations have little relevance to Bowers' overall position. For instance, he asserted that the decision to terminate publication of the *Frontiers of Democracy* in 1943 (formally *The Social Frontier*) actually rejuvenated the reconstructionist influence among educators. The sudden cancellation of this journal freed restless reconstructionists "from the constraint of participation in an organized group that had been indelibly associated in the public mind with radicalism" (p. 201). Given this new freedom, the reconstructionists were only connected by their general view that the schools should be used to help define and accomplish necessary social change. Without the encumbrance of a radical image they could appeal to a much wider audience. Bowers also maintained that the reconstructionists' power was further enhanced by the decline of the Progressive Education Association which had tended to be dominated by child-centered educators. Given all this, the reconstructionists were placed in a position to influence teachers who rejected Marxist theory but "were more receptive to the idea of a community-centered school that fostered democratic living" (p. 204).

Bowers insisted that this new approach to reconstructionism was still radically at variance with the traditions of our culture's mainstream educational philosophy. Those he defined as proponents of this latter form of reconstructionism included H. Bruce Raup, George Axtelle, Kenneth Benne, and B. O. Smith. These "reconstructionist" educators cloaked their radicalism in a revised philosophical rhetoric. Whereas earlier reconstructionists tended to "disparage individualism" and promote a collectivist social orientation, the "new" reconstructionists argued for a new society based on an "uncoerced community of persuasions" (p. 207). To Bowers, this was clearly a "logical extension" of the earlier reconstructionist views. It meant that social policy would be based on the collective analysis and consensus of *all* who were affected by it." It was the application of the method of intelligence to social problems and, thus, the ideal representation of democratic planning. This interpretation indicates why Bowers saw little significant difference between Dewey and the reconstructionists.

According to Bowers, the "new" reconstructionist's were as utopian as their predecessors. They assumed that total agreement could be reached on social issues and "without resorting to compromise" (p. 207). They rejected compromise as a basic goal, because it contains the major faults of compulsion, that is, it does not promote the growth of intelligence and character via intercommunication. And Bowers reminds us that, to the "later reconstructionists, 'growth' meant giving up one's own individually held values and ideas and adopting instead the collective judgments of the group" (p. 207).

According to Bowers, to implement the reconstructionists' democratic planning ideal would require a "radical" restructuring of our basic political and economic institutions. This process of change would entail the "endless polling" of those involved as well as a massive reeducation campaign. Bowers claims that the new reconstructionists "were deeply suspicious of the individual who refused to go along with the decisions of the group" (p. 208). By regarding such individuals as undemocratic, the meaning of truth and social consensus became indistinguishable.

Bowers also argued that this latter variant of reconstructionism was more "seductive" than the earlier more direct attacks on capitalism. Pleas for democratic living, planning, and cooperation all "expressed loyalty to the ideals of the country" (p. 212). This was particularly true of the wide appeal of the "life-adjustment" curriculum. Bowers claimed it would be incorrect to see the life-adjustment movement as an approach to curriculum significantly different from reconstructionism. The "basic tenets of life-adjustment educators and...moderate social reconstructionism" were similar and several reconstructionists (as defined by Bowers) served on commissions that supported the life-adjustment curriculum (p. 214). Bowers acknowledged some "slight," nonsignificant differences between the two approaches. The life-adjustment groups tend to emphasize the "4-H" dimension of education, for example, practical training for family membership, dating, child rearing, health, etc., while the reconstructionists placed more emphasis on community membership. However, the life-adjustment position is "easily derived" from reconstructionism. Both groups shared a commitment to democratic problem solving, a group orientation, the value of "immediate" verses "historical experience," and the priority of general rather than specialized education. Both groups sought to help shape their students character "in accordance with their own vision of the good society" (p. 216). Bowers believed that the widespread implementation of the life-adjustment curriculum would have been a significant "transformation" of our society.

Thus, despite the rhetoric for democratic consensus, the new reconstructionism was ultimately a program of psychological and social pressures to bring about group agreement and a disguised form of social engineering. Education was seen as an "ideological weapon" to gain the individual's adherence to the group as opposed to the earlier forms of education which sought to "emancipate" the individual. According to Bowers, this new form of reconstruction reached its zenith between 1948 and 1951 (p. 238).

In the 1950s, there was a renewed reaction to the reconstructionist philosophy by writers such as Mortimer Smith, Arthur Bestor, Robert M. Hutchins, Frederic Lilge, and others. Bowers claimed that the influence of the new forms of reconstructionism had largely ended by 1954. Even so, the persistent view that our schools can help solve social problems (including race relations, foreign policy, technology, etc.) indicates that at least this aspect of reconstructionism has become a "conventional" part of educational wisdom (p. 253). This was an unfortunate development, in Bower's view, since all such approaches amount to variants of Dewey's instrumentalist educational philosophy. This approach to curriculum posed "a fundamental threat to a society that depends upon a citizenry that understands its past traditions and yet is free from prejudice and popular misconceptions" (p. 254).

For Bowers, we still had a viable alternative to reconstructionism, that is, to enable the individual to become intellectually free in the sense of escaping the unconscious influence of society. Instead, the reconstructionists have sought to replace education with politics. Rather than a "countervailing force" defending and promoting the individual's capacity for intellectual freedom, reconstructionism urged educators to take sides as another faction competing to influence students (p. 254).

Bowers' analysis of reconstructionism appears to be incorrect in several respects. For one thing, the criteria he uses for identifying reconstructionists or reconstructionist groups are suspect. In his critique, collectivism becomes a pejorative code word for any educators who seemed to emphasize the "group" in any significant way. To begin with, as Dewey, Brameld, and others have argued, the group versus the individual or student versus society are false dichotomies. Neither of the terms in these dichotomies can exist without the other in both a figurative and a literal sense. The individual is produced by groups and, obviously, all groups are composed of individuals who help shape group behavior. The interaction is reciprocal but can be out of balance. As the split among the progressive educators illustrates, the dispute over how much relative emphasis the group and individual should receive had been going on long before the development of reconstructionism. Furthermore, it is quite possible that one could use an emphasis on the group in education to help reinforce the status quo (e.g., nationalist education). Thus, reconstructionism had to be far more than an educational program emphasizing the group, community, and collective action in order to consider it a "radical" threat to our democratic culture.

The same is true of the focus on social problems. Here Bowers neglects or underestimates the very real differences between instrumentalists like Kilpatrick or Bode and reconstructionists like Counts or Brameld. As indicated earlier in this chapter, there is even some significant tension between Dewey and more moderate reconstructionists like Rugg. Such differences are not trivial. In a superficial sense, most (if not all) educators, regardless of their ideology, hope our schools will help to improve the social order. The critical question is how one conceives of the school's role in this regard. Ironically, Bowers' approach, that is, to free the individual's intellectual capacity so that he or she is free of unconscious social pressure, seems very similar to Dewey's method of intelligence. Why would Bowers want such intellectual freedom if it could not be used to critique the social order and consider the possible need to improve on it? And is this position not similar to Dewey's view? Dewey recommended no specific "blueprints" for a new society, only the method of intelligence so that students themselves would have the capacity to examine critically the current social order to help create a better world. Yet Bowers places Kilpatrick, Bode, Counts, Brameld, and Dewey in the same category and describes the life-adjustment curriculum as a continuation of their thought.

The issue is not so clear-cut in all cases. Bowers does point to certain similarities between reconstructionists, moderate progressives, and life-adjustment educators. These similarities do need to be explored and discussed. But Bowers has failed to link all these educators in any significant way. His notion that a widespread adoption of the life-adjustment curriculum would have radically transformed our society is not substantiated. How would it have accomplished this? In what fundamental ways would our society have changed? The superficial and innocuous nature of the life-adjustment curriculum seems only to have posed a threat to educational quality. Perhaps the radical transformation feared by Bowers was akin to the "rise of mediocrity" alleged by the recent educational reform report such as *A Nation at Risk* by the National Commission on Excellance in Education (1983). But he does not make this sort of claim and hints at a darker, totalitarian potential in what he calls "new" forms of reconstructionism.

Bowers' conclusions are even more puzzling given his critique of the reconstructionists' naivete regarding the potential power of teachers to change society. It is true that teachers alone have a relatively limited chance of causing radical social change. Historically, schools and teachers have served the dominant forces in the social order and, by and large, continue to do so. How then would life-adjustment educators affect radical social change? Bowers argues that the reconstructionists' appeal was directly proportional to the extent that they moderated their views. Paradoxically, then, if one follows Bowers' logic, the more successful the reconstructionists might have been the *less* significant or radical would be the changes implemented. But Bowers argues that this was really a pseudomoderate, reconstructionist program which disguised its radical dimensions in order to gain popular support. In essence, it remained a radical approach that sought to change our society as we knew it. Yet Bowers never makes clear how this would or could happen.

Bowers also argues that this new reconstructionism reached its apogee between 1948 and 1951, one of the most reactionary periods in U.S. history. He makes no mention of McCarthyism or its impact on education and other institutions. This analysis is also insensitive to the politicization of education by dominant conservative groups, a phenomenon documented by Counts and others since the 1920s and 1930s. The reconstructionists understood and accepted that education was a thoroughly and essentially political institution. In this sense, education generally functioned in the interests of some group or class and was never neutral.

Bowers suggested that education could be neutral in the sense of emphasizing the individual's right to acquire the intellectual capacity essential for a "free life." He also recommended that all students be well-grounded in the knowledge of history, particularly the history of their culture. These are both reasonable (albeit limited) positions, but they are also political and ideological, not neutral. Furthermore, there is a tension between these two views; a necessary tension, but one never articulated by Bowers. It would seem that a grounding in one's history provides an orientation to help the individual make decisions and solve "social problems." Otherwise, what is the point of transmitting this knowledge? The reconstructionists too wished to provide students with an orientation. Their program would involve a thorough grounding in history and the human sciences as well as an effort to develop a student's critical disposition and competence. And it would focus on the future with tentative suggestions (defensible partialities) for constructing a better social order. Rather than dealing directly with the subtleties of these issues, Bowers has overgeneralized based on questionable criteria and dismissed reconstructionism, progressivism, and life-adjustment as mere variations on a radical theme antithetical to our culture and society.

RECONSTRUCTIONISM AND RECENT DEVELOPMENTS
IN MAINSTREAM SOCIAL EDUCATION

Curriculum Theory

Of all the curriculum areas, one might expect that traces of reconstructionist thought or influence would most likely appear in social (or social studies) education. And so we will confine most of our analysis in this section to the social education curriculum as it has developed over the past four decades. However, the boundaries of social education are not always clear, and this analysis takes place against a background of persistent debate and lack of consensus regarding what social education is or should be (e.g., Shaver 1967; Barr, Barth, and Shermis 1977; Hertzberg 1981; Morrisett and Haas 1982; Dougan 1983; Stanley 1985a; Jenness 1990). In some instances, therefore, we will often draw on related mainstream sources some might not usually see as part of social education.

Although a main purpose of this study is to discuss the links between reconstructionism and recent developments in radical educational reform, it is also useful to examine the recent development of mainstream reform in this process. For one thing, an analysis of mainstream curriculum theory and reform in social education helps reveal those elements of radical reform that have penetrated educational discourse. In addition, we can examine the radical utopian potential in mainstream social education rhetoric and rationales. These mainstream approaches often share some of the same concerns raised by the reconstructionists. In short, an analysis of mainstream theory provides a background to better illuminate the complexity of radical approaches to educational reform and to place it within the context of the wider discourse on education.

It is necessary to qualify the use of the term "mainstream" in this context. This term is not used here in any definitive sense, but it does describe certain tendencies in the field of social education regarding what is considered important as well as the prevailing methods of investigation (e.g., see Newmann 1984; Stanley 1985a). Mainstream social educators can be contrasted with radical or critical types. Those in the mainstream have tended to analyze and develop social education curriculum within the limits of a dominant discourse that has prevailed throughout most of this century. This discourse contains conservative and liberal elements but generally accepts the major institutions and values of the culture and society, as well as prevailing methodologies for research. In contrast, critical social educators have challenged the very nature of the mainstream discourse and its methods of inquiry. So while neither the mainstream nor radical positions are definitive and disagreement exists regarding who might be included in each category, the terms do provide useful analytic categories that point toward two significantly different approaches to rationale building, criticism, and research.

The Crisis Metaphor[1]

One major focus of reconstructionism was the view that we were in a "crisis" situation which demanded immediate and radical changes. This metaphor was applied to our social, economic, political, and cultural formations. It is interesting to note the continuing and pervasive use of this metaphor in recent decades. I have made no attempt to document this usage from 1945 to the present; however, a variety of examples dating from the 1960s should suffice to illustrate that the metaphor is alive and well.

We could start with Silberman's *Crisis In the Classroom* (1970), although readers might prefer some earlier starting point, perhaps the antiprogressive reaction of Adler, Bestor, Connant, Rickover, and others in the 1950s. In any case, Silberman did perceive a crisis, but he explained it mainly in terms of "mindlessness." If only our educators took a more rational approach and availed themselves of the model provided by the British open schools, our educational system could be so much better. While his analysis and recommendations were too superficial and reductionist, Silberman did document some very serious problems similar to those pointed to by the reconstructionists. The key point is that he perceived public education to be in a state of "crisis" which required major changes.

Silberman's relatively simplistic analysis aside, the so-called "crisis" in education must always be understood in terms of the larger society and culture. Despite the postwar prosperity and military power of the United States, many intellectuals continued to express a deep anxiety and concern for our future, and this was often represented in terms of the crisis metaphor. For example, C. P. Snow (1959) spoke of the dire threats to our society and the illusion that we had much time left to make necessary changes. Others echoed these sentiments and argued that because our world had become so dangerous, only utopian conceptions of change were relevant and capable of making a meaningful difference (e.g., Platt 1966; Brown 1968).However, for many, the threats to our very survival were so great that acute pessimism was the most rational view (Clark 1968; King-Hele 1970). For example, the gloomy report of the Club of Rome (Meadows et al. 1972), presented what the authors held to be empirical verification for the sense of global crisis and pessimism. Indeed, they predicted a global economic collapse unless the nations of the world acted quickly to take measures toward a zero level of growth.

---

1. The work of John Lucas (1984) has informed much of the analysis in this section.

In a similar way, H. G. Vonk (1973) argued that we had lost control of our own technology which now threatened to destroy its creator. Ironically, we had the technological capacity to change our destiny for the better, but we appeared to lack adequate "social know-how." Ultimately, this lack of social analysis could result in the triumph of technical means over social ends. Yet our society remained committed to an outmoded curriculum focused on the past. This mode of thinking created a nonthreatening situation, since most people tended not to concern themselves with past controversies. And in those cases where they do, this only serves to divert their attention from the very real problems of the present.

One explanation for our failure to fully appreciate and react to our present crisis was its unbelievable nature. For example, the threat of nuclear war, while real, was almost incomprehensible (Lens 1976). Over time we have lost oursense of urgency regarding this issue and become numbed to the state of "permanent emergency." We seem to be confronted by an irrational lunatic process, wherein every individual's behavior appears to be sane but their collective behavior is psychotic. This behavioral process seems to be self-sustaining and beyond our control.

Nielson (1977) described a similar phenomena that he labeled "psychic overload," resulting from our sense of crisis. People, more and more, feel overwhelmed and powerless. This is not merely a case of apathy, as some have argued, but the result of deep confusion and cynicism. What we seem to fear is that "in our society, we have lost the capacity to shape our collective destinies, to control our lives together as social beings, or even, in any proper sense, to understand them so that we can see where we are going and try to forge a rational. . .society where human beings can flourish" (p. 46). We sense that "our collective lives are out of control." The causes of this existential doubt are so complex, deep, and obscured that we can barely grasp any of the process. The result is a sense of acute anxiety and the prevailing sense that we cannot act in any effective way to save ourselves. Or as Nielson put it, we hold "no rational hope for changing society and, indeed, we would not even know how to change it if we could" (p. 47).

In the face of such threats we appear to "take refuge in the hope that the holocaust won't happen, and turn back to our individual concerns. We deny the truth that is all around us" (Schell 1982, 230). Perhaps the single best account of this modern sense of crisis and its effects is found in Christopher Lasch's *The Culture of Narcissism* (1979) and *The Minimal Self* (1984). It should be clear that the sense of crisis posed by the reconstructionists in the 1930s has continued to the present. Certainly Brameld never gave up this metaphor, and while others might differ with his educational views, many shared his deep sense of threat to our society and culture.

The crisis metaphor has been used by educational critics from the right and center as well as the left. One could contrast Brameld's views in the 1950s with those of Bestor, Rickover, Connant, Hutchins, and others. In the present debate over educational reform we have conservative critics like Bennett, Bloom, Hirsch, Ravitch, and Finn who, if nothing else, seem to share a sense of educational crisis with left critics like Apple, Freire, Giroux, and Shor. Indeed, some have argued that the right has co-opted much of the left's rhetoric and effectively turned it against radical reform in the current debate (Giroux 1988c). It is instructive to examine the recent development of mainstream social education rationales in this context. What we seek are traces of reconstructionist thought.

Mainstream Rationales for Social Education

In 1960, Engle argued that the following rationales were most typical of the field of social education. First, there was the view of social education as the social sciences "simplified for pedagogical purposes." The rationale has roots which can be traced to the work of Edgar Bruce Wesley in the 1930s (Wesley and Wronski 1958). The social science rationale was given increased credibility by the early work of Jerome Bruner. He sought to make the structure of the scholarly disciplines (that is, the concepts, generalizations, theories, and methods) the focus of curriculum and instruction. Bruner (1960) believed that such structures could be taught in some intellectually defensible form to students of all ages (p. 14). This knowledge was of most value, because it could be transferred to new situations and provided the best means for dealing with social problems (p. 7). The work of William T. Lowe (1969) is among the best examples of this approach as applied to social education.

A second rationale described by Engle (1960) was social education as primarily concerned with the development of "good" citizenship. Engle argued that this rationale was further subdivided into three different approaches. One served to synthesize and apply the content of the social sciences to analyze "broad social problems of the society" (p. 46). A second focused on the process of decision making (often referred to as problem solving or the reflective method) as it applied to the "practical circumstances" faced by citizens. Within this framework, content would be that "data which is relevant to the problems which citizens confront and to the exercise of the process by which information (and perchance values) is brought to bear on these problems" (p. 46). The third approach to citizenship referred to the unreflective inculcation of content and values deemed essential. More specifically, this involved "content (including myths as well as facts) by which budding young citizens may be indoctrinated with the 'right' beliefs and attitudes believed to be necessary for the unity of the nation and the loyalty of her citizens" (p. 46). Those advocating this approach assumed that they knew what knowledge and values were essential and saw little need to focus on developing the skills necessary to chose among competing values. Engle (1964) rejected indoctrination and argued that we should promote decision making abilities as the central rationale for social education. He emphasized the development of one's reflective abilities to "maximize the opportunities for students to make intelligent and thoughtful decisions with respect to what to hold valuable, what to believe, what guiding ideas or principles to accept, and what course of action to follow" (p. 41).

A decade after Engle's analysis, there was another major effort by Barth and Shermis (1970) to describe and define the field of social education. A more complex elaboration of their position was published seven years later by Barr, Barth, and Shermis (1977). These authors described three major rationales that largely determined how content is selected, organized, and taught. The three rationales were somewhat similar to Engle's description of the social education field but more detailed. In their initial analysis, these authors argued that each rationale they described was conceptually distinct and prescribed a different model of curriculum and instruction (Barth and Shermis 1970; Barr, Barth, and Shermis 1977). They referred to these models as the "three traditions" which included social education as (1) citizenship transmission (CT); (2) social science education (SS); and (3) reflective inquiry (RI).

Like the indoctrination approach described by Engle, the citizenship transmission rationale was based on the assumption that social educators have an obligation to inculcate certain basic knowledge and "self-evident values" that are fundamental to a democratic society. In practice this tends to be a rather conservative view of democracy and does not provide students with the capacity to deal with value conflicts (Stanley 1981c, 1985a). For the most part, the citizenship transmission rationale involved the unreflective inculation of knowledge and a value system that served the interests of dominant groups in society.

The social science tradition was an extension of the Wesley and Wronski (1958) position as described by Engle (1960). This rationale gained wide support during the 1960s and early 1970s, the high point of social studies projects.[2] For our discussion of this approach, we will treat history as if it were a social science discipline, although this oversimplification neglects some serious differences in theory and method (Shaver and Berlak 1968). Nevertheless, in the majority of the social studies projects developed during the 1980s, the content and methods of history were treated much

---

2. See, for instance, the November 1972 issue of *Social Education* wherein twenty-six projects were analyzed and only four were not based directly on social science disciplines.

like social science content. Students were to learn the essential knowledge (concepts, generalizations) and methods of the particular discipline studied. While some argued that we should seek to integrate, synthesize, or "orchestrate" history and the social science disciplines (e.g., Lowe 1969; Senesh 1971; Kuhn 1971), others held that a particular discipline should provide the basis for, or, at least, a central focus of social education (e.g., Morrissett 1967; Krug 1967; Bestor 1969; Morrissett and Stevens 1971; Wiggins 1972).

The social science rationale remains influential but often in superficial ways, for example, the typical K–6 elementary social studies curriculum and the various social science requirements or electives offered at the secondary level. It has also received considerable criticism. Shaver (1967) has noted two serious problems. First, the social sciences lack adequate concern for those analytical concepts necessary to inquire into public issues. A scientific approach is appropriate for description but not to application in practical circumstances, and the latter is "a prerequisite to citizenship training" (pp. 588–89). A second serious problem is the tendency of social science classes and programs to limit the focus to the induction and training of members of a professional "guild" (p. 590). This is a serious shortcoming, because "social studies education" should be "general education" and not limited to the interests of the college bound.

It is not that the social sciences do not have much to offer the process of social analysis and citizenship education. What was lacking, in Shaver's view, was a systematic approach and the necessary concepts for dealing with value dilemmas. Many educators have held the naive assumption that the scientific method (often inadequately reduced to the process Dewey posits in *How We Think*) is appropriate to solving all problems including value disputes. But in fact "there is nothing in social science methodology that will help the citizen decide the latter" (p. 590).

Newmann (1967) questions the very relevance and existence of separate social science disciplines with unique structures as suggested by Bruner and others. For Newmann, this "resembles a quest for a transcendental intellectual natural law" (p. 593). We have not yet defined or identified such structures, and inquiry in the disciplines appears to be governed by abstract concepts of structure which await our discovery. Even if structures were identified (a doubtful prospect), we lacked the principles to guide the selection of which structures apply in concrete situations. These principles must be found via philosophical analysis and cannot be derived from the social sciences themselves (p. 594). To date, we have no clear evidence that exposure to social science has given us greater control over our destiny or resulted in social progress. Indeed, the social sciences have often been applied to thwart human progress. The central point is that we cannot use the social sciences in our unresolved quest to define "what constitutes the good life, progress or social improvement" (p. 595).

We should also recall that curriculum theorist Joseph Schwab (1968), a leading proponent of studying the social science disciplines, also emphasized the study of the syntax of the disciplines. By syntax, Schwab referred to the "variety of modes of inquiry, of patterns of discovery and verification. . ." (p. 301). Without a sufficient understanding of the syntax of the disciplines, students would be unaware of the various conceptions of truth which result from "the context, the structure of problems, evidence, inference, and interpretation which constitutes the syntax of discovery behind each statement. . ." (p. 301). To learn the syntax of a discipline, therefore, is to be aware of the different forms of inquiry employed to arrive at conceptions of knowledge.

Schwab (1968) also emphasized the changing nature of a discipline's substantive structure. The concepts, generalizations, and theories of one period often become outmoded as new knowledge and new ways of looking at knowledge develop (pp. 302–04). Consequently, to teach the structure of the social science disciplines is to teach more than the awareness of a fixed body of facts, concepts, generalizations, and theory. It is also to enable students to understand a process of change in which one structure often provides the very beliefs and questions which lead to its destruction and replacement by another and so on. Educators, therefore, must not only choose which facets of a given structure are to be taught, but also the tentative nature of every structure and the process by which it changes.

In the early 1970s, Bruner (1971), a leading proponent of teaching the social science disciplines, began to question the relevance of his views of the structure of the disciplines concept to the real social problems faced by citizens in their daily lives. He wondered if a focus on the study of social problems might not be a better way to organize the curriculum (p. 20). More recently, Bruner (1986) has even rejected many of the grounds for his original position on curriculum and turned to a more phenomenological, narrative, and interpretivist analysis of society and knowledge.

We can see that neither the dominant citizenship transmission rationale nor the social science alternative appear to deal adequately with the issues raised by the reconstructionists. The former amounts to unreflective indoctrination and generally assumes knowledge and values to be unproblematic, while the social science tradition emphasizes value neutrality (except for valuing the scientific method itself). Thus, both rationales for social education ignore the reconstructionist's claim that knowledge can never be selected or presented in an unproblematic, value-neutral way. Certain things are included and others excluded from any curriculum, and this content selection necessitates some reflective process to establish value criteria and goals.

What about the third tradition identified by Barr, Barth, and Shermis, (1977), that is, reflective inquiry? This tradition might seem to have the greatest potential to incorporate the "radical" concerns raised by the reconstructionists, but a close examination of this rationale reveals some basic conflicts between the two positions. A wide variety of social educators have advocated some variant of this rationale (e.g., Hunt and Metcalf 1955, 1968; Massialas and Cox 1966; Oliver and Shaver 1966; Newman and Oliver 1970; Nelson 1974; Nelson and Michaelis 1980; Fraenkel, 1980; and others). While this approach has much progressive potential, in the main, the proponents of reflective inquiry have been resistant to some of the fundamental aims and practices of reconstructionism. In part, this is because the reflective inquiry tradition is closely linked to the work of Dewey (Barr, Barth, and Shermis 1977; Barth and Shermis 1980b; Shermis 1982; Shermis and Barth, 1980, 1982, 1983). As noted earlier, while the reconstructionists were strongly influenced by Dewey, there were important differences in their respective positions. Those differences and several other powerful cultural influences, for example, our cultural conceptions of individualism, political pluralism, and a market economy, form an intellectual environment in which the development of reflective inquiry has diverged from reconstructionism (Stanley 1979, 1987; Whitson and Stanley 1988).

Some examples of specific reflective inquiry rationale proposals will help illustrate the tension between reconstructionism and reflective inquiry. Brubaker (1967) and Goldmark (1968) are among the very few social educators who directly acknowledge some of the contributions of the reconstructionists, specifically Counts and Brameld. Like these reconstructionists, both Goldmark and Brubaker accepted the need for some level of indoctrination in education. But in Brubaker's (1967) view, the best solution is to indoctrinate "students to accept the view that inquiry into all matters is absolutely desirable" (p. 120).

Goldmark (1968) agreed with this argument and was critical of Counts and Brameld for overemphasizing the ends of society above the *means* for achieving those ends (p. 41). She proposed the teaching of the inquiry process itself as a sufficient rationale for social education, because it reinforced a central aim of education, that is, to develop responsible, scientific methods of judgment, including the analysis of values (p. 2). Goldmark argued, somewhat like Dewey, that this process "should lead to a reconstruction of values to meet the demands of a rapidly changing world" (p. 2). Reflective inquiry was more than a mere cognitive process. It also involved affect, since it emphasized a basic *"commitment to a way of behavior*—to doubting and questioning" (p. 7). Such behaviors, then, constituted the goals of the reflective inquiry rationale. Social "problems" were too vague to serve as the core focus of social education, and we cannot predict with any certainty the specific knowledge students will require in the future. The only point that seemed certain was that students "will probably always need a *method for making judgments* about problems—for evaluating alternatives and making decisions" (p. 43). Students should also be taught "to *want* to cope with problems" (p. 43). Subject matter could serve as a means to this end but was "never an end in itself."

Other advocates of a reflective inquiry rationale have made a rather different argument. These social educators usually combined a focus on the inquiry process with the study of social problems and the democratic ethos or core values of our political culture. Hunt and Metcalf (1968), for instance, argued that our people were so divided over which parts of the culture are of most value that our society was in "turmoil, transition and crisis" (p. 45). This is quite similar to the social and cultural crisis posed by the reconstructionists. To confront this crisis, Hunt and Metcalf recommended that schools should teach reflective inquiry into the "closed areas" of our culture, that is, those areas generally excluded from critical examination. These include such areas as social class, sexuality, nationalism, religion, and certain economic issues, among others. By avoiding analysis of closed areas, schools tended to concentrate on trivial subject matter and deprived students of learning how to cope with inter- and intrapersonal value conflict within a democratic culture. As a result, our present forms of schooling could contribute to the growth of totalitarian beliefs (p. 28).

Hunt and Metcalf argued that content, inquiry processes, and values could be imposed, because individuals often did not see the connection between their personal problems and the "broader social maladjustments in which they are rooted" (p. 287). In other words, the severe conflicts present in the culture frequently remained hidden or closed to investigation. At best, such conflicts might be perceived by students as aberrations in an otherwise sound social system. It was the task of reflective inquiry to help students penetrate such illusory modes of thought. But Hunt and Metcalf warned that doing so might either "fortify or undermine" basic social beliefs, because we cannot predict the future outcome of decisions made on the basis of reflective inquiry (p. 289). Nevertheless, this is the only way to make social, political, and moral decisions in a democratic culture.

Another significant variant of the reflective inquiry approach to social education is the "jurisprudential" rationale developed by Oliver and Shaver (1966). Oliver and Shaver accepted the need to use education to impose the core values of our culture, or what Gunnar Myrdal referred to as the "American Creed" (pp. 11–12). This creed included the basic rights and freedoms outlined in our major political documents like the Declaration of Independence and the Constitution. While Oliver and Shaver believed the schools should inculcate a fundamental commitment to the creed, they also acknowledged that this cannot be justified in any "ultimate sense" (p. 9). The most persuasive reasons for adopting this rationale appeared to be culture bound and consistent with the Western value of human dignity or the "belief in man [sic] as an end in himself [sic]" (p. 10). Oliver and Shaver also believed we must avoid moral relativism and that people were likely to "intuitively" agree on what best constitutes "civilized" behavior (p. 51). In the end, people must learn to live by "tentative conclusions about ultimate moral meaning" (p. 27).

Oliver and Shaver's approach to social education would have students use an inquiry process to examine various social issues of significance within the framework of the American Creed. They argued, like Hunt and Metcalf above, that social cohesion is not possible without some basic normative commitments (p. 14). To avoid the worst effects of indoctrination, Oliver and Shaver defined the American Creed on two levels. The first level, including the general tenets of the creed, must be imposed on students in an effort to secure their commitment. However, on the second level, that is, the translation of the creed to actual issues or situations, the specific solutions or applications of the creed were to be decided by individuals and groups confronted with particular, concrete problems (p. 14). At this second level the government must guarantee a pluralistic process of choice. The only necessary conditions are that choices must be made via an open inquiry process and the results should not violate the general values of the creed.

As Newmann (1975), another advocate of this approach, has argued, it is never correct to convince students to endorse specific policies (p. 72). This caveat was necessary, because it was seldom clear which policies would best achieve our ends, and for teachers to advocate specific policies might eventually limit a student's opportunity to openly inquire into issues and policy formation. At most, educators should teach the core democratic values and the skills required to make decisions. Other than the commitment to democratic ideals and inquiry, the schools should remain neutral. For example, teachers should never try to persuade students to support specific goals such as the eradication of poverty (p. 166). Furthermore, as Oliver and Shaver (1966) argued, the classroom was not an appropriate place to seek to subvert the basic ideals of our society, since students are not sufficiently autonomous enough to deal adequately with such efforts (p. 14). Educators had a professional obligation to use "our culture as an operative basis for curricular decisions" (p. 26).

Like the reconstructionists, Oliver and Shaver and Hunt and Metcalf have made an effective case for the educational importance of indoctrination. These liberal social educators recognized that schools were not and should not be neutral. They were also aware that knowledge was socially constructed and derived from particular cultural contexts. Such views on social education were a major advance beyond either the impoverished rhetoric of citizenship transmission or the more sophisticated social science education rationale. Still, there are problems that limit the critical potential of either of these particular approaches to reflective inquiry. The limits of the jurisprudential rational of Oliver and Shaver are the most obvious. Oliver and Shaver appear to take the value of our contemporary culture and institutions for granted. True, there remain serious social problems to resolve, but there is little discussion of the possible systemic or structural causes of such social problems. They also appear to assume that our current social structure and institutional arrangements are basically adequate—perhaps even the best system humans could conceive. And given the restrictions they place on educators, students are unlikely to consider radical alternatives to the current system. From a reconstructionist perspective, Oliver, Shaver, and Newmann's work lacked a sufficiently specific theory of social welfare or a utopian vision beyond the rather vague guidelines of the American Creed. For example, why couldn't we oppose poverty on the grounds that it violated the aims of the creed? Thus, Oliver, Shaver, and Newmann have not really solved the problem of moral relativism that they fear. For if, in the end, the application of the creed to specific situations must be determined on the basis of a vote influenced by the relative power of dominant interest groups, how can it serve effectively as a guide for social decisions to bring about cultural transformation?[3]

In contrast, Hunt and Metcalf (1968) argued that we are in a crisis situation and took a more critical view of our sociocultural system. Their proposal to study "closed areas" seems more likely to have students examine controversial alternatives to our current system. They also recognized that there was no way to ensure that this process of social education would not "undermine" certain basic social beliefs or practices. They clearly supported using the schools to help improve the social order and even allowed for the potential for educators to transform the culture. But Hunt and Metcalf's rationale stopped short of the more radical aspects of reconstructionism. Like Oliver and Shaver, they did not urge educators to support goals more specific than the basic democratic ideals and processes. And though their vision was more critical than the jurisprudential rationale, it still lacked a focus on building a "new social order." Much like Dewey, Hunt and Metcalf would leave the future to the method of intelligence, although they did seem less sanguine than Dewey regarding the likelihood that such an approach would lead to a better

---

3. In Chapters 5 and 6, we will examine some other critiques of neo-Kantian theories grounded by the assumption of a priori values.

society. There are also some potential problems with the type of pragmatic theory employed to ground the process Hunt andMetcalf prescribed (Stanley 1989). We will discuss some of the limitations of pragmatic theory further in Chapter 5. There have been many other "inquiry" oriented approaches to social education (see Haas 1981; Stanley 1981a, 1981c, 1985a; and Hertzberg 1981 for more complete surveys), but none seem to have significantly more in common with reconstructionism than those we have examined. However, there are other recent developments in the mainstream literature that address concerns raised by the reconstructionists. While these may be somewhat narrow or limited in scope, they do relate to the reconstructionist project.

Citizen Action and Social Education

Newmann (1975), a leading proponent of citizen action as a major goal of social education, contends that most citizens feel like they lack any significant control over their destinies or even their everyday lives. This reflects many of the views discussed earlier in this chapter by those who hold that our society and culture are in a state of crisis. Newmann posed three possible reasons for this general sense of alienation and powerlessness. First, one could subscribe to some form of power elite theory in which the majority of people are exploited to maintain the position of powerful groups (p. 1). A second possible explanation for powerlessness was rooted in factors that resulted in the oppression of certain groups. This included all forms of discrimination, for example, racism, sexism, and attitudes prejudicial toward youth, the mentally ill, the physically handicapped, the poor, the elderly, homosexuals, ex-convicts, etc. The third explanation for powerlessness holds that social issues "are inherently so complex that man [sic] will never solve them through deliberate rational intervention" (p. 2). Indeed, so many variables seem to be involved that attempts to change the system, at best, result in the temporary illusion of control. We must, therefore, accept that our lack of control is basic to our existence (p. 2).

Newmann accepted that each of these interpretations was partly true, but he insisted that none was sufficient to account for the widespread inability of people to affect public policy (p. 2). Therefore, it made sense to focus on improving citizen competence as a necessary requirement for exerting one's influence in public affairs. Furthermore, if lack of citizen competence could be eliminated as a variable, the other alleged impediments to action could be better tested for actual effect.

Newmann made an effort to distinguish between his approach and most other citizenship programs in social studies education. In his estimation, the other programs tended to emphasize "thinking critically about" or "taking an active interest in" citizenship, while Newmann's emphasis was on exerting influence via action. Furthermore, the current emphasis on developing knowledge of the disciplines, the political-legal structure, decision making, analysis of social problems, and voting were all inadequate to develop the skills necessary to exert influence (pp. 4–5).

For instance, our schools tended to teach students to support such values as democracy, majority rule, equality, due process of law, and so forth. The development of these attitudes was presumed to be the basis of a vigilant and active citizenry. Yet, though these concepts are relevant to the issue of citizen influence, they also tended "to communicate unworkable notions of citizen participation" (p. 6). The net effect was to emphasize the students' need to understand rather than to exert influence. Or put another way, to debate whether or not one should jump in a lake to save a drowning person is no more than an abstract exercise unless those debating the issue know how to swim.

In Newmann's (1975) view, too much emphasis has been placed on abstract reflection at a general level, and he recommended more analysis at specific and concrete levels. Hence, we should focus on local rather than national or global issues, since the former had a far greater probability of solution (p. 6). The key, in Newmann's view, was not mere action but action to exert influence. Thus, much out of school student activity, such as trips to nursing homes and police stations or simulated career experiences, would not meet Newmann's criteria. He used the term "environmental competence" to describe his basic educational goal. He defined competence as "the ability to behave in such a way, or to use one's efforts in such a manner, as to produce the consequences that one intends" (p. 12).

Newmann also believed that by developing the student's environmental competence we can help strengthen the democratic consent ideal, a primary goal of our public education system (p. 46). Without the ability of all persons to participate in the political process, some groups will be better able to subject others to their will (p. 47). Newmann noted that, at present, various forces (including powerful elites and the complexity of issues) often make action difficult or impossible (p. 54). However, he also argued that consent should not be seen as an end that will ultimately be achieved by all, but rather as an ideal goal we continue to strive toward. Indeed, to do less might result in the realizations of a self-fulfilling prophecy of citizen incompetence (p. 54).

Regarding the political role of schools, Newmann maintained that they ought to be as neutral as possible. Since truth cannot be determined unless we are able to examine a wide range of alternatives, school should be committed to a pluralistic model that exposes students to a great "variety of political philosophies and cultural styles" (p. 64). However, the school must not be neutral in its commitment to the democratic consent ideal. Newmann did acknowledge that a focus on improving student's environmental competence might better serve certain more advantaged students in some instances, but he saw this as similar to any curriculum program, for example, foreign languages or sports. In any case, this possibility did not cause him great concern, since any student would be relatively better off with increased environmental competence.

Prosocial Behavior, Imposition, and Social Education

A related but rather different concern was raised by Pearl Oliner (1983) who has criticized mainstream approaches to social education for failing to focus on the development of prosocial behavior. Oliner lamented the decline in our culture of a sense of community and suggested that social educators could help to remedy this situation by integrating the "concept of 'community' into their citizenship education programs" (p. 65). Current approaches were inadequate because they focused almost exclusively on our relation to the nation-state. Oliner acknowledged that this is a critical relationship that helps to create a sense of national cohesion among the very different groups in our heterogeneous population. This traditional focus on nationalism did not, however, function sufficiently to develop relationships among people. What is worse, current approaches to social education often encouraged feelings of alienation antithetical to a sense of community (p. 66). Oliver believed that an increased focus on prosociality could help to begin the process of "community" building.

More specifically, the excessive focus on a citizen's relationship with government often had the following effects. First, this focus on the state encouraged "feelings of impotence and alienation," because it was too complex and remote from most people's daily experience. It also tended "to externalize the locus of responsibility by minimizing personal accountability" (p. 69). Consequently, there was relatively little left for the average citizen to do other than vote and follow the laws. Finally, the current emphasis on the student's relationship to the state failed "to direct student's towards those citizen behaviors which build emotionally satisfying relationships and integrative community linkages" (p. 70).

Thus, the missing element in all contemporary approaches to citizenship education was "that the *relationships of students to each other* are not of primary importance," especially personal relationships (Oliner 1983, 73). Many social educators did emphasize cooperation and reciprocal relationships. But cooperation was generally viewed as an abstract goal, rather than specific forms of individual behavior, and approaches to reciprocity were most often concerned with "the commodity or behavior being exchanged." These typical approaches to social relationships in mainstream social education have resulted in alienation and exclusion. Consequently, an integrated society also requires social interactions in which the basic relationship is persons to each other, and which are characterized at least some of the time by "self-transcendence". (p. 73)

Prosocial education was concerned with direct student relationships in which they were encouraged to act on behalf of others without expecting reciprocation or reward. The focus was on helping, sharing, giving, caring, concern, and altruism. These behaviors went beyond forms of cooperation and were based on mutual benefit or conceptions of interdependence "based on reciprocal satisfaction of need or exchange" (p. 73).

Such an approach to education would not neglect the growth of cognitive competence, because cognitive skills were critical to making competent decisions regarding prosocial behavior and avoiding misguided efforts. Oliner saw such decisions in terms of both a cost/benefit type of analysis, that is, the ability to determine if a situation exists that requires prosocial behavior) and identification of the best contacts (persons) to help us act in a prosocial way.

Oliner believed that one way to achieve her goals was to add prosocial standards "to the normative criteria by which the behaviors of national and global 'heroes' are measured" (p. 75). We needed to provide students with opportunities for face-to-face participation and teach them that (like greed and ambition) altruism and care can also serve as the basis of our political behavior. We could help facilitate this by "personalizing" the study of government, which normally is portrayed as abstract and impersonal to students. In addition, we could try to increase student's awareness of the prosocial activities of ordinary people to give them models for everyday social behavior (p. 76).

In an interesting and complex argument, Leming (1981) has also expressed a concern with the lack of emphasis on prosocial behavior in social education. Like Oliner (1983), Leming was interested in teaching students the value of prosocial behaviors such as caring and altruism, but he went beyond this to argue that we should also teach students to commit to specific moral injunctions or norms "e.g., not stealing, honoring contracts," and so forth (p. 24).

Although Leming's primary focus was on moral education, his views bear directly on the general concept of citizenship education. In reality, one cannot speak of moral and citizenship education as if they were separate entities. As Leming noted, programs "hiding moral education under more appealing labels" (e.g., citizenship education) did not establish a firm foundation for long-term success (p. 24). He also agreed with Aristotle's view that "moral education is fundamentally political education, and moral and civil law represents a systematic and concrete expression of the moral idea; that is, a tested conception of the good life" (p. 30).

Leming's main complaint was that, to date, there has been little evidence to support the effect of contemporary approaches to moral education. In particular, research regarding approaches such as values clarification, values analysis, and cognitive development suggested "that student growth which occurs as a result of these programs is unrelated to social behavior." In short, they have failed "to yield socially significant results" (pp. 7–8).

According to Leming, one major cause for this lack of effect was the overly narrow focus by social educators on individual choice and rational decision making. Most current approaches to moral education (e.g., Raths, Harmin, and Simon 1978; Newmann 1970; Fraenkel 1977; Kohlberg 1975; Nelson 1974; and Metcalf 1971) shared the following features.

1. The development of decision-making skills applied to problematic content.
2. The assumption that reason played the key role in motivating one to act morally.
3. The perception of the morally educated person as independent and autonomous, i.e., "subordinate only to the dictates of...reason and...decision-making principles."
4. A view that the advocacy of specific moral content should be avoided. Certain forms of deliberation were preferred but not specific moral injunctions.
5. The teacher should function primarily as a facilitator in an open, nonjudgmental environment and should use great "caution before advocating any specific moral content."
6. The assumption that moral education generally took place in discrete lessons within the overall curriculum.
7. As a general principle, students should not to be evaluated in terms of the outcome of their moral decisions but only on the quality of their reasoning. (Leming 1981, 12–13)

In sum, the prevailing approaches to moral education eschewed moralizing. Leming believed this behavior was consistent with the ethos of our political culture, but it also has placed social educators in a position that severely limits their potential effectiveness.

Leming relied on current research on prosocial behavior and the earlier work of Durkheim to argue "that the child is not initially led to moral behavior through training in decision-making processes." The challenge, therefore, was to find a means to "initiate children into life in society governed by moral rules while at the same time...not (closing) the door on the development of independent rational moral judgment at a latter point in the child's development." The key point was that the current emphasis on rationality can be dangerous to the child and his/her society "to the extent that it develops in the child the expectation that he/she exists independent of society with no restraints on his/her behavior other than what his/her reason dictates" (pp. 18–19).

For Leming, the foundation of moral education must reflect a commitment to the "rules of collective life within a given society" (p. 19). We must go beyond the emphasis on decision-making skills and consider the role of nonrational processes and the climate of the school to facilitate moral education. While research indicates that reasoning has little impact on the development of prosocial behavior, modeling, empathy, or sharing emotional responses does seem to have a significant influence on the development of such behavior. In addition, there is reason to believe that moralization, properly practiced, could also be effective in increasing prosocial behavior.

Unlike the prevailing approaches to moral education, moralization could provide specific examples of moral behavior to be "learned in naturally occurring social contexts" in which reinforcement would generally be "immediate and derived from what individuals perceived as significant" (Leming 1981, 13). Furthermore, thought often follows action; that is, reasoning "frequently arises out of behavior to explain, interpret, or rationalize experiences" (p. 14). Thus, giving reasons for moral injunctions can also have an important influence on behavior. The point is that while changes in thought can influence behavior, the reverse is also true and too often ignored in current approaches to moral education.

Leming believed that the work of Durkheim provides a theoretical basis for changing our approach to moral education. Durkheim was a structural functionalist who promoted the view that, in general, "existing forms of society serve an essential role in the maintenance of that society's equilibrium and continuing survival" (p. 15). Morality, therefore, consists of systems of specific rules that have been "justified by their efficacy in maintaining a stable environment in which the individual can live with dignity and freedom" (p. 15).

To effect moral development, the school and the teacher must set out to reinforce and model specific moral behavior, especially in the early years. Here the school can play a unique role "because it represents an intermediary step between the affective morality of the family and the more impartial morality of the society" (p. 17). It is critical to the child's full development to acquire the competence to function as a morally responsible member of the society.

Leming recognized that some current approaches to moral education (e.g., Oliver and Shaver 1966) do accept teaching a commitment to higher order principles such as justice, freedom, and human dignity, but these "are stated so generally that they do not suggest specific actions for specific situations" (Leming 1981, 18). What we lack is a willingness to teach students to commit to "specific first order principles—principles containing the content of moral beliefs, e.g.,...always tell the truth, never take what doesn't belong to you, etc." (Ibid.). The latter smacks of moralizing, and has been argued against by most social educators on theoretical grounds, thereby depriving us of a "necessary and essential dimension in the moralization of youth" (p. 19).

Leming (1981) understood that it was not possible to remove all moral ambiguity and that consensus regarding specific moral prescriptions will be difficult. Nevertheless, it was possible to reach a good deal of consensus in terms of what a community held as morally correct behavior, and the community and school should work this out jointly. Those areas where agreement could not be reached should be pointed out and discussed with the students. Some ambiguity notwithstanding, it was "socially preferable to have individuals approach social life deeply committed to specific norms and reluctant to break norms...than to have a citizen capable of reaching elegant and refined decisions in situations of moral uncertainty but lacking any allegiance to a socially-based morality" (p. 24). Of course there are some limits on what the community can promote as moral behavior. For instance, specific injunctions must not violate the basic values embedded in our American Creed. For example, Leming would not accept a community decision to teach students to be racists.

Leming rejected the charge that his approach to moral education would be indoctrination. In his view, indoctrination "refers to attempts to influence others which distort, through oversimplification, misrepresentation, and/or one-sided presentation..." (p. 25). He used the term "directive moral education" to describe his approach. In a manner similar to reconstructionism, Leming argued that we must never distort information or refuse to consider alternative viewpoints, but one can "forcefully assert in a reasoned manner what the right behavior may be for students in a specific moral context" (p. 25). This approach also required that social educators must gradually but consistently expand the role of rationality in moral education as it relates to the child's development as the child moves from lower to higher grades.

One might argue that while current approaches to moral development based on decision making have had little effect, neither have attempts at direct moral instruction been effective. Leming accepted this contention and noted four possible reasons for the limited impact of direct moral education thus far. First, moralizing approaches have often gone to the extreme and neglected the necessary shift to moral reasoning where appropriate. Second, not enough attention has been devoted in research to identifying the specific behaviors that would enable a teacher to have an impact on the development of moral behavior. Third, the constant flux in our value systems in this country has undermined all approaches to moral education but is especially problematic for directive moral education.

Finally, "the societal demand for self-chosen identity as the cultural task of adolescence necessarily involves a degree of moral redefinition with the emerging identity" (p. 28). This emphasis on individual moral choice runs counter to attempts to impose general values. We had little control over the last two variables, but the others could be addressed by social educators to help make direct instruction more effective.

Finally, Leming rejected suggestions that a structural functionalist approach to moral education entails either "uncritical transmission of all existing contemporary moral standards," or developing students with a "slavish and unreflective acceptance of current moral norms" (pp. 28–9). The end of moral education must be "enlightened allegiance" to the moral system. But this must be a just system, and changes will need to be made to the extent it is not consistent with the higher principles of our culture. Teachers can teach the moral order and also point out examples of violations of our normative structure.

One further point: Leming rejected "the social reconstructionist view that schools should play a central role in the social and moral transformation of society" (p. 29). He believed that history demonstrated the reconstructionist's clear lack of effect in this area. Furthermore, he agreed with Oliver and Shaver (1966) that a teacher must operate from the ideals of society and not act to subvert them in the classroom. Clearly Leming presents an interesting approach to social education which, like reconstructionism, does not fit neatly into the three social education traditions posed by Barr, Barth, and Shermis (1977, 1978). But Leming also rejects the reconstructionist program and argues for a far more conservative rather than transformative orientation.

From another vantage point, Shaver (1977) has criticized social education for its frequent "mindlessness." Specifically, he referred to the general failure to develop rational justifications for practice. Shaver and Strong (1982) have continued to explore the process of social education rationale building in an effort to help social educators develop better justified rationales. They make clear that developing the competence to do the philosophical analysis required for building social education rationales is necessary if we are to avoid the mindless selection and application of content and methods. One of the more important functions of a good social education rationale was "to avoid the unthinking imposition of your beliefs on your students." Of equal concern was "the need for a systematic, well-grounded basis from which to explain, even defend, your instructional behavior to administrators and parents" (pp. 10–11).

Shaver and Strong (1982) recognized that *no* curriculum is ever truly value-free, and the values held by social educators will, consciously or unconsciously, shape the way they approached their work. Most importantly, social educators in the United States functioned in a culture oriented

to a basic value set or ethos, that is, the American Creed. Social educators
need to have a commitment to this creed; yet they must also recognize
that these basic values "conflict with one another by their very nature."
Because of this inherent conflict, "we cannot fully attain all of the basic
values at any one time" (p. 50). Thus, a commitment to pluralism was
an essential ingredient of our democratic culture. Pluralism ensures that
those decisions we need to make to apply the creed to specific situations
will be conducted with a full consideration of all information and options.
Unfortunately, the available research indicated that the value of expressing
unpopular opinions is probably the least understood and valued
constitutional right.

Some have argued that our cultural commitment to pluralism more likely
indicates that Americans do not hold any single set of values, and, in part,
this is correct. However, in a vital sense this contention was also wrong,
because "at the affective, emotional level there is a commonality of
commitment to a set of values that allows us to speak of an American
Creed" (Shaver and Strong 1982, 57). As Gunnar Myrdal (1944) concluded,
"It is difficult to avoid the judgment that this 'American Creed' is the
cement in the structure of this great and disparate nation" (p. 3). R.
Freeman Butts has made a similar case (1979, 1980). The creed is in a
process of continual flux and any fixed view of it would be dogmatic and
maladaptive in a democratic culture. Still, "the Creed with its cognitive
vagueness and emotive solidarity, does provide a viable context for
confrontations over fundamental issues as we adapt to tomorrow's
realities" (Shaver and Strong 1982, 62).

For Shaver and Strong, this commitment to core values has certain clear
implications for both rationale building and the professional behavior of
social educators. Social education must be related to developing citizens
who have internalized the creed and developed the knowledge and
competencies to apply it in decision making. This requires that social
educators clearly understood and supported the creed. In addition, they
had "an obligation to try to shape the expectations of . . . the students,
parents and, more broadly, the community—to help insure that schooling
does take place in a context of democratic commitment" (p. 79).

A social educator who is not committed to the ethos of the creed should
not agree to work in public schools.

> The school is not a legitimate place for subversion in the sense of encouraging
> or advocating the destruction of the values and basic governmental forms
> set up—with all their theoretical and practical limitations—to protect our
> evolving conception of human dignity. (Shaver and Strong 1982, 79)

But the notion of subversion requires clarification. For example, one might
legitimately examine the relevance of violent methods for social change

as an issue. "But to *advocate* violence as a form of political action clearly falls outside the proper role of a public school responsible to a democratic society, and would be legitimate grounds for dismissal" (p. 80). Nor should one use the classroom to advocate other political positions, as "teachers are not hired to carry out partisan political indoctrination" (p. 80). This does not proscribe the teachers' right to express personal views, identified as such, in the classroom. In fact, to do otherwise would seem unauthentic to students.

Shaver and Strong noted that members of the community "often fail to distinguish between what is subversive in their eyes and what is subversive to a democratic society" (p. 82). Thus, teachers had a professional "right and obligation to act in a context broader than that of the local community" (p. 82). This does not negate the value of local control, but it does mean that "decisions about what the schools should teach ought to be made in the light of the school's role as an institution of a democratic society" (pp. 82–83).

Questions related to the use of imposition have been a major issue in social education throughout this century. Shaver and Strong argued that a reasonable case can be made for the imposition of certain core values and knowledge within a democratic society. Leming (1981), as noted earlier, went somewhat further than Shaver and Strong and supported the imposition of a number of specific behaviors. In my earlier work (Stanley 1981a, 1981b, 1981c), I supported the reconstructionist position that imposition is both an inevitable and desirable part of social education. But I also insisted that while we must make rational decisions regarding what to impose, we must simultaneously use critical methods to block the reification of current knowledge and values.

SOCIAL CRITICISM AND SOCIAL EDUCATION

The definition and role of social criticism in education is a complex issue. For Berlak (1977), consciousness, social criticism, and civic education should be the primary goals of social education. He cited the dilemma of continuity versus change as the central question for social educators. If we do not teach students the skills and values necessary to be thoughtful social critics, it will not really matter what content we select or which approach to values education we employ. One approach may be more effective than another, but the important point was to encourage "students to examine the relationship of social/political/economic arrangements past and present to the ways in which people live their everyday lives. . ." (p. 35).

Berlak rejected simplistic Marxist or socialist-revisionist critiques as too extreme in their contentions that our schools will reproduce society.

Perhaps these warnings (e.g., Bowles and Gintis 1976) were "a useful corrective to the naiveté revealed by liberal school reformers" in the 1960s (Berlak 1977, 36). However, this was no longer necessary, and, in fact, both radicals and conservatives have been naive in assuming we could easily accomplish social change. The point was that "any conception of political education rests upon an assumption that experience...is capable of altering the way a person views the world." Berlak assumed that by focusing on social criticism and raising student consciousness "they may be capable of acting differently" (p. 36). He believed that most recent reform proposals in social education have not been directed toward this end. While it might seem ironic, Berlak argued that, contrary to suspicions that such an approach is seditious, the call for social criticism is consistent with our constitutional ideals.

Nelson (1980a; Nelson and Michaelis 1980) has argued that social criticism should be the major focus of social education, but he took a somewhat different position than Berlak. Nelson believes that our schools tend to reify the status quo and he is skeptical of any attempts to impose knowledge on students. Some research (Naylor 1974; Nelson 1977, 1982; Palonsky and Nelson 1980) indicates that a great deal of self-censorship goes on in our schools. This censorship occurred despite claims by school officials and teachers that there should be freedom to discuss controversial issues.

Although the student teachers in one study felt more restraint than did the administrators, the apparent differences between them faded in the reality of their mutual commitments to prevailing ideology and classroom practice (Nelson 1982). Both student teachers and administrators accepted the abstract right to discuss controversy and present personal views, yet they tended not to exercise these rights in practice, because they saw such behavior as inappropriate and unprofessional. The main concern of both student teachers and administrators was that all sides of an issue must be presented. They seemed unaware that certain specific dominant viewpoints were continuously being transmitted uncritically to students.

A major cause of such behavior on the part of teachers and administrators was the dominant functionalist ideology that rationalized schooling in general and social education in particular (Besag and Nelson 1984). Functionalist sociological theory held that our present institutions had evolved because they were the most effective, and thus, functionalism rationalized "what is" as "what ought to be." This tended to stifle creativity, autonomy, and criticism as well as to reproduce existing social inequalities.

Nelson (1980a; Nelson and Michaelis 1980) has also argued that since change is an inevitable part of social life, a functionalist-oriented social education program with its class-based, nation-specific, past-oriented, passive, conformist, and static dimensions was dysfunctional by definition.

Nelson's views amount to a rejection of most of Leming's (1981) positivist and functionalist arguments discussed earlier. We require instead an approach related to the problems inherent in social change. Some (e.g., Newmann 1975) have suggested an increased emphasis on social activism as a possible solution. But this was an inadequate approach in Nelson's view, because activism has no necessary rationale and can be used for a variety of conflicting purposes (Nelson 1980a).

There are a number of models available to orient social criticism, including Dewey's philosophy, Critical Theory, and reconstructionism. Nelson (1980a) discusses each model in brief, but does not take a clear stand in favor of any particular approach. His main point was to emphasize that social criticism as a central approach to social education can be justified, because it: (1) dealt with change, (2) contributed to informed decision making in a democratic system, and (3) facilitated basic learning and skills.

Newmann (1981b) has taken a different position from Nelson's and raised some questions regarding the possible effects of social criticism. He believed that a fundamental problem in social education was "the absence of an adequate ideology on the nature of citizenship in a modern, pluralistic culture, nested within an exosphere, with a presumed mandate to work toward democratic forms" (p. 1). Thus, we often attempted to construct social education programs without: (1) developing any means of resolving the fundamental conflicts related to different group loyalties, (2) attempting to balance individual liberty and group needs, (3) considering the need to develop a substantive conception of justice, and, (4) balancing social criticism against the need for some nonrational social attachment.

An area of particular concern to Newmann (1981a) was the development of "collective identity." Newmann agreed that this

> should be pursued as an educational goal largely to counteract the American preoccupation with individual choice, liberty, rights, consumption, skills, development, and fulfillment that is destructive to culture and to individuals. (p. 11)

Newmann (1981a) agreed that our cultural concern for individualism was important, but he also believed that it has been overemphasized. Our failure to promote adequately the importance of collective attachment conveys a distorted view of individual dignity to students. Dignity is critical to the full development of every person, but individual dignity requires situations "where individuals contribute to and receive from others, i.e., contexts of productive group life" (p. 11). The same can be said of justice, for while it is defined in terms of how we treat individuals, "the point is to recognize that constructive forms of group life are necessary for justice to be done" (p. 13). Thus, collective identity is important because it helps us achieve so many other worthwhile goals.

Although students spend a great deal of time in groups, Newmann (1981a) doubted that this developed a strong sense of collective identity, especially given the tendency of the norms of social education "to undermine the promotion of group life" (p. 14). In particular, current approaches to social education promoted the following assumptions: (1) our history is the story of the progressive development of individual freedom, (2) our political system provides the means to express and reconcile conflicting individual interests, (3) the American economic system ensures the delivery of important goods and services along with providing incentives for individuals to acquire more, and (4) our legal system "protects the individual from abuse by the state and offers fair mechanisms for resolving private disputes among individual parties" (p. 15). For Newmann, this represented a general obsession with individual interests. Indeed, many critics of social education tended to "sanctify individual liberation as an ultimate end" (p. 15). In part, such critics were overreacting to the view that knowledge is socially constructed.

Newmann (1981a) also had reservations about the general efficacy of social criticism. "Collective identity can be strengthened through critical rationality, but it cannot be sustained if all beliefs...are subject to continuous critical questioning." Thus, there are times when criticism must be restrained to "avoid weakening the nonrational basis of social cohesion" (p. 16). Most social educators failed to address these issues, and social education tended to remain a process of socialization in conformity to adult norms. If we are to make progress in this area we need to develop a new ideology to help resolve the inherent conflicts related to individual liberty, social control, and multiple group membership (Newmann 1981a).

Newmann (1981a) has also reviewed the research on adolescent development as it relates to constructing group identity. He found "no conception of growth or adaptation which recognizes collective identity as a central issue," (p. 29). In fact, most theories of adolescent development view collective identity as "dangerous to psychological health because of its potential threat to individual autonomy" (p. 29). Perhaps most important, there was no research to indicate that adolescents had any psychological limitations on their capacity to develop a strong sense of collective identity. Newmann concluded that it must be the social structure and culture that block this development. Social education had the potential and responsibility to help correct this condition, and some other social educators appear to have made efforts in this area (e.g., Butts 1980; Leming 1981; Nelson 1980a, 1980b; Oliner 1983; Oliver and Shaver 1966; Shaver and Strong 1982).

Our brief look at various rationales for social education clearly indicates that citizenship *is* a central concern in most all of them but that the concept remains conflicted and blurred. As Nelson (1980a, 1980b; Nelson and Michaelis 1980) has argued, the focus on citizenship education as the core of the social education curriculum is of limited value since we hold widely divergent conceptions of what citizenship means or should be. The concern with providing a clear account of citizenship remains a critical part of the quest for radical reform (Giroux 1988c). Part of the problem can be accounted for by the gradual devaluation of this concept in modern industrial society.

Ophuls (1980) contends that, in a practical sense, citizenship no longer exits in the modern industrial world. Few persons, if any, actually enjoy the status of citizen, and we seem to have lost our historical conception of self-government. Thus citizenship has deteriorated to a spectator activity and citizenship education has become a study of what others (those in government) do (p. 217). Ophuls traced this level of apathy to a confusion over values in our culture. Modern conservatism has roots in nineteenth-century liberalism, the core ideas of which were: atomistic individualism, innate selfishness, and the role of government limited to a referee in the struggle for private ends. Indeed, privatism and liberalism are intrinsically linked in our past. We have come to accept that "the ends of man [*sic*] are *private* ends—that is, ends that are privately determined, privately attained, and privately enjoyed. The community was seen as little more than a necessary evil, nothing but an arena for the ego's quest" (p. 223). Thus, even on those occasions when we do participate in public life, it tends to be as a means for pursuing private ends. To the extent this is so, citizenship is diminished.

This impoverished conception of citizenship was further damaged by the pressures and complexity of modern society (Lasch 1979, 1984). In part, this effect was related to the anonymity of our expanding urban culture and the widening psychological gap between significant political behavior and the reality of our daily lives. Furthermore, the most generally prevailing view was that political issues have become so complex as to be beyond the grasp of most people. Believing that we lacked the under-standing and skills necessary to influence political events, the world of politics has become progressively more incomprehensible and divorced from reality. In effect, individuals have been relegated to the status of hapless consumers in both the political and economic marketplace (Lasch 1984; Ophuls 1980). But the typical political consumer must devote so much time to economic survival and private interests that little time or energy remained available for informed citizenship.

A disturbing dimension of our current political culture was a negative attitude toward the use and consumption of community resources. In the present sociocultural context,

> It is always rational for individuals to abuse the commons even when they
> are fully aware (and they rarely are) that this will cause long-term ruin. . . . If
> an individual exploits, he [sic] stands to receive all the gain, but others absorb
> most of the resulting environmental damage. (Ophuls 1980, 228–29)

And conversely, to fail to exploit was to risk that others and you will absorb
the damages without any benefit. So most individuals opted to exploit,
even if the long-term effects would be detrimental to all. We assume this
will be postponed until a future generation—if we even think about it at
all. But in a world of growing resource scarcity and increasing pollution,
this sort of behavior appeared more and more irrational.

Our educational response to these problems seemed designed to
exacerbate them. School curricula generally emphasize the knowledge,
skills, and values required for bureaucratic and technological expertise.
This materialistic and functionalist approach to curriculum spent little time
or effort on developing the competence for social and political discourse
required to realize effective citizenship. Instead, the focus on technical
efficiency and economic rationality tended to promote political passivity
(Bellah, et al. 1984; Lasch 1979, 1984). Ophuls (1980), like the reconstructionists, believed that the schools functioned in the interests of powerful
groups, and our current school curriculum was unlikely to produce many
students with an interest in challenging the social order (pp. 237–39).

Other mainstream critics of social education have pointed to general
failure of our schools to focus on the study of the future. Alvin Toffler's
(1971) work is a case in point. Some of his books have been best-sellers
and for some time he was a major celebrity subject to a great deal of
attention. Toffler's connection to reconstructionism is located in his
discussion of our failure to address adequately the rapid nature of social
change in modern society, the result of which is "shattering stress and
disorientation." Yet our current curriculum continues to look "backward
toward a dying system, rather than forward to the emerging new society"
(Toffler 1971, 399). While our curriculum might have been well-suited to
our industrial age, it is increasingly irrelevant to the emergent post-
industrial order (p. 400).

For Toffler, like the reconstructionists, education must now focus on the
rapidity of social change by having students study these developments
and learn how to project or place themselves in the future society. Only
by expanding their temporal horizons in this way could they begin to
develop the capacity to deal with such rapid change. The current dilemma
for social educators is that students seem to either become apathetic,
thinking that social change is all beyond their control, or conversely assume
that we can resolve all these problems by some type of "technological fix"
(Smith 1981; Lasch 1979, 1984).

The critical assumption, from a reconstructionist vantage point, is that social change has proceeded so rapidly in modern industrial society that our major institutions and theories (including educational theory), have tended to lag far behind such changes and become increasingly irrelevant. The net effect was to create a very dangerous gap between social reality and educational rhetoric and practice, a point emphasized by various mainstream educators (Besag and Nelson 1984). A prevailing assumption on the part of the reconstructionists and many mainstream social educators is the belief that the technology *is* available to resolve our basic problems such as adequate food, clothing, shelter, etc. (e.g., Combs 1981, 371–72). Those who accept this assumption tend to shift the focus to changing the social or value dimension of human society. As we will discuss in more detail in the next chapter, the "technological fix" is not so available or obvious as we might think. This is a point often made by Lasch (1979, 1984) and others.

Finally, some critics have serious doubts about the value of using the future to guide social policy. Since the future is most difficult to predict, there is a high probability that our current visions of what the future will be like are erroneous. We remain in constant danger of deceiving ourselves. Indeed, several hundred years of apparent success in the natural sciences has tended to promote an unwarranted belief in human progress and the potential of the human sciences to realize such progress. The reconstructionists were prone to this line of thought. It might be the case that we have a very limited capacity to anticipate or shape future events.

In other words, it might be more reasonable to think of human potential as far more limited than reconstructionists have supposed. The reconstructionist recommendation to use our schools to effect progressive social change could be understood as an idealistic fantasy rooted in our rational-democratic traditions. If anything, the reconstructionist assumption that schools serve to transmit and reify our society and culture seems a more accurate description in both an empirical and normative sense. This seems an unduly pessimistic account; one critical pedagogy has sought to overcome as we shall see in Chapter 4.

CONCLUSIONS

The persistence of reconstructionist ideas in liberal and some conservative mainstream social education curriculum studies and programs gives some credibility to the centrality of certain reconstructionist claims regarding the role of schools in society. In this sense, reconstructionism can be viewed as a significant component of the current mainstream curriculum. But this hypothesis must be qualified. First, reconstructionism (in its most developed form, e.g., Brameld's work) called for thoroughgoing cultural, social, and educational reform. The vast majority of liberal mainstream curriculum theorists call for far more modest changes, and most appear to believe that necessary reforms are possible without radically altering our culture or major institutions. Second, the reconstructionists insisted that education could and should be a primary and activist agency for social transformation. Mainstream curriculum theorists tend to be far more cautious regarding the reform potential of education. Indeed, some (e.g., Bowers, Newmann, Kohl) convey a view that suggests that the impact of education is quite limited. While education might be able to help improve the general level of knowledge, human action through other institutions would be required for significant change. In fact, there is a prevailing tone in much of mainstream curriculum theory that suggests it is quite naive to think education could or should have a significant impact on social transformation.

Nevertheless, mainstream curriculum theory does echo several of the reconstructionist's key concerns. First, the sense of a cultural and educational "crisis" (however unfocused that metaphor might be) looms large in the mainstream literature. Second, the use of critical thinking to study social problems has become an accepted component of mainstream social education curriculum proposals. Third, both conservative and liberal educators see the school as a principal agency for social change and improvement, although they generally differ regarding goals and methods. In spite of these apparent parallels with reconstructionist thought, reasons for concern remain.

Morrissett and Haas (1982) note the persistent dominance of a social education curriculum focused on conservative cultural continuity. This curriculum orientation aims at transmitting the "core" values, norms, and mores of the society. Morrissett and Haas put it this way:

> precisely because education and socialization are united in the social studies, the dominant approach tends to be a conserving and preserving one, designed to socialize the young to the current status quo and to educate students via an extremely restricted and romanticized interpretation of history, politics, and economics. (p. 20)

The conservative cultural continuity approach to social education is suited to transmitting a view of history as a natural process of growth and progress. It perpetuates social myths regarding celebrations of our political, social, and economic status quo, that is, "the current concepts of growth and progress and an extreme gradualism as the preferred mode of social change" (p. 21). Morrissett and Haas (1982) emphasize that the schools are social agencies and as such represent the basic interests of the society and culture. There are occasions where the schools are used to promote change or ameliorate social problems, but there seems to be little support for this position among teachers (Stake and Easley 1978). Even among academics, the support that does exist is mainly limited to reforms within the limits of existing cultural and institutional arrangements (Stanley 1981c; Giroux 1983b).

The "hidden curriculum" of the school also appears to reinforce the conservative socialization function (Fielding 1981; Giroux 1981). As Fielding (1981) asserts, the hidden curriculum is very powerful and operates to emphasize "passive acceptance" as opposed to "active criticism." In sum, "the voice of authority is to be trusted and valued more than independent judgment" (p. 118).

Given the prevalence of the conservative socialization goal, it is quite possible that most parents and teachers see the main purpose of social education as socialization via the overt and covert indoctrination to our society's norms and values. In fact, a number of studies indicate that this is the most popular perception or justification for social education (e.g., Stake and Easley 1978; Haas 1979, Stanley 1981b; Fetsko 1979; and Shaver, Davis, and Helburn 1979). Thus, there may be a de facto consensus on a rationale for social education, that is, conservative cultural transmission to reify and reproduce the status quo of society and institutional arrangements. If so, this would help explain the resistance to radical social education reform movements, and it would also account for much of the indifference toward the rationale-building process. After all, if there is a de facto consensus on the purpose of social education, why continue to examine other rationales?

There is evidence to support this last contention. As studies by Stake and Easley (1978) and Shaver and others (1979) reveal, rationale building is an intellectual activity mainly confined to the academic community. As Morrissett and Haas (1982) note, "few social studies educators...are concerned about such seemingly esoteric issues" (p. 63). Mehlinger (1981), Shaver and others (1979), have pointed to the gulf that separates social studies academics from classroom teachers. Haas (1981) agrees and believes that much of the debate over rationales is unrelated to the goals of effective classroom practice. Shaver (1979) has argued that teachers willingly accept the schools' function to socialize youth and that socialization is "an inevitable part of the school's role" (p. 43). Yet the social studies intelligentsia "ignore or reject teachers' socialization goals." Their bias is "toward critical thinking and inquiry—an orientation which, of course, implies another socialization agenda" (p. 43). This discrepancy in views has limited social studies academics' abilities to help teachers improve their instruction. Indeed, "a utopian view of social studies that does not take into account the legitimate nonrational citizenship education duties of the school has provided a dysfunctional basis for research aimed at influencing practice in social studies education" (p. 44). The concerns of those like Barr, Barth,

and Shermis (1977) notwithstanding, defining the social studies appears
to be a nonproblem for most teachers. In practice, social studies teachers
seem to exhibit a great deal of autonomy and tend to be practical and
eclectic rather than to hold consistent rationale positions (Wiley 1977; White
1982; Morrissett 1979). This gap between social studies intellectuals and
social studies teachers might amount to what Leming (1989) calls "the two
cultures of social studies education."

Finally, one could consider Shaver's (1977) explanation that much of what
goes on in social education reflects a "mindlessness," that is, a failure to
think about purpose and to link it to practice. This could help explain the
current lack of consensus regarding rationales. For instance, Morrissett
(1979) believes that many approaches to citizenship education are
unrealistic, because they expect high levels of altruistic behavior as well
as large commitments of time and energy. In addition, it is not realistic
to pretend that democracy can be practiced in classrooms that are typically
authoritarian in nature. "Finally, citizenship education is typically
unrealistic in its presentation of how democracy works, ignoring or
glossing over the nature of social conflict, special interest groups, political
survival, and 'national voter ignorance' " (Morrissett and Haas 1982, 33).
In the next chapter we turn to the radical approach to education called
critical pedagogy to examine another view of the "crisis" in public
education and the links between reconstructionist and current radical
approaches to curriculum.

4

CRITICAL PEDAGOGY AND RECONSTRUCTIONISM

Over the past two decades, we have witnessed the emergence of a radical challenge to the dominant liberal and conservative approaches to curriculum. This challenge involves a number of alternative positions that might be subsumed under the term critical pedagogy (Giroux 1988b). Critical pedagogy draws on various sources including neo-Marxism, Critical Theory, phenomenology, feminism, structuralism, poststructuralism, and postmodernism. As such, there has been no simple way to define critical pedagogy. Furthermore, there is considerable disagreement among many of those identified as critical pedagogues (e.g., Beyer and Apple 1988; Cherryholmes 1988; Ellsworth 1989; Giroux 1988c; Pinar 1988b).

Despite the significant growth of critical pedagogy, some maintain that it has had a relatively limited impact on mainstream curriculum theory (Giroux 1988b; Apple 1988b). But a more optimistic account is provided by Pinar (1988c, 1989) and Grumet (1989) both of whom argue that by 1980 the mainstream curriculum field had incorporated what Pinar has called the "reconceptualist" critique, thereby indicating a significant reduction in the field's traditional resistance to critical approaches. What is not in dispute is the persistent development of critical pedagogy as manifested in books, scholarly journals, and presentations at professional conferences. The development of critical pedagogy has passed through several recent stages or schools of thought. We will briefly review some of the more influential perspectives. Our purpose here is not to present a definitive summary but to explore the connections between various approaches to critical pedagogy and the reconstructionist legacy.

REPRODUCTION OR CORRESPONDENCE THEORIES

Reproduction or correspondence theories have tended to present schools as agencies of the dominant culture which functioned to reinforce existing power relations, asymmetries, and forms of domination. This analysis emerged in the 1970s and was somewhat reminiscent of the earlier orthodox Marxist view of education. But reproduction theory is, in many ways, a more complex account than orthodox Marxism and one that takes the role of education more seriously. In many respects, reproduction theory also presents a better theoretical and empirical account of education than the critique raised by the reconstructionists in the 1930s. On the other hand, reproduction theory seems far more pessimistic than reconstructionism regarding the potential of schooling to help transform society.

Reproduction theorists have been critical of both liberal and conservative efforts to shape educational practice (Apple 1979; Bowles and Gintis 1976; Giroux 1983b; Sarup 1984). Mainstream liberals have espoused an egalitarian democratic rhetoric and viewed education as a vehicle to provide for both individual development and social mobility for the disadvantaged. For liberal educational theorists, state apparatuses like public education are conceived as basically neutral institutions that are intended to operate in the interest of all the people. This relatively atheoretical position gives little attention to the possibility of deep structural causes (e.g., cultural and institutional arrangements, including the state apparatuses) for current inequality.

Conservatives, in contrast, actually supported a version of reproduction theory that would preserve the traditions of the dominant culture and the conditions required to support a market economy. Indeed, conservatives (and many liberals) assumed that a market economy was a necessary condition for the very survival of democracy. Public education must be used in terms of its capacity to transmit effectively the knowledge, competencies, and dispositions required to maintain the dominant socioeconomic order. More recently, conservatives have argued that our failure to transmit such knowledge and values has led to cultural and economic decline (Bennett 1989; Bloom 1987; Finn, Ravitch, and Fancher 1984; Hirsch 1987; Ravitch and Finn 1987). These conservative scholars tend to accept that education might ameliorate some instances of inequality, but it will never eliminate social stratification since such stratification was the result of the natural variation in talents among various groups and individuals. A more reasonable goal would be the creation of a meritocracy wherein education would help all students to reach their "natural" potential.

Critical educators contend that most liberal and conservative educational reformers have tended to emphasize poor teacher training, faulty curriculum design, "mindlessness," and a widespread lack of cultural knowledge and skills as the fundamental problems we need to address. They assume that if only we could design better curriculum materials and deal with the cognitive needs of students, we might have successful educational reform (Giroux and Penna 1979, 21). Consequently, most mainstream reformers have emphasized content mastery, testing, basic skills, computer literacy, and teacher accountability. This mainstream approach to reform also tends to link the desired outcomes of education to the needs of the business sector and our national quest for economic and military superiority (Apple 1986a; Giroux 1984, 1988c).

In sharp contrast, reproduction theorists hold that our schools work all too well to reproduce the dominant social order. It is not possible to understand how this reproductive process functioned without first analyzing schooling within a sociocultural, economic, and historical context. Reproduction theorists, like the reconstructionists, rejected the liberal inclination to view schools as neutral agencies. Instead, reproduction theorists held that schools mainly functioned to reproduce the ideology of the dominant classes by transmitting particular forms of knowledge and an unequal distribution of skills and competencies in accordance with existing social asymmetries. According to Giroux (1983a), schools reproduce the dominant order in three basic ways: 1) by providing differential knowledge, competencies, and dispositions to those likely to hold different places in the social order; 2) by the distribution and legitimation of the dominant culture; and 3) by transmitting and legitimating the economic and ideological components required to support the political power of the state (p. 259). Apple and Weis (1983a), in an argument similar to Giroux's, have also sought to document how schools contribute to capital accumulation, legitimation, and production consistent with the status quo.

Giroux (1983a) has presented a good summary and critique of the reproduction theorist's work and their major contributions to curriculum theory. He describes the way Bowles and Gintis (1976) developed an economic reproduction model and produced the most influential statement of reproduction theory in the United States. Bowles and Gintis viewed power as a property used by dominant groups to reproduce and legitimate their position and ideology. They posed a correspondence theory of education wherein schools mirrored the dominant social structure including its values, preferred skills, and forms of knowledge. The schools sought to inculcate directly such knowledge, skills, and values, but different kinds of knowledge were imposed on different groups in accordance with the likely role they would play in the stratified social order. For Bowles and Gintis, the most effective aspect of this process was the hidden curriculum that exercised its influence through the organization of schooling and day-to-day classroom social interaction. In fact, the messages of the hidden curriculum were so powerful precisely because they appeared to be natural and universal aspects of life in schools. Very early in schooling, children come to know what is considered high verses low status knowledge. For example, intellectual work was preferred over manual work, hierarchical over democratic forms of organization, and individual competition over collective sharing and cooperation. The indirect imposition of these ideas helped form the subjectivities of students, that is, they were part of the conscious and unconscious dimensions of experience that shape one's behavior.

Giroux (1983a) explains how Althusser's (1969) conception of ideology has been used to reinforce and extend the Bowles and Gintis argument. For Althusser, ideology is to be found in the material practices of daily life, including routines, rituals, classroom seating arrangements, and school architecture. Ideology is so pervasive that it does not produce conscious compliance so much as appear to reveal meaning located in the concrete daily practices that shape our consciousness. In this way, ideology promotes an "imaginary relationship" to the actual conditions of one's existence. Thus, ideology does not involve intentionality, and the conventional understanding of ideology as a worldview or false consciousness were not what Althusser had in mind. As he put it, ideology had little to do with consciousness. In most cases it is "profoundly unconscious" and functions as part of a system of representations in "perceived-accepted-suffered cultural objects" that act functionally on individuals while also escaping their attention (Althusser 1969, 233).

Another variant of reproduction theory is found in the cultural reproduction model of Pierre Bourdieu (1977a, 1977b, 1979; Bourdieu and Passeron 1977). Giroux (1983a) believes Freire's work in *Pedagogy of the Oppressed* (1969) was an early statement of this position. Bourdieu, like Bowles and Gintis and Althusser, argued that humans participated in their own domination. But Bourdieu's theory held that schools did not simply mirror the dominant culture. In fact, schools were described by Bourdieu as relatively autonomous institutions that are influenced directly and indirectly by other powerful institutions. Schools were not involved in the direct imposition of the dominant order but functioned as one part of a wider group of symbolic social institutions. The process of social reproduction was real but very subtle.

Bourdieu employed the concept of "symbolic violence" to signify the process by which the knowledge and dispositions consistent with the interests of the dominant order were portrayed as both natural and necessary. Schools have considerable power, in Bourdieu's view, because they appear to be neutral transmitters of the best and most valuable knowledge. This enables schools to promote the unequal aspects of our society while appearing to be objective and fair. Indeed, it is the school's relative autonomy that lets them "serve external demands under the guise of independence and neutrality" (Bourdieu and Passeron 1977, 178).

The culture transmitted by schools is actually made up of various cultures and subcultures within our society. Bourdieu used the term "cultural capital" to describe the different kinds of linguistic and cultural competencies students acquire in schools and other institutions. The actual nature of the cultural capital one acquired was constrained by the student's class boundaries. Cultural capital came first from one's family which gave children a collection of meanings, styles, ways of thinking, and dispositions, each of which have an assigned social value and status. The important point is that the value assignments regarding cultural capital were made in terms of the dominant cultural orientation. Schools played an important role in this process by transmitting and legitimating the value structure of the dominant classes. This was accomplished by endorsing certain forms of knowledge, ways of speaking, styles, behavior, and worldviews as having high or low status and value. Students from subordinate groups had a relatively poor understanding of the dominant culture and entered school at a considerable disadvantage since the culture of most schools is very similar to the culture of the dominant groups in society. So while lower class students may try to acquire the dominant culture, they were always at a disadvantage compared to middle-class students for whom the school culture appeared natural because it *was their* culture.

Schools promoted what Bourdieu and others have called the hegemonic curriculum, that is, a curriculum that simultaneously legitimated the dominant culture while marginalizing or rejecting other cultures and knowledge forms. Other cultures were not merely portrayed as different within a multicultural framework but as both different *and* inferior. In our present social order, high-status knowledge was necessary for entry into the professions and this fact further legitimated and reinforced the purported superiority of such knowledge. These circumstances helped explain why the dominated often participated in their own domination.

Bourdieu employed a dual conception of history to help explain the subtle process of domination he described. First, there was the *habitat*, an objectified form of history that developed over time and was manifest in actual things including architectural forms, knowledge forms, customs, books, and so forth. A second conception of history was the *habitus* or embodied form of history. The habitus encompassed the various needs and competencies internalized by subjects. In other words, individuals developed internalized ways of understanding and relating to the world that were grounded in their very bodies. Consequently, the habitus was very durable. It was generally reinforced by objective conditions but often persisted long after such conditions were altered. Different groups develop a different habitus which became the main determinant for organizing individual behavior in practical activity. Domination was forged, in part, by the correspondence between one's habitus and the objective structures, interests, and practices (habitats) of major institutions such as schools.

According to Giroux (1983a), Bourdieu's notion of embodied learning in the habitus is a valuable addition to our understanding of the hidden curriculum. Bourdieu called our attention to the role that emotion, sensuality, and physiology play in socialization. He explained how, when organized in terms of a group or individual's class-structured cultural activities, learning proceeded at an unconscious level in the body. Such knowledge was quite resistant to intentional attempts to transform its effects. It was difficult, if not impossible, to make this form of knowledge explicit so that it might be examined and contested.

A final form of reproduction theory discussed by Giroux (1983a) is what he calls the *hegemonic-state reproduction model*. This model is reflected in some of the work of Apple (1979), Dale (1986), and Sarup (1984), but Gramsci's (1971) work is critical to understanding how the model worked. Gramsci argued that the concept of hegemony must be understood as a constantly changing condition wherein force and consent were related in various combinations. Hegemony was a process of domination employed by dominant groups who used intellectual and moral influence as well as coercion. It was effective to the extent that the dominant groups were able to persuade subordinate groups to understand their interests in a way that was consistent with the interests of those who had the power to dominate. While coercion was an important and often necessary strategy, hegemony must always be maintained by more than coercion. It involved the continuing struggle to structure and control the consciousness of subordinate groups. Therefore, production of knowledge, and hence schooling, was a key component in the state's construction of power.

According to Gramsci, the state should not be understood as merely the repressive organ of dominant groups. The state also used private and public institutions, including schools, to maintain a system of meanings that serve to universalize the ideologies of the dominant groups and limit the development of opposition. This was a constant struggle that took place within the context of the continual change of historical conditions and the complex reactions of human beings. Furthermore, the process was filled with contradictions, since neither the dominant groups nor those dominated were homogenous entities. Still, there existed what Poulantzas (1975) referred to as a dominant class grammar or short-term consensus on maintaining the fundamental conditions designed to preserve the basic capitalist social order. In this process, the state often used liberal-sounding appeals to democratic rights, social mobility, and happiness to justify its policies, while also taking action to contain or eliminate significant opposition.

Giroux's (1983a) analysis is important, because he reminds us of the very valuable insights of reproduction theory and how it can contribute to the construction of an effective theory of critical pedagogy. But as Giroux also makes clear, there were also basic flaws in reproduction theory that might function effectively to block efforts for radical educational reform. First, it overemphasized the process of domination. For the most part, reproduction theory was derived from structural-functionalist versions of Marxism wherein history was made "behind the backs" of citizens. This perspective neglected the very important role of human agency in making history and thereby either dismissed or underestimated the potential for resistance to domination. Second, reproduction theory gave inadequate attention to how the actual practice of schooling worked to reproduce conditions of existence within a specific historical context (Giroux 1983a, 259). Unfortunately, these theoretical limitations often led to reductionist reproduction models of analysis that became a form of radical pessimism (p. 265).

Even Bourdieu's complex cultural reproduction model was overdeterministic and left little room for human agency. Where actual resistance might occur, that is in those instances where one's habitus and institutional position are mismatched, the contradiction was understood as a structural accident and not grounded in critical self-reflection by human objects. Bourdieu also presented a rather monological view of cultural domination that greatly underestimated the complexities of culture, especially working-class cultures. In addition, he did not emphasize that culture both structures and transforms the social environment (Giroux 1983a, 272). Giroux also criticized Bourdieu's (and by implication Gramsci's) conception of ideology as primarily relegated to the unconscious. Giroux argues that ideology is also imposed and consciously resisted or only accepted with reluctance. Giroux maintains that hegemony is more than just winning approval; it also involves avoiding rejection. Thus, schooling could never be merely an agency to serve the interests of dominant groups. It was also an active part of such groups or organic to them in the sense of both conserving and constructing their identity (p. 273).

Bourdieu's primarily cultural theory also neglected the concrete aspects of economic domination that produced real constraints beyond the limits of symbolic violence. Domination is always grounded in more than ideology and depends as well on material conditions. Conversely, the state reproduction models of Poulantzas, Gramsci, and others tend to underestimate the autonomy of culture and its capacity to function as *both* the subject and object of human resistance. In the state reproduction models, only culture as an object of resistance is emphasized (Giroux 1983a, 281).

RESISTANCE THEORY

Over the past fifteen years a variety of new approaches to critical pedagogy have built upon the insights of reproduction theory while simultaneously trying to counter its most serious limitations. This recent work has been loosely referred to as resistance theory (Apple 1982, 1986a, 1986b; Apple and Weiss 1983; Freire 1970a, 1970b, 1970c, 1970d, 1973, 1985; Giroux 1983a, 1983b, 1985, 1988c; Shor 1979, 1986; Willis 1977). The shift to resistance theory has helped reinvigorate the analysis of schooling and to stimulate the critical reform potential in education.

The work of the resistance theorists is guided by several basic assumptions. While resistance theorists accept most of the insights provided by reproduction theory, they are more optimistic regarding the potential for education to offer a significant challenge to the sociocultural forces of domination. From the perspective of resistance theory, schools can be understood as contested terrain, that is, sites of numerous structural and ideological contradictions. For although our schools operate within the limits and asymmetrical conditions set by dominant groups, they remain relatively autonomous institutions with the capacity to help change those limits (Giroux 1983a, 260). Given these circumstances, students should be understood as far more than mere passive participants in the educational process. For example, as Willis (1977), McRobbie (1978), McNeil (1983), and others have documented, students often consciously reject the dominant ideology that orients so much of schooling. But beyond this phenomenon, the ideology dominant groups seek to impose via schooling is itself a source of contradictions that contain the potential for opposition. This is quite different from the conservative educational theorists' explanation of resistance as a form of deviant or inferior behavior, an analysis that amounts to a rationalization of the status quo.

Apple and Weis (1983a, 1983b) also explain school curriculum as a complex discourse that simultaneously serves the interests of domination while also providing possibilities for opposition and emancipation. In other words, there are contradictions inherent in the most basic functions of schooling in our society. For example, schools can produce a surplus of educated students at a time when economic conditions severely limit employment opportunities. When this happens, it tends to breed dissatisfaction and loss of public faith in the legitimacy of the government. In fact, recent Marxist studies demonstrate that the "correspondence between what is allegedly taught in schools and the needs of a hierarchical labor market is not that clear" (p. 12).

Apple and Weis (1983b) caution that we must be careful not to romanticize resistance theory. While it does provide a framework to examine how oppositional cultures arise and how race, gender, and ethnicity are involved in the process of schooling and socialization, resistance theory is a recent development and further research is required to document its true potential (p. 28). For instance, some of the key studies conducted by resistance theorists demonstrate that what appear to be genuine instances of resistance (e.g., Willis 1977) have had the long-term effect of reproducing, at a deeper level, the dominant order (Apple 1982, 66–90). In the study conducted by Willis (1977), students rejected the dominant ideology that held mental labor as higher status, but also discounted the potential of critical thinking for social transformation.

Paulo Freire (1970a, 1970b, 1970c, 1970d, 1973, 1985; Freire and Macedo 1987) has developed an influential approach to curriculum theory which is focused on resistance to dominant forms of education that reinforce the status quo. Indeed, Freire's early work was a precursor of what later came to be called resistance theory. Freire has referred to traditional approaches to curriculum as "banking education," or a process whereby teachers deposit official knowledge in the minds of passive students. By using banking education methods, schools function primarily to maintain the status quo. According to Freire, teachers should challenge this prevailing system by helping to enlighten students concerning those things that prevent them from having an accurate conception of reality. Such awareness gives students the knowledge they need to help transform that reality (Freire 1970b, 452–77).

Freire calls his educational process *conscientization*. His main efforts have been in the area of reading and literacy, but there are clear implications for social education. The general goal is to disrupt the attempts to accommodate students to the dominant culture by providing them with the means to challenge the social order (Freire 1970b, 205–225). Freire's basic assumption is that for literacy to empower students it must enable them to become critical questioners of social reality. The mainstream conceptions of literacy in most societies promote skills that are not adequate to challenge the dominant social order. Consequently, Freire describes the mainstream view of education as a threat to true democracy. We need instead a critical conception of literacy to enable students to help transform oppressive social relations.

Ira Shor (1986) has been strongly influenced by Freire's views, and points to the need to develop a pedagogy of "desocialization" to counteract the dominant form of banking education. Teachers need to initiate some form of desocialization, since students, despite their alienation, cannot do it on their own. Shor believes that this will be extremely difficult to accomplish, given the powerful influence of dominant educational forms and the general level of student resistance to formal education, including emancipatory approaches. Indeed, a teacher who wants to help empower students might, "ironically find herself or himself forced back into traditional roles by student resistance" (p. 186). And, as noted above, it is often the case that student resistance itself can function to limit student potential to challenge the social order (e.g., Willis 1977; McRobbie 1978; Giroux 1983a, 1983b).

Shor also calls our attention to the potential conflict between student and teacher resistance. Furthermore, those teachers who seek to promote a form of critical literacy in students by refusing to deliver "pre-packaged batches of knowledge" tend to "do so with some risk of career suicide" (Shor 1986, 186). Even many mainstream educational critics have provided evidence to demonstrate the domination of passive models of instruction and teacher control that inhibit or block attempts at reform (e.g., Cuban 1984; Goodlad 1984; Sirotnik 1989; Sizer 1984).

Giroux (1983a) has explored some other ways a critical pedagogy might help enable students to resist the dominant forces of society. He urges us to educate teachers to become aware of the political nature of education. Teachers can use education to help create a genuine democratic society by enabling students to evaluate society "against its own claims" and to function in ways that might create different social possibilities or ways of living (p. 202). Teachers and students must acquire and display the civic courage "to act as if they were living in a democratic society" (p. 201).

Critical pedagogy, as proposed by Giroux, would stress student participation in the learning process with the intention of enabling students to challenge the social order. Teachers could help to render mainstream knowledge problematic by revealing "its objective pretensions." The purpose would be to have students learn how they came to acquire a particular worldview and how it limits their understanding. Students must also "learn why certain values are indispensable to the reproduction of human life" (p. 203). Finally, students need to develop the competencies required for collective action to help transform the social order as well as the "passion and optimism" necessary to conceive of the possibilities for creating a better world (p. 203). In sum, resistance theorists have sought "to demonstrate that the mechanism of social and cultural reproduction are never complete and always meet with the partially realized elements of opposition" (Giroux 1983b, 259). Consequently, resistance theory has provided a necessary corrective to pessimistic and, generally, one-sided views of reproduction or correspondence (political economist) theory.

Like reconstructionism, the advantage of a critical pedagogy oriented toward resistance lies in its demonstration of and insistence on the moral/political nature of teaching and the need to radicalize the process of critical thought to inform social action. But I believe we must clarify an important point neglected by some critical pedagogues. It is not just a case of adding a moral/political dimension to schooling. Indeed, to do this would only reinforce the positivist fact/value dichotomy. As Christopher Lasch (1979) has argued, values are not to be grafted on to education or other professions to make up for some perceived lack. Instead, we need to conceive of professional activities like education as essentially moral enterprises that operate within the social fabric.

Giroux (1983a) has pointed to some important theoretical weaknesses in contemporary resistance theory. For example, these theorists often "do not adequately conceptualize the historical development of the conditions that promote and reinforce contradictory modes of resistance and struggle" (p. 285). Thus, they often fail to explain that not all oppositional behavior has "radical significance" or involves a clear-cut response to domination. In fact, some oppositional behavior may even be an "expression of power that is fueled by and reproduces the most powerful grammar of domination" (p. 285). For example, student violation of school rules might only reflect racist or sexist values learned in other contexts.

Another problem has been the resistance theorists' tendency to overemphasize class as an explanatory variable and to neglect the analysis of race and gender as modes of domination (Giroux 1983a; Apple and Weis 1983a; Apple 1986a, 1986b, 1988a, 1988b). More recent work by feminists (Ellsworth 1989) and others (e.g., Giroux 1988a, 1988b, 1988c; McCarthy 1988) have called our attention to these limitations. According to Giroux (1983a), resistance theorists have also focused too much on the overt acts of rebellious student behavior and ignored the less obvious forms of resistance such as reduced student participation, humor, digressions, collective student pressure on teachers, and so on. Less overt student behaviors could be perceived as resistance if they emerged "out of a latent or overt ideological condemnation of underlying repressive ideologies that characterize schools in general" (p. 288). These are important considerations, since, given present school conditions, some students will not see overt rebellion as a reasonable response. Finally, resistance theory has not yet given "enough attention to the issue of how domination reaches into the structure of personality itself" (p. 288). A critical psychology is needed to explore how socially developed needs are produced in the psyches of individuals to tie them "to larger structures of domination" (p. 288).

In sum, the limitations discussed above undermine the power of resistance theory to offer an adequate critique. Still, if these weaknesses can be addressed, we might construct a more adequate theory of resistance to orient radical pedagogy. Nevertheless, resistance theory has helped restore the role of human agency and the hope for a radical transformation of schooling and society, as espoused by reconstructionists. This element seems to be absent from many radical theories of education that appear to be unduly limited by a theoretical pessimism (Giroux 1983a, 1983b, 1988a, 1988c). To bring about necessary changes in a critical theory of education will require a rigorous definition of "resistance" as an analytic concept. Given such an analytic framework, we can begin to explore ways to draw on the limited potential of students to resist domination and reaffirm their own cultures and histories. As Giroux (1983a) concludes:

Schools will not change society, but we can create in them pockets of resistance that provide pedagogical models for new forms of learning and social relations—forms which can be used in other spheres more directly involved in the struggle for a new morality and view of social justice. (p. 293)

This does not quite capture what George Counts (1932) apparently had in mind when he challenged the schools to "build a new social order." On the other hand, Counts eventually moderated his position, and perhaps Giroux displays a more realistic assessment of the power of education to change society than the early claims of the reconstructionists.

It is clear that both reproduction and resistance theory have much in common with reconstructionism. All three theories argue that schools are not neutral institutions but agencies that attempt to transmit and legitimate the structure and ideology of the dominant social order. But reproduction and resistance theorists have provided a richer and more complex theoretical and empirical account of the role schools play in the process of domination. However, reproduction theorists, much like the orthodox Marxists of the 1930s, have presented a relatively pessimistic account of schooling which is very qualified concerning the power of education to help effect radical sociocultural transformation. Conversely, resistance theory, like reconstructionism, seeks to illuminate the role of human agency and the real potential for schools to help develop opposition to the dominant order.

THE NEOCONSERVATIVE REVIVAL

Any analysis of recent developments in critical pedagogy must be understood in relation to the success of the neoconservative revival over the past two decades. There are several detailed treatments of this topic available (e.g., Shor 1986; Apple 1986a, 1986b, 1988a, 1988b; Giroux 1985, 1988c; McLaren 1988b, 1988c), and I will restrict my analysis to those developments most relevant to the present discussion.

For Shor (1986), the point of the conservative restoration is to "teach the right words." Of course this entails displacing the wrong words such as civil and equal rights, feminism, black power, and other terms of an oppositional culture. Shor argues that these oppositional terms were gradually replaced by others such as accountability, back-to-basics, career goals, competence, literacy/illiteracy, computer literacy, merit pay, excellence, and so on. The focus of debate moved away from an open conception of curriculum oriented by democratic values to a standardized, measurable curriculum for cultural conformity and vocational skills. Students preoccupied by career goals and competitive self-interest are less likely to find relevance in social concerns. According to Shor, the conservative conception of curriculum was a technical approach in which science was defined in terms of its utility for economic productivity and technological development, thereby either eliminating or trivializing the critical study of society (p. 53). This view of conservative schooling was the anthesis of the liberal arts conceived as having the potential to educate students for competent, critical citizenship.

Conservatives have often misrepresented the nature and cause of the alleged educational "crisis" they defined. While there is evidence in our society of economic decline, rising crime, drug abuse, and deteriorating educational conditions, many conservatives have too conveniently and simplistically attributed such conditions to poor teachers, mediocre students, and the decline of a core curriculum. The educational reforms of the 1960s are seen as having a particularly pernicious effect on schooling. The possibility that our severe social problems might be the result of dominant economic, social, and cultural institutions and structures is either not discussed or simply dismissed. Liberal educational theory and reform are posited as convenient scapegoats for most of our current educational ills.

In addition, the nature of the educational crisis described by conservatives is confusing. Declining Scholastic Aptitude Test (SAT) scores have been used to illustrate the decline in literacy and educational quality in general. Again, the gender, race, and class issues related to the SAT decline are either denied or ignored by most conservative critics of schooling. Furthermore, evidence for the decline in writing skills cannot be linked to the SAT scores since, in the main, the SAT tests have not evaluated writing. Conservatives also appear to assume that there is a single correct discourse representing literacy, one that just happens to coincide with the discourse of dominant groups.

Shor makes another important point regarding the current conservative emphasis on excellence or what he calls the new "super-basics" or ultra-literacy". This emphasis on excellence is packaged under the guise of egalitarianism in the sense of being extended to all students. The new super-basics would include the original basics (the three R's) plus communication skills, so-called higher-level problem-solving skills, computer literacy, foreign languages, and relevant forms of scientific and technological literacy. Perhaps this approach is best illustrated by Mortimer Adler's *The Padia Proposal: An Educational Manifesto* (1982). Two important points were lost in all this neoconservative rhetoric: 1) there was a shift from education for competent citizenship to a focus on traditional (read dominant) academic and technical skills, and, 2) the new focus on excellence still functioned as a "sorting machine" despite the veneer of egalitarian rhetoric. Indeed, the excellence in education movement was a perfect match with the growing bipolar economy described by Apple

(1986a, 1986b, 1988b). What this amounts to is a cynical misrepresentation, since the direction our economic and political system is taking cannot incorporate large increases in traditional higher education. While some new occupations require extensive education, most new positions are in service occupations requiring relatively modest educational levels.

Like the reconstructionists, Shor did not believe that education had the capacity to transform society without a concomitant reform of the current sociocultural matrix. But he did believe that a radical program for education could play an important role in this regard. Shor agreed that liberal educators like Boyer, Goodlad, and Sizer had offered some worthwhile reform proposals. In particular, Shor endorsed their recommendations for major changes in the conditions of teachers work, particularly less teaching time and smaller classes to free teachers to play a more active role in the process of education. But reform must go further than the programs proposed by liberals.

Shor believed it was of critical importance to develop a Freirean program for critical pedagogy. This would be a dialogical approach to teaching that would challenge the monological curriculum of domination. As Shor argued, if schooling were as powerless as some of its critics suggest, it "would be more ignored and less troubled than it is" (p. 185). In fact, it is because schools are at the center of our culture that they have such potential to unsettle it. Shor believed the contradictions of the conservative ideology make it vulnerable, and a critical pedagogy should exploit this opportunity.

Apple (1986a, 1986b) has also pointed out several indicators of recent change in a conservative direction. One is the significant increase of censorship and controversies involving the threat of censorship in schools. Apple believed the present situation to be similar to the conservative movement that supported the censorship of Harold Rugg's reconstructionist social studies textbook series in the late 1930s and early 1940s (p. 172). A second development was the rapid increase in fundamentalist Christian schools, most of which promoted a conservative ideology. Third, there has been a growing movement to educate children at home. Apple argued that all of these developments reflected a decline of state legitimacy in the area of public education. This decline was part of the right's successful effort to construct a complex political alliance held together, in part, by several "seemingly anti-statist themes" (p. 172). Gradually, the right has been able to portray public education, rather than economic, social, and cultural policies, as responsible for economic decline, cultural illiteracy, and the breakdown of traditional values and institutions.

Apple (1986a, 1986b, 1988b) explained the recent neoconservative rhetoric as an instance of the historic conflict between *property rights* and *person rights*. The latter are based on conceptions of liberty and freedom that have supported policies which extend democratic rights to previously disenfranchised groups, including women, people of color, and the poor. Over time, the arguments for person rights have been extended to include equal treatment in economic relationships. In the current debate, dominant conservative groups have acted to shift the focus away from person rights to the prerogatives of property (Apple 1988b, 169). The neoconservative goal has been to redefine equality outside the context of historical instances of oppression, and this new conservative discourse conceives of equality as "guaranteeing *individual choice* under the conditions of a 'free market' " (Apple 1988b, 170).

The results of the neoconservative influence on the current educational debate can be observed in the popularity of recent policy recommendations and positions such as: 1) free-market proposals including voucher plans and tax credits, 2) state legislation to raise standards and specify minimum competencies for teachers and students, thereby further centralizing curriculum content, 3) an intensive critique of school curriculum for its secular humanism, insufficient patriotism, and anti-free enterprise bias, and 4) the increasing use of corporate interests and needs as a ground for educational policy and reform (p. 170).

Apple (1986a, 1986b, 1988a, 1988b) cautioned that the effect of the neoconservative restructuring of the educational, social, and cultural debate cannot be reduced to an instance of false consciousness. In fact, the effectiveness of the neoconservative position derived in large part from its direct connection to the real and contradictory experiences of a large percentage of the population (Apple 1988b, 172). In this sense, the debate has always been more than a cultural struggle, since our experiences are constantly shaped by concrete structural constraints including racism, sexism, class exploitation, and other forms of inequality and domination "generated by the economy and the dual labor market, and by government policies that largely reproduce these conditions..." (Apple 1986a, 179). Those on the right realize that the maintenance of such forms of domination (although the right would certainly define it otherwise) required that dominant groups win the allegiance of civil society in political, moral, and intellectual areas (Apple 1988b, 172).

The right has built a wider following around a new form of *authoritarian populism* that combined a variety of themes—e.g., nationalism, family, duty, authority, standards, tradition, self-interest, competitive individualism, and antistatism—all of which served to create "a reactionary common sense" (Apple 1988b, 172–73). The neoconservative arguments to portray an "educational crisis" have succeeded in undermining even the limited commitments to equality of opportunity enacted during the 1960s and 1970s. As Apple explains, because "so many parents *are* justifiably concerned about the economic futures of their children...rightist discourse connects with the experiences of many working-class and lower-middle-class people" (p. 173). Many people do feel a real loss of economic security and the disintegration of the very values and institutions schools would normally pass on to succeeding generations. Such sentiments promote a we/they vision of the world in which "they" or the others are explained as those who deviate from the normal view of culture as defined by the dominant conservative groups (pp. 178–79). The term "others," of course, generally refers to those groups most subject to oppression and domination.

Giroux (1988c) has also called our attention to the real problems caused by the neoconservative resurgence. He reminds us that patriotism is not intrinsically antidemocratic, but the current conservative position in the debate over education treats patriotism as unproblematic and strips the concept citizenship of its critical democratic dimension (p. 3). The conservative view of citizenship lacks any significant emphasis on the historical struggles of oppressed groups for equal treatment. Instead, citizenship is defined by conservatives in terms of nationalism and moral fundamentalism. For Giroux, the ideology of the new right consists of: 1) a neoliberal emphasis on market economics as a prerequisite to political freedom, 2) a neoconservative commitment to a nineteenth-century view of society and political order, and, 3) a combination of "traditional elitist-libertarian ideology with a strain of popularist ideology that focuses on social issues such as abortion, school prayer, taxes, and other concerns that resonate with the daily experience of working people and other groups generally ignored by the old conservatives" (p. 4).

Giroux (1988c) believed that among the right's greatest successes were its response to the moral relativism at the heart of the most popular forms of educational and political theory and the rapid growth of a political program that has induced the spread of mass political illiteracy. Conservatives have tried to fill the current moral and political vacuum with simplistic forms of individualism, consumerism, and scientific rationality. But Giroux argued that it has been the right, not the left or liberals, that "recognized the need to develop a language of morality in its struggle to redefine its ethical and political vision of schooling, the family, and community life" (pp. 41–42).

The neoconservative ideology of schooling utilized three related narratives. First, they have posited an unproblematic and nostalgic view of history in which schools once functioned successfully to transmit the best of our cultural traditions including moral values. For many conservatives, this amounts to an unapologetic endorsement of indoctrination (Giroux 1988c, 43). Giroux cited the work of Edward A. Wynne, Kevin Ryan, William Bennett, and others to illustrate his argument. He believes that the knowledge and values supported by such individuals were those central to the ideology of dominant groups in our society.

Second, the most direct threat to the conservatives' nostalgic conception of an ideal form of schooling is traced to the liberal reforms of the 1960s and early 1970s. The activities of liberal reformers in this period allegedly diluted educational standards that in turn brought on, or at least exacerbated, widespread cultural illiteracy and the decline of workplace skills and economic productivity. We need to make clear that those developments of the sixties that conservatives attack for their alleged negative effects include far more than educational proposals for more open classrooms or curriculum proposals for multicultural and values education. Conservatives also criticized the effects of the civil rights movement, feminism, gay liberation, and countercultural movements, including the drug culture and new forms of popular music and art. All of these developments were feared by conservatives as a direct challenge to our basic institutions, cultural values, and traditional forms of authority. A major goal of the conservative restoration in education was to restore endangered forms of traditional authority and values. Giroux (1988c) cites the following comments by Kevin Ryan (1986) to illustrate this point.

> In the Eighties, culture is once again viewed as a human achievement that should be transmitted to the young. To transmit the culture, however, we must introduce the young to its ethical principles and moral values. In other words, much of schooling should be vigorously devoted to teaching the young those things that the society has learned about how to live together in a civilized fashion. (Cited in Giroux 1988c, 43)

Giroux (1988c) notes a peculiar irony here. Ryan, the advocate of an approach to education committed to transmitting an unproblematic conception of the "best" in our culture, also laments that the anti-authority spirit of the sixties undermined the influence of teachers and helped reduce their role to that of a mere technician. But as Giroux notes, "Ryan forgets that much of the deskilling that has characterized teacher work in the 1980s has had little to do with the reforms of the 1960s and a great deal to do with the increased centralization of public school systems and the loss of teacher's control over the conditions of their work" (p. 45). This loss of teacher control has been documented by Apple and Weiss (1983a, 1983b), Apple (1986b, 1988a, 1988b), Aronowitz and Giroux (1985), Giroux (1983b, 1988c), McNeil (1983), and others and includes the institution of accountability models, teacher-proof curricula, and sanitized textbooks.

At a less obvious and deeper level, teacher control over education has always been limited by the dominant influence of certain cultural themes such as the link between market economic ideology and individual political freedom; the prevalence of racist, sexist, and class oppression; and the scientism that permeates social theory. It is also important to point out, as Giroux (1988c) does, that the conservative nostalgia for a "golden age" of schooling is a myth. An analysis of our educational history throughout this century and before reveals no such period (pp. 46–47).

None of these comments should be read as a denial of the significant limitations of the educational and cultural developments of the 1960s and early 1970s. Certainly, many of the proposals of this period were unreflective or worse. The expansion of the drug culture helped make an existing problem more severe. There was also a good deal of anti-intellectualism that did threaten educational standards, as well as mindless forms of pluralism, nihilism, and vacuous approaches to values education such as values clarification. So the conservative critique of the sixties is not without some merit. However, far more rigorous critiques of the sixties reforms have been made by liberals and radicals (e.g., Clacek 1983; Lasch 1979, 1984; Shor 1986; Gitlin 1987). Moreover, Giroux (1988b) is largely correct when he maintains that a careful examination of the conservative critique of the 1960s reveals "a thinly disguised attack on the notion of equity itself" (p. 46). This is part of the more general antidemocratic thrust of the neoconservative restoration grounded by a belief in cultural uniformity and preservation of dominant groups and ideologies.

CRITICAL PEDAGOGY AND ETHICAL THEORY

One reason the neoconservative revival has been so successful is because its rhetoric is consistent with major cultural themes and the common-sense perceptions of its relevance to the concrete problems faced by many working and lower middle class people. But of equal importance to the neoconservative revival is the failure of liberal and radical discourse to provide an adequate response to the neoconservative challenge. Giroux (1988c) argues that "the liberal faith in reason, science, and instrumental rationality has played a decisive role in shifting liberal discourse away from the politics of everyday life while simultaneously grounding its analysis in the celebration of procedural rather than substantive issues" (p. 53). This tendency is exacerbated by the culture of empiricism and scientism that dominates education and the social sciences.

Apple (1986b) is also concerned that critical approaches to the study of schooling have often been too abstract to have significant impact. He calls our attention to the political dimensions of the textual analysis of education. We always write for an intended audience, about something, and from within a specific context that shapes the writer/reader relationship. All of these dimensions of critical scholarship involve choices that are motivated by political values and have political consequences. For example, Apple believes that much of the critical scholarship in education has been elitist, because it is written for a narrow academic audience (p. 199). The overly theoretical and abstract tone of so much critical scholarship tends to make it either irrelevant to most classroom teachers or helps increase their alienation by talking down to them. Apple understands the importance of theory, but he fears that for too many critical educators, theoretical writing has become their only form of political activity. This amounts to an escape into theory disconnected from the concerns of real world teachers and students (p. 264). Obviously an escape into theory is not an adequate response to the neoconservative revival.

There is another important dimension of the failure of critical pedagogy to cope with the neoconservative revival. While critical pedagogy has frequently offered a penetrating critique of how education plays a key role in the reproduction of various forms of inequality and oppression, it has failed to produce a well-defined ethical theory or substantive vision of a preferred social order. We should recall that this was a central concern of the reconstructionists in the 1930s. In other words, the moral indignation of radical educators has too often been expressed in a language that reflects a deep skepticism and is limited to describing the failures of schooling in the United States.

The failure of radical educators to construct an adequate moral theory has enabled conservatives to gain the moral "high ground." In part, this is the result of the failure of most educators on the left to illuminate those historical traditions that would provide a moral vision to guide current efforts toward individual and social transformation (Giroux 1988c, 38). With the loss of a "deep grammar" of moral responsibility, critical "historical inquiry has had a tendency to collapse into an overly determined view of social control in which schools are viewed primarily as reflections of capitalist domination" (p. 38). This had the net effect of removing most radical educators from the center of the current debate over schooling. According to Giroux (1988c), the focus of the current debate should be on the growth of moral relativism, the decline of a democratic public sphere, and the increase in forms of oppression. There is no effective way to contest these phenomena without an adequate moral theory and discourse.

Giroux argues that a radical conception of morality or ethics would include a critique of domination and development of a language of protest or counterlogic to challenge the dominant order. But it must also include a conception of ethics that is linked to a vision of a preferred community wherein democracy is conceived as an ongoing struggle to improve the quality of human life. For Giroux (1988c), a radical moral theory should reject the essentialist and unproblematic conservative conception of morality as well as the "antifoundationalism" of some forms of postmodern and poststructuralist thought (p. 40). In contrast, radical educators must

NEED FOR MORAL THEORY

construct a "provisional" conception of morality, a form of morality that is grounded is those historical referents or instances when people have resisted forms of oppression. Such instances of resistance "provide a priori examples of what principles have to be defended and fought against in the interest of freedom and life" (p. 40). Utilizing these historical examples, radical educators can create an emancipatory discourse of possibility and hope. This provisional morality must not be confused with orthodox Marxist views of history with their assumptions of linear and inevitable progressive development. A radical theory of provisional morality posits no certain future. It takes a partisan standpoint, seeking to understand history as viewed by its victims. This involves an interpretive bias favoring democracy and justice. This "selective reading" of the past assumes a potential for human agency in the face of oppression. Such a radical approach to moral theory also poses a direct challenge to the anti-utopian discourse of both liberal and conservative educators (p. 41).

Apple (1986a, 1986b) is in agreement with the views of Giroux (1988b, 1988c) and McLaren (1988a) that critical pedagogy must provide both a "language of critique" and a "language of possibility." And like these scholars, Apple would ground a language of possibility in a sense of history, especially the often neglected history of struggles against oppression. Like the reconstructionists, Apple (1986a) believes that, as educators, our first task is to educate ourselves concerning social inequality and the ways we might help to enable students, teachers, and others in society to understand and act to create a better world (pp. 178–79). We are unlikely to move away from a society grounded in privatization and greed toward a reconstruction based on the principle of the common good until a sufficient number of people are "convinced that the current and emerging organization of a large part of our economic, political and cultural institutions is neither equal nor just" (p. 178). Indeed, for an analysis of society to hold any potential for change, it must contain the ability to judge social realities against a conception of social justice and morality. This form of thinking helps stimulate resistance and can be a form of resistance in certain contexts (pp. 180–82).

As educators increase their understanding and competence to resist, they can draw on the experiences of various groups that have already established educational sites for radical reform. For example, Apple (1986a) points to the work of the Public Information Network and their reform proposal "Education for a Democratic Future: Equity and Excellence." The main goal of this proposal is to use schools to create sites and forms of "counter-hegemony." Apple also believes that the past struggles over education have been at least partly successful is documented by the fact that schooling itself tends to be more equally distributed than, for example, economic capital, income, or employment status (p. 198).

For Apple (1986b), another critical aspect of educational reform is the restructuring of teacher's work (much like Shor's [1986] proposals) so that they have more time to engage in the reflective analysis necessary to develop modes of resistance. This change would also serve to help reduce the current gap between academics and practioners as well as better clarify the connections between theory and practice (p. 191).

GIROUX'S APPROPRIATION OF SOCIAL RECONSTRUCITON

Giroux (1988c) is one of the few critical educators who has paid serious attention to the social reconstructionists and their relevance to current radical projects to reform education. For Giroux, the reconstructionists represented an important historical movement that sought "to demonstrate the importance of a discourse of democracy and ethics as central elements in the language of schooling" (p. 80). This concern is part of Giroux's challenge to the historical "amnesia" of conservative ideology and an effort to use history as a source of "liberating remembrance" (p. 81). In this sense, history can serve as both a record of specific struggles for liberation and a source for building a theory of political ethics and possibility. Radical traditions like social reconstructionism created communities of "responsible defiance and action" which provide a subversive discourse that can be employed in an emancipatory pedagogical project.

Giroux believes the social reconstructionists were seeking to illustrate the connection between citizenship education and the empowerment of individuals and groups. This required a curriculum committed to developing critical reasoning motivated by the need and possibility of transforming the culture and social order. Giroux (1988c) relies primarily on the work of Dewey, but also on Bode, Childs, Counts, Newlon, Rugg, and Kilpatrick to summarize the relevant aspects of reconstructionism. As noted in Chapter 3, there is some difficulty in reconciling the views of Dewey, Bode, Counts, Childs, and Kilpatrick. Giroux does acknowledge that the reconstructionists were divided over some important issues (p. 86). However, two major concerns remain. First, to what extent is it meaningful or helpful to categorize such disparate personalities as Kilpatrick, Bode, Counts, Childs, and Dewey as reconstructionists? I am not positing a definitive test to determine who was or was not a reconstructionist, but while all of these scholars might be considered "progressives"—even if we accept Kliebard's (1986) reservations concerning the disparate meanings of this term—it might dilute the theoretical power of reconstructionism to stretch its membership too widely. This is especially true in the case of Kilpatrick who was opposed to much of the reconstructionist curriculum rationale. On the other hand, Giroux's attention to the work of John Childs is important. In my earlier work on reconstructionism, I consistently neglected or underestimated Childs' contributions.[1]

Dewey is a more difficult case. Certainly Giroux is correct to include those dimensions of Dewey's work that are consistent with reconstructionism, but as indicated in Chapter 3, Dewey was ambivalent toward the reconstructionist program. Beyond this ambivalence, he was, on occasion, a formidable critic of some of the central positions of reconstructionism. By failing to note this, Giroux runs the risk of misrepresenting the very real tensions and contradictions between pragmatism and social reconstructionism. This is especially important if the writers cited by Giroux as representing reconstructionism would oppose significant elements of his own approach to critical pedagogy. Dewey, for example, might have had some difficulty with Giroux's views regarding provisional morality and authority.[2]

A second and related concern is Giroux's relative neglect of Theodore Brameld's work as central to an understanding of reconstructionism. In Chapter 2, I tried to suggest reasons why Brameld could be considered the most radical of those considered reconstructionists. Indeed, I believe it is Brameld's work that most closely supports Giroux's claims regarding the relevance of reconstructionism. Giroux (1988c) does include references to Brameld in the introduction to *Schooling and the Struggle for Public Life* (pp. 8–10), but he does not include Brameld in his more detailed discussion of reconstructionism in the third chapter of the book (pp. 80–87).

Despite these reservations, I still believe Giroux has made a significant contribution to critical pedagogy by pointing out the importance of social reconstructionism as a genuine instance of democratic resistance to domination as well as an early example of radical curriculum theory in the United States. Let us summarize what Giroux sees as the main legacy of reconstructionism.

First, reconstructionists believed it was essential that educational philosophy be connected to a wider social philosophy grounded in a democratic form of life. This involved a normative orientation or moral ideal which could be used to help critique and guide the reconstruction of community and social practice. Regarding this point, Giroux reminds us of Dewey's understanding of experience as having the potential to produce a "scientific" process which provides the only dependable "authority" to help direct the course of new experiences. This process has the potential to improve upon the past by constructing democratic practices that had not existed previously. This was a critical issue for Dewey, since

---

1. I am indebted to Spencer Maxcy of Louisiana State University for helping me to better understand Childs' work as it related to reconstructionism.

2. The question of provisional morality will be discussed in more detail in Chapter 6.

any community that did not live up to its democratic potential limits the variety of opportunities to critique experience in an effort to enlarge and enrich it. Since this process will continue as long as human experience continues, democracy's task is ongoing sociocultural reconstruction toward a more humane social order (p. 82).

Second, by using democracy as an ideal to orient social criticism and the construction of social policy, schools would become a key institution in the process of social transformation. As Giroux points out, this was an extension of the narrower liberal view of democracy as the context of elections, interest-group politics, and governing. For the reconstructionists, it was essential to connect democracy, ethical theory, and educational theory and practice in order to challenge the dominant social order. As such, schools neither could nor should become moral or politically neutral institutions. For example, the central purpose of schooling, in Dewey's terms, was to develop individuals with the reflective intelligence to act as socially responsible citizens.

Third, based on the assumptions noted above, a reconstructionist approach to education must conceive of intelligence within the context of a theory of social welfare and not as a mere competence to be developed for its own sake. Thus, education could never be limited to epistemological or cognitive dimensions, because it was always bound up with a moral discourse related to the wider sociocultural context (Giroux 1988c, 83–84). It is this relation between intelligence and morality that reveals the "utopian impulse" essential to the construction of democratic communities. In other words, human intelligence holds the potential to imagine a preferred social order or more desirable future and to conceive of means to realize this possibility. According to Giroux, Dewey believed the survival of a democratic culture requires that we must cultivate and extend our faith in this human capacity.

Fourth, democracy required more than a faith in human intelligence linked to ethical theory; it also involved lived communal experiences. Democratic behavior is learned and extended in practice, that is, in face-to-face experiences that help produce subjectivity or "a politics of the body" that is internalized. The importance of such experiences makes clear the necessary connection between schools and the community. The failure to stress this aspect of democracy was one of the central limitations of child-centered progressivism in education.

Fifth, Giroux (1988c) also sees reconstructionism as contributing to "a politics of difference" (p. 85). The reconstructionists feared the totalitarian attempt to produce a monological discourse of homogeneity. Within a totalitarian context, genuine difference is viewed as deviant and a threat to the social order. In contrast, the reconstructionists insisted on open dialogue as essential to the construction and maintenance of a democratic community. In this sense, differences or what we have come to call the "other" is seen as essential to a dialogical process.

Finally, reconstructionists viewed teachers as transformative intellectuals. This role required that teachers "be given the ideological and material conditions necessary for them to make decisions, produce curricula, and act out of their own point of view" (pp. 85–86). For Dewey, giving teachers such power enabled them to help create the conditions for students to experience democratic forms of life. Teachers would find their identities in the mutually supportive activities of democratic curriculum building and forms of social activism. Indeed, Childs insisted that both activities were essential to the practice of a teacher as moral agent (p. 86). These ideas are also evident in the work of Brameld, Counts, and Childs wherein each writer calls for teachers to help build a new democratic social order (e.g., Childs 1936, 277).

THE MAINSTREAM AND LEFT CRITIQUE
OF CRITICAL PEDAGOGY

Although critical educators have tried in various ways to construct a radical educational theory that redresses the weaknesses of more orthodox neo-Marxist critiques of schooling, they have, in turn, provoked critical reaction by mainstream as well as other radical educators. A brief survey of this critical reaction helps illuminate the continuing conflicts, contradictions, and unresolved problems that characterize the development of critical pedagogy over the past two decades.

Among the more prominent mainstream critics of critical pedagogy are C. A. Bowers (1982, 1987) and Kenneth Strike (1989). These two scholars claim that radical educators have, for all practical purposes, abandoned Marxist theory. Strike (1989) has focused on the work of Apple, Bowles and Gintis, Giroux, McLaren, and Willis, among others. In Strike's view, this group of radical educators increasingly exhibits idealist and liberal tendencies. This turn toward liberalism reflects the growing awareness that Marxism is a "degenerate research program" (p. 167). According to Strike, the problems that generated a Marxist research program in education cannot be resolved unless radical educators abandon the central assumptions of Marxism.

C. A. Bowers (1987) makes some similar claims in his critique of Paulo Freire's work. Bowers claims that Freire's views would be understood (and scorned) as a form of "democratic humanism" and "revisionist liberalism" by those who would "rely upon a more scientific Marxism as a basis for their social organization" (p. 37). According to Bowers, there are four basic assumptions that Freire's work shares with liberalism: the view that 1) change is inherently progressive, 2) the individual is the basic unit of society and the source of rationality and freedom, 3) human nature is either naturally good or susceptible to social manipulation toward progressive ends, and 4) human rationality serves as "the real basis of authority for regulating the affairs of everyday life" (p. 2).

Bowers (1982), not surprisingly, has also been a critic of Giroux's work. He has praised Giroux's grasp of neo-Marxist theory and his ability to apply neo-Marxism to a critique of positivist influences on educational theory and practice. But Bowers also claims that Giroux has failed to understand the extent to which the Enlightenment epistime forms a common tradition his version of critical pedagogy shares with positivist and instrumental approaches to education. Specifically, this shared tradition includes the

> anthropocentric university, the efficacy of reason in controlling man's [sic] future, a view of time and change as essentially progressive, a privileged position assigned to intellectuals and experts, and the absence of any real insight into the psychological and sense of the tragic. (p. 420)

Bowers believes that Giroux's failure to understand that his analysis is limited to categories derived from the Enlightenment is evident in much of his writing. For example, he notes Giroux's emphasis on making explicit the origin and purpose of taken-for-granted knowledge and using critical theory to help free individuals from the domination of history. But this sort of analysis neglects the extent to which "culture, as a symbolic schemata, is reproduced through communication and lived as a tacit form of knowledge" (p. 421). Consequently, Giroux tends to "overestimate the power of rational thought...while underestimating how people are psychologically and linguistically rooted in their unconscious history" (pp. 421–22).

Although Giroux has said he is opposed to any form of dialectical critique that would impose a formula for social change, Bowers believes Giroux inadvertently acts as if he had discovered such a formula when he "assumes that acts of resistance are always progressive, that substituting explicit forms of rational thought for the tacit knowledge rooted in tradition is more enlightened, and that people want to make their own history" (p. 422). By dealing with such issues within the framework of the Enlightenment tradition, Giroux ends up misunderstanding the nature and power of culture. Giroux's views also limit his ability to recognize "the way teachers and students are embedded in the language environments that make up culture" (p. 422). All things considered, Bowers believes that Giroux is not truly radical, since he fails to examine critically those basic categories of our Western tradition that have become increasingly problematic.

The critique of critical pedagogy made by Strike and Bowers is puzzling. While it is true that many critical pedagogues have modified their earlier Marxist orientation, this obvious point fails to describe the nature of this process. First, we should recall that radical educators like Apple, Bowles and Gintis, Freire, Giroux, McLaren, Willis, and others have been neo-Marxists, that is, their earliest work already amounted to a significant break with orthodox Marxism. Indeed, the very conception of a critical pedagogy is at odds with orthodox Marxism's tendency to minimize the role of education in the process of sociocultural change. Like the reconstructionists, proponents of critical pedagogy have constructed a theory of education for sociocultural transformation. In addition, the earliest work by many radical educators focused on the cultural as well as material conditions of domination. Freire had developed many of his ideas on education as a form of resistance by the late 1960s. Giroux's early work was strongly influenced by Critical Theory, a neo-Marxist critique that had rejected much of early Marxist theory. Bowers and Strike seem to ignore or underestimate these and other neoMarxist origins of critical pedagogy. In addition, they appear to posit a sort of Marxist litmus test for critical pedagogues, that is, either you are a Marxist or you must be a liberal humanist. This either/or mentality precludes serious consideration of how elements of Marxism, liberalism, and other theoretical positions might be combined in productive ways. Thus, in many respects, both Bowers and Strike have taken a stance that reduces critique to caricature.

As noted earlier, Freire holds out no guarantee for the success of his project, therefore, he does not assume that *all* change (even when intended) is inherently progressive. Furthermore, since dialogue is central to Freire's theory, social group interaction, not the individual, is at the center of planned social change. Freire, like many liberals, is optimistic regarding the potential of education to change human behavior. But as a radical educator, he criticizes liberals for their general failure to understand or acknowledge the deep structural and cultural constraints that reinforce the power of dominant groups. Thus, he rejects as inadequate traditional liberal solutions to social problems. And while Freire does have a modernist faith in the liberating potential of human rationality, he also is sensitive to the real limits on rationality and the constant struggle necessary to secure a public space for genuine rational discourse.

Bowers' specific critique of both Freire and Giroux raises some interesting questions but ultimately ignores the complexity of their work. Like Freire, Giroux does not assume that all acts of resistance are progressive. As pointed out earlier in this chapter, Giroux has been critical of some resistance theorists for failing to analyze sexist, racist, and other anti-democratic aspects of student resistance. Also Giroux has shown an appreciation for the formidable limitations on the exercise of human rationality as well as the importance of the psychological and linguistic dimensions of culture. It seems that Bowers is critical of Giroux for continuing to have faith in the potential of human rationality despite acknowledging the serious obstacles to genuine critical praxis. On the other hand, Bowers' suggestion that critical pedagogy shares traces of the positivism inherent in the very Enlightenment tradition it criticizes is worth further discussion. However, Bowers does not make the best case for this claim, and we will postpone further discussion of the issue until Chapters 5 and 6.

A rather different critique of Giroux's work is made by Reitz and Martin (1984). Although directed at Giroux, much of this critique could be applied as well to other critical pedagogues. Reitz and Martin believe that, despite his intentions, the flaws in Giroux's work probably help "to serve political interests opposed to that for which it was originally intended" (pp. 163-64). For example, Giroux has substituted amorphous notions of resistance and civic courage for the traditional and more "rigorous doctrines" of class struggle, party activism, and revolutionary socialism. Reitz and Martin also contend that Giroux's scholarship is often shallow or incorrect. For instance, Giroux's critique of Bowles and Gintis (and orthodox Marxism as well) is far too mechanistic and materialistic. A careful reading of *Schooling in Capitalist America* (1976) does not sustain Giroux's claim that the book neglects the subjective, individual capacities to effect social change. Half of the book deals with the question of change, and Bowles and Gintis make clear that "simple mechanistic relationships between economic structure and educational development" were not likely to correspond to the available evidence (Reitz and Martin 1984, 167). Furthermore, Bowles and Gintis were not unduly pessimistic since they emphasized revolutionary optimism and activism.

Reitz and Martin also claim that Giroux has misunderstood and incorrectly applied the views of Althusser and Marcuse. Since he relies so heavily on Althusser and Marcuse in his work, this misunderstanding tends to undermine Giroux's own theoretical development. Giroux also posts "civic courage" (i.e., acting *as if* one lived in a democracy) as having emancipatory potential. Yet he has not developed an adequate theoretic base for this claim. According to Reitz and Martin, the philosophy of "as if" or utopian fiction is derived from the work of Hans Vaihinger, but Giroux seems unaware of this or the non- and anti-Marxist aspects of this theory. In short, Giroux's views are closer to some form of radical neoliberalism than to a Marxist theory based on a call for praxis to orient the underclass's struggle against oppression (pp. 170-71).

Finally, Reitz and Martin argue that Giroux's form of radical individualism is often expressed in terms that are so vague they do not constitute a concrete proposal of any kind. This amounts to a fundamental neglect of the need to develop in students a collectivist character oriented toward altruism, cooperation, and social concern for the welfare of others. Anything short of these goals will only serve to aid the interests of educational reactionaries (p. 173).

Giroux has been a prolific writer and, not unexpectedly, his work is not free from error. One well might cite particular passages wherein Giroux has oversimplified or distorted the positions of Althusser, Bowles and Gintis, Marcuse, or others. But to overgeneralize from such possible faults, as Reitz and Martin do, is to miss the constant modification and development of Giroux's thought and his intellectual willingness to incorporate new knowledge and modify or discard untenable positions. In contrast, the Reitz and Martin (1984) critique of Giroux appears to be mired in a reductionist variant of orthodox Marxism that unduly privileges the variables of class and collectivism. It also completely ignores Giroux's efforts to ground critical pedagogy on a theory of social welfare to help orient student concern for wider social problems and the importance of a democratic culture.

The sort of critique raised by Reitz and Martin is only one instance of a wider reaction by some educators on the left who feel that, too often, proponents of critical pedagogy have neglected, distorted, or moved too far from orthodox Marxist insights. A good example is Daniel Liston's (1988) *Capitalist schools: Explanation and ethics in radical studies of schooling.* A major part of Liston's critique is focused on the earlier work of several scholars discussed in this chapter, for example, Apple, Apple and Weis, Bowles and Gintis, and Giroux. In Liston's view, these radical scholars have frequently presented weak arguments with poorly defined goals, inadequate explanations, poor methodology, and a general failure to provide rigorous empirical assessment of their claims. He also contends that while radical educators are critical of functionalist approaches, they nevertheless rely on functionalist assertions in their own work (p. 101).

Liston is concerned with the ethical dimension of critical pedagogy. He observes that the radical educators he examined tend to "claim that the structure of the larger socioeconomic system is unjust and that the schools contribute to the reproduction of the unjust system" (p. 123). According to him, a careful reading of Marx indicates that he found concepts like justice and equality to be problematic. "Marx viewed (and a consistent Marxist tradition would construe) justice as a deficient standard. Marx criticized capitalism morally but his standard was freedom (not justice), a standard embedded in the naturalist ethic" (p. 168). Thus, freedom should serve as the basis for critique of the dominant social order, including curriculum and educational practice. Liston claims a general sympathy with the aims of critical pedagogy, but he is concerned that the problems he has illuminated could result in the failure of this movement.

McLaren (forthcoming c) has rejected Liston's argument as another example of a reductionist orthodox Marxist critique. In particular, McLaren characterizes Liston's arguments for empirical validation as a revival of a discredited empirical position rooted in a conception of objective knowledge and "Truth" as the goal orienting science. McLaren also claims that Liston has misrepresented critical pedagogy (particularly Giroux's work) and posed an analysis that serves to undermine the radical critique of education.

Burbules and Kantor (1988) pose a somewhat more sympathetic critique of critical pedagogy focused on Michael Apple's recent work. In their words, "Explanations in current radical studies in education have, in our view, taken an overwhelmingly culturalist turn, to the neglect of issues concerning political dynamics and the foundation of changing belief structures in changing material interests" (p. 187). Burbules and Kantor hope "to move the point of emphasis a bit further toward an analysis of political economy" (p. 187). They are also much less sanguine than Apple regarding the practical value of promoting more democratic approaches to curriculum and instruction (p. 190). Burbules and Kantor would place more stress on strategies to redress economic and political inequity by giving disenfranchised groups more control over their destiny. Radical school reform is not so much a question of curriculum change but more of finding ways to change the process of school funding and policy-making consistent with a vision of social justice and democracy.

Similar and related concerns have been expressed on other occasions by these and other left education critics (e.g., Liston 1985, 1986, 1988; Burbules 1985, 1986a, 1986b; Dale 1986). These critics function to help keep the debate honest by constantly reminding us of the valuable insights of Marxism and the very real evidence for class inequality and domination. Apple (1988a) is certainly sympathetic to such concerns, but in a direct response to Burbules and Kantor, he makes the following comments.

> To underplay the truly constitutive role of the cultural/ideological is to risk losing some of the gains we have made in recognizing the importance of ideological and cultural processes in conflicts over power. To separate it out as epiphenomenal is also to risk falling back into the trap of base-superstructure models we have moved away from. Not to see the constant and contradictory interactions among economy, culture, and politics—to treat the realism of ideology as merely "ideas" rather than social practices—is to fall prey to the same kind of errors that led us to create separate domains of cognitive, affective, and psychomotor behavior in educational theory and practice....(pp. 193–94)

Class leadership can only be effective in complex industrial societies by winning public consent via some hegemonic accord. Like other material conditions, "[p]opular beliefs and lived culture 'are themselves material forces' and have a major impact on human existence" (p. 194). To focus too much on class is to neglect the significance of race, gender, and other critically important determinants of oppression simply because they do not fit within the rather narrow framework of orthodox Marxist theory.

A very different sort of critique is raised by other critical educators (e.g., Ellsworth 1989; McCarthy 1988; Roman, Christian-Smith, and Ellsworth 1988; Sultan 1989) who pose serious questions concerning the capacity of neo-Marxist critical pedagogy to account for issues of domination related to gender, race, ethnicity, lifestyle, and other considerations. Sultan (1989), in a summary of some of these critical reactions, acknowledged the considerable achievements of the neo-Marxist educators, including Apple and Giroux. Such critics have mounted a successful challenge to the dominance of behaviorism, scientism, and psychologism. They have also helped to shift the focus from a pervasive preoccupation with education as a mental process to a concern with the cultural, social, economic, and political dimensions of schooling. Despite these considerable achievements, Sultan believes that neo-Marxist educators have failed to address adequately those identity-related issues regarding gender, race, and sexuality (p. 13).

Sultan argues that the theoretical language of neo-Marxism is a major cause of its present limitations. Like all theoretical positions, neo-Marxist critical theory is historically conditioned, and the historical conditions of advanced capitalism have exposed the inadequate aspects of neo-Marxist approaches to curriculum (pp. 13–14). Sultan points to a number of transformations in advanced capitalist societies that have resulted in complex and contradictory consequences, including the recent growth of cultural neoconservatism, rapid technological development—especially our increasing dependence on communications media and computers—the expansion of multinational corporations, the spread of welfare-state intervention, the erosion of state sovereignty, genetic research and the growth of biotechnical impact on the individual, the expansion of nuclear and space technology and weaponry, and the growth of new social and political movements concerned with issues of race, gender, ethnicity, alternative lifestyles, and the environment. The effect of these changes cannot be understood solely in terms of domination or a top-down relationship, because in contemporary mass culture the subcultural influences of marginal groups are frequently more influential than more traditional mainstream cultural forms.

Furthermore, the growth of new political movements, such as religious fundamentalism or the neoconservative revival, are often driven more by cultural or social concerns (e.g., school prayer, flag desecration, abortion) than the social relations of production. Indeed, such movements are frequently at odds with mainstream state policy. Sultan concluded that sociocultural issues related to preferred social values, norms, and knowledge forms cannot be understood adequately via "objective" scientific method or "even a critique of the political economy of education—whether from the Right or the Left. In this sense, neo-Marxist analysis has lost most of its value" (p. 14).

In the United States and other industrialized, capitalist/welfare-state societies, the complex multiplicity of groups, institutions, discourses, and modes of association reflect the asymmetrical differentiations of power and inequality linked to class, race, gender, ethnicity, age, and sexuality. For Sultan (1989), the loss of theoretical certainty, the rising plurality of social movements, and rapid technological developments all warrant a pragmatic response. Of the available pragmatic perspectives, Sultan recommended the Critical Theory of Jürgen Habermas as offering the best potential for developing a critical pedagogy (p. 19).

Sultan's description of the rapidly changing historical context and the problems it creates for critical pedagogy is accurate, and I agree with his attempt to emphasize the importance of Habermas to the current debate. However, he does not give adequate consideration to the following: 1) the extent to which critical pedagogy has already begun to incorporate the theoretical insights of feminism, cultural studies, postmodernism, poststructuralism, and neopragmatism, and 2) the controversy and limitations associated with Habermas' project. For all the complexity of his analysis, Sultan opts too soon for a reductionist solution. Habermas' work should not be neglected by critical pedagogy, but we are certainly not at the point where it is evident that Habermas provides the core theoretical ground for the "correct" critical approach to curriculum. Yet this latter point seems to be Sultan's claim.

James Paul Gee's (1988) work on critical literacy helps to illuminate some of the problems we must confront in developing a theory of critical pedagogy. Although his critique is somewhat oblique, it poses fundamental questions for any emancipatory project. Gee has been influenced by the work of Harvey Graff (1987a, 1987b), Cook-Gumperz (1986), Scollon and Scollon (1981), and Scriber and Cole (1981), all of whom have questioned the basic assumption regarding literacy made by most mainstream educators. These mainstream assumptions amount to what Graff (1987a, 1987b) has called the "literacy myth." According to Graff, there is very little historical evidence for our belief that literacy leads to a public better able to think logically and analytically; the construction of complex government structures and an increase in political democracy; increased wealth and productivity; a more innovative, cosmopolitan, and politically aware society; increased political stability; less crime; and so on. Gee (1988) argues that the available evidence indicates that the "literacy myth" is losing its support and that the attention of the educational community is turning, more and more, to an investigation of the ways in which mainstream approaches to literacy work to undermine the interests of marginal groups and reinforce inequality while simultaneously claiming to reduce it (p. 196).

Gee traces the controversies over literacy in Western culture to Plato's critique of writing and preference for the spoken word. For Plato, writing was a threat to real knowledge because it relieved us of the need to know by allowing knowledge to be stored in an external location, the text. Plato believed this would lead to a deterioration of human memory and the inclination to take the words of written texts at face value. Writing, unlike oral dialogue, could not be interrogated or made to explain itself. Over time it would take on the character of authoritative self-sufficiency. True knowledge, for Plato, occurred in oral dialogue wherein one had to explain what he or she meant. Of course, Plato was sophisticated enough to know that certain forms of orality (e.g., the epic poetic tradition) could have the same effects as writing, causing us to take for granted the contents of our cultural traditions (p. 198). So in the end, "Plato's deeper attack is against any form of language or thought that cannot stand up to the question, what do you mean?" (p. 198). This question, much like the work of Bakhtin (1981), is an attempt to critique any language form that tries to influence us by claims based on authority or traditions as opposed to "a genuine disinterested search for truth" (Gee 1988, 198). So only dialogic thought, speaking, and writing were considered authentic by Plato, and he understood writing to be inherently inclined to function in an antidialogic manner.

This summary of Plato's views make him appear to be a precursor of progressive education—that is, one who favored process over product. But, we must also consider another more political dimension of Plato's thought. Plato was an opponent of the prevailing political system in Athens. He was a revolutionary who had proposed a utopian blueprint for a preferred social order in his *Republic*. But Plato's utopian conception was based on an authoritative reading of society wherein people were born into natural social positions. Understood in this way:

> Plato's attack on writing takes on additional meaning. His objection that the written text can get in the wrong hands, that it cannot defend itself, is an objection to the fact that the reader can freely interpret the text without the author ("authority") being able to "correct" that interpretation; that is to stipulate the correct interpretation.... Plato wants the author to stand as a voice behind the text not just to engage in responsive dialogue, but to enforce canonical interpretations. (Gee 1988, 199–200).

Obviously, this impulse is contained in the current "correct" view of the canon and the culture reflected in the neoconservative thought of Alan Bloom, William Bennett, Diane Ravitch, E. D. Hirsch, and others.

Gee (1988) sees Plato as presenting two basic functions of literacy, that is, as liberator and as weapon. In this sense, Plato seems to want it both ways. On one hand, he wants to guarantee that the "text" can respond dialogically. On the other hand, Plato hopes to ensure that the voice of the text "is not overridden by respondents who are careless, ignorant, lazy, self-interested, or ignoble" (Ibid.). Thus, Plato has posed a genuine dilemma. His authoritative view of text is capable of ending dialogue by specifying what would count as a correct response. Yet there is no simple solution to this problem for: "if all interpretations (re-sayings) count, then none do, as the text then says everything and therefore nothing. And if it takes no discipline, experience, or 'credentials' to interpret, then it seems all interpretations *will* count" (Ibid.). Gee believes there is no easy way out of this dilemma, although there have been many attempts to do so. Indeed, the literacy myth has been one of the most recent attempts.

The history of literacy documented by Graff illustrates how Plato's dilemma has been acted out. As Gee (1988) explains, there is a striking continuity in Graff's historical research regarding how "literacy has been used. . .to solidify the social hierarchy, empower elites, and ensure that people lower in the hierarchy accept the values, norms, and beliefs of the elites, even when it is not in their self-interest (or 'class interest') to do so" (p. 205). In fact, literacy has proven to be a most effective technique to support Gramsci's concept of hegemony. There is considerable evidence that lower class speakers denigrate their own local forms of speech in favor of the ostensibly normal standards imposed by the middle class. This has the effect of making middle-class speech appear normative when in reality it represents "the historical empowering of one set of localized, community-based conventional behaviors over other sets" (p. 206). This hegemonic domination is also effective in a wide range of behaviors beyond language. In effect then, social stratification has not been preserved so much in terms of different group levels of literacy as by controlling "a certain type of school-based literacy. . .associated with the values and aspirations of the middle classes" (p. 206).

But Gee also raises questions concerning those who seek to promote the liberating or emancipatory side of Plato's dilemma, for instance Paulo Freire (1970a, 1970b, 1970d, 1973, 1985). Freire and his supporters believed that literacy could empower the masses to the extent it enabled them to become active questioners of social reality. Freire sought to develop the individuals creative, critical spirit as opposed to passive acceptance of the dominant culture. However, Freire remains caught in Plato's basic dilemma. Gee (1988) demonstrates this by citing numerous instances where Freire spoke of helping people "to learn to think correctly" or to understand the "correct sense of political militancy" as a characteristic of "the new man and new woman" (pp. 207–208). There is a great irony in a radical pedagogy which focused on questions and was "less certain of 'certainties' " that also knew what it means to *think* correctly. In the end, Freire also has his *Republic* and does not escape Plato's dilemma. As Gee concludes, nothing necessarily follows from literacy, but much can follow from the values and norms that must accompany different approaches to literacy and schooling. In fact, Gee believes that there is no way to promote literacy without an ideological commitment (p. 208).

This analysis begs the question, is a truly emancipatory approach to literacy even possible if every approach must have a built-in perspective? First, we need to try to make our assumptions explicit, since implicit assumptions continue to serve political ends under the guise of neutrality. The research regarding the insidious effects of current mainstream approaches to literacy is a case in point (e.g., Cazden 1987; Cook-Gumperz 1986; Heath 1983). Second, we need to reexamine the prevailing emphasis on schooling to enable individuals to think for themselves (Gee 1988). This individualistic approach tends to neglect the *social* nature of human understanding and interpretation. To illustrate the point, consider that there are many types of texts and each can be read in a variety of ways. The various types of texts and kinds of readings possible are derived from social and historical conditions. Gee holds that we "always and only learn to interpret texts of a certain type in certain ways through having access to, and ample experience in, social settings where texts of that type are read in those ways" (p. 209). Consequently, one never really thinks for oneself "rather one always thinks for (really *with* and *through*) a group— the group which socialized one into that practice of thinking" (p. 209). In our lifetime, we are typically socialized into several different groups, and the sort of group thinking we employ tends to vary in different contexts.

If we accept Gee's arguments, then true literacy requires that we learn about those different groups and institutions involved in our socialization and the socialization of other groups with whom we are likely to come in contact. This would involve far more than studying the linguistic behavior of such groups. In short, literacy for emancipation must be conceived in nontraditional ways. In the end it "comes down to whether the social groups and institutions that underwrite various types of texts and ways of interpreting them can be changed" (p. 210). Schools are a key social institution to assist in such a project, since they socialize us beyond the home and peer group, ostensibly in an attempt to enable us to participate in the public sphere.

Gee's (1988) critique of Freire should not be read as a rejection of Freire's pedagogy but rather as an attempt to illuminate a fundamental problem (or universal dilemma) for all critical educators: that is, given the persuasive arguments against the possibility of transparent or objective knowledge, how do we establish the authority for an emancipatory curriculum theory to help transform our sociocultural environment. Gee does point out that Freire acknowledges that no educational program, including his approach to critical literacy, can be politically neutral (p. 208). Left unexamined, in Gee's essay, are the attempts by Freire to struggle with the authority for a critical pedagogy.

McLaren (1986) has examined this issue and provides us with a view of Freire that relates to the dilemma posed by Gee, although he does not comment directly on Gee's argument. McLaren (1986) reminds us that Freire viewed critical literacy as a critical engagement with a world in process, not a given world (p. 397). Freire does claim that a critical pedagogy requires a utopian orientation. But the suffering of the oppressed forms Freire's reference point to ground his project, and this is a concrete rather than a transcendental fiat which nevertheless compels our affirmation of our humanity and our solidarity with victims of oppression (p. 397).

Freire's language of emancipation, therefore, does not exist outside of concrete instances of human action and struggle. Yet it "speaks to a univocal and sovereign concern: common human suffering that must be alleviated and transformed" (p. 397). While he offers no guarantee for the success of his pedagogical project, Freire does argue for a program that gives priority to ameliorating oppression. Beyond this, Freire presents a strong case for the fundamentally dialogical nature of human existence. On this point McLaren acknowledges the similarity of Freire and Rorty's views inasmuch as both understand truth as "conversation" as opposed to "reflection of essence" (p. 400). Thus, Freire claims no final answers but does point to the need for a process of continual struggle with specific concrete situations as well as multiple theoretical positions. There can be no closure for truth or transcendental justification, since history is always a process of becoming via human praxis. In this sense, Freire's conception of utopianism involves implementing counter discourse to contest oppression and illuminate the contingency of forms of domination (p. 400).

Freire's use of the term "correct thinking" is unfortunate to the extent that it obscures the complexity of his pedagogical theory and his grasp of the dialogical and contingent nature of truth. Indeed, as McLaren (1988b) explains, Freire's approach to critical literacy provides a direct critique of the authoritarian and prescriptivist approach to literacy taken by Bloom (1987) and Hirsch (1987). Freire has said that he refuses to write texts that give recipes for action as this tends to domesticate the mind. His critical approach to literacy assumes literacy is both multivocal and characterized by its own surplus of meaning. Freire understands that meaning (regardless of the author's "intent") can never be essentialized outside the historical context in which such meanings were generated or those in which readers interact with the text.

FEMINIST CRITIQUE OF CRITICAL PEDAGOGY

Over the past two decades, a substantial body of critical feminist scholarship on education has emerged. This feminist educational scholarship is one part of the much wider production of feminists work on philosophy, gender, cultural studies, social theory, history, and science. The relationship between critical feminist work on education and critical pedagogy is complex. The two movements overlap and are mutually reinforcing in several ways. Feminist educators have made important contributions to both critical pedagogy and the general critique of mainstream schooling (e.g., Arnof 1984; Arnof and Weiner 1987; Brennan 1989; Bunch and Pollack 1983; Culley and Portuges 1985; Gilligan 1982; Grumet 1988; Kenway and Modra 1989; McRobbie 1978; Noddings 1984; Pagano 1990; Roman, Christian-Smith, and Ellsworth 1988; Shrewsbury 1987a, 1987b; Weiler 1988). However, there are also serious tensions between elements of the feminist critique of education and discourse of critical pedagogy, and recently, some feminist educators have posed a direct critique of the theory and practice of critical pedagogy (e.g., Ellsworth 1989, 1990; Luke, unpublished manuscript).

We should recall that feminism, like critical pedagogy, is a general term that refers to a wide range of theory and practice. While feminists do share common concerns such as sexism and the use of gender as a basis for domination in a patriarchal society, they differ significantly in terms of how they analyze and seek to explain such phenomenon. It is more accurate, therefore, to speak of *feminisms* rather than feminism (Brennan 1989; Christian 1988; Harding 1986; Jagger 1983; Harding and Hintikka 1983; Hooks 1984; Nicholson 1990; Pagano 1990).

So there is no "feminist" critique of critical pedagogy; rather there are a range of questions and criticisms raised by different feminist educators. Among the criticisms posed by feminist educators, some stand out more than others. First, radical male (and mainly white) educators are frequently criticized for being gender blind in their work and either ignoring or failing seriously to study feminist scholarship. Second, the theoretical orientation of critical pedagogy is often framed within epistemologies (e.g., neo-Marxism, Critical Theory) that are understood as essentially masculinist and patriarchal. Finally, various feminists believe that critical pedagogy has failed to address adequately issues related to difference, otherness, and authority as explicated in poststructuralism and postmodernism.

It is the case that most critical pedagogues (as well as social reconstructionists) have been male, white, and middle class. Such educators likely experience a very different sociocultural environment than women, people of color, or other minorities working in the same profession. Moreover, almost all of the major theoreticians whose work provides the intellectual base for critical pedagogy—for example, Aristotle, Marx, Freud, Dewey, Counts, Adorno, Horkheimer, Gramsci, Habermas, Bourdieu, Althusser, Freire, and others—are white males whose work has frequently been gender blind or even sexist. Carmen Luke (unpublished manuscript) argues that the discourse of critical pedagogy has primarily constructed a masculinist subject and been driven by a concern to resolve problems rooted in male experience. By failing to engage in a coherent and systematic theorization of gender, critical pedagogy ends up restating and valorizing the great patriarchal metanarratives of history. In Luke's view, women's issues have, for the most part, been marginal to critical pedagogy. Until critical pedagogy makes a serious effort to critique its own gender blindness and reexamine the masculinist epistemology at its core, it will lack true emancipatory potential. Luke is a rather harsh critic of critical pedagogy and we will give more attention to her arguments shortly. But even a feminist like Weiler (1988), who is sympathetic to the project of critical pedagogy, has argued that, with few exceptions, critical pedagogy has "simply failed to consider the question of gender to any serious extent at all" (p. 4). Weiler recommends a synthesis of critical pedagogy and feminist analysis as the basis for a more effective pedagogy oriented toward emancipation.

Like Weiler, other feminist educators that have called our attention to the importance of gender and the evidence for the persistence of masculinist epitemologies have done so without the wholesale rejection or condemnation of critical pedagogy. For instance, Grumet (1988) has developed a feminist perspective on the question of reproduction in education. Both social reconstructionism and critical pedagogy have tended to view social reproduction as a major problem for critical educators. In other words, reproduction has been criticized as characteristic of the transmission model of mainstream education, an approach that functions to reify the forces of domination. But for Grumet, "[w]hat is most fundamental to our lives as men and women sharing a moment on this planet is the process of reproducing ourselves" (p. 8).

Reproduction can be understood in several ways. First, there is the literal sense of the biological reproduction of our species. But more relevant to schooling is the metaphorical conception of cultural reproduction, that is, one generation extending the traditions that shaped it to the next. It is this second conception of reproduction that has most concerned radical educators. But Grumet argues that cultural reproduction need not degenerate into mere ideology. "For reproducing ourselves also brings a critical dimension to biological and ideological reproduction by suggesting the reflexive capacity of parents to reconceive our own childhoods and education as well as our own situations as adults and to choose another way for ourselves expressed in the nurture of our progeny" (p. 8). It is this third critical conception of reproduction that Grumet believes should be expressed in curriculum. Indeed, the parent/child relation is the most fundamental subject/object relationship, and the biological and cultural mediation of this relationship has resulted in the evolution of distinct feminine and masculine epistemologies. Grumet's views on pedagogy are strongly influenced by the object relations theory of Nancy Chodorow (1978, 1985) as well as other feminists such as Dinnerstein (1976) and Kristeva (1982, 1984).

Chodorow (1978) has argued that child-rearing practices provide an essentially different experience for males and females. In the case of males, their identity as subjects is formed, to a great extent, by the process of separating from the mother. Males, so this reasoning goes, are preoccupied with boundaries and differentiation. Females, in contrast, develop a sense of self that is relational. This early development of male and female orientations toward the self and knowledge is further shaped and highlighted by our patriarchal society and culture.

In a related argument, Pagano (1988) claims that the "ambiguity of paternity" has also functioned to provide an impulse and foundation for patriarchal society. Since paternity cannot be established with certainty, it has been institutionalized via law and language, such as taking the name of the father and laws related to private property rights and inheritance. Certainly linking sexuality and property is a principal factor in mixing production and reproduction.

Neither Grumet (1988) nor Pagano (1988) believe we should be forced to choose between male and female epistemologies or approaches to curriculum. According to Grumet (1988), the paternal approach to curriculum seeks compensation for the inferential nature of paternity and tries to claim children by teaching them to master and assimilate the language and authorized texts of the father. The object relation's orientation is sustained by a capitalist system "that draws men away from parenting and into institutions that require behavioral obedience and an orientation to external authority, thus reinforcing the repressions of the preoedipal experience" (p. 18). This argument is similar to positions taken by some critical theorists, but Grumet finds the latter critique too "skewed in the weight it gives to the labor and love of the fathers in determining the character and culture of our world" (p. 18).

A masculinist epistemology reflects a search for means to influence and control an orientation toward productivity. Subjects and objects are not viewed as mutually constituting each other but related in terms of cause/effect, activity/passivity (Grumet 1988, 22). This orientation has led us to some of the most positivist and mindless educational reform, in particular those associated with back to basics, competency testing, and process/product research and programs. Nevertheless, Grumet also sees a commendable courage in the paternal curriculum's attempt to accept the political dimensions of schooling and willingness to try to shape the future (p. 23).

In contrast, a feminist epistemology reflects the dialectical interdependence of subject and object. The child's achieving independence is facilitated by the earlier satisfaction of the need for intimacy, dependence, and nurturance (p. 27). This reproductive labor is also a fundamental part of the process of civilization. The point is to appropriate the valid insights of the masculine curriculum without denying the equally critical elements of feminist epistemology. Making a similar point, Pagano (1988) argues that as production and reproduction get mixed up in the process of education, we often lose sight of what she calls the "claim of philia," that is, "the claim of affiliation that helps bind us together as an educational community. To seek affiliation is to temper our need for proof to make tolerable the ambiguity for paternity" (p. 524). Pagano seeks to contradict patriarchal culture without denying it.

> There is no conflict between nurturance and authority. If we think so and assert the value of mom's world over dad's, we have entered the nexus of exchange. We become sexless, ironically at the very moment when we assert our sex. As ourselves and no other to ourselves we must see each as giving point to the other to engender a new thing. (p. 527)

Patriarchal forms of curriculum were authoritarian, but that is not to be confused with authoritative. The problem with a patriarchal orientation is its failure to acknowledge the importance of reproduction. The claim of patriarchy then becomes a "single-sided concern with totalizing discourse" that tends to convey knowledge into another commodity to be exchanged within a capitalist economy. Yet the "[r]omanticized, ritualized, sentimentalized, theatricalized, privatized claims of matriarchy similarly wedge knowledge into the cramped corners of commodity relations" (p. 528).

The claim of philia presents an alternative in which knowledge holds a use as offered to an exchange value. This claim also defies abstraction, since we can only affiliate with particular subjects. It is a claim on both men and women. Our attention is directed not only to texts but to textuality and the process of reading texts. The claim of philia understands that our reading of texts will always be potential and unauthorized but that such reading provides the basis for our authority.

> The trick is to let the unauthorized inform the authorized without distorting it. This is the root sense, the radical sense of information—to form and shape. Authority comes from our willingness to claim the shapes we make and to lend our bodies for a while to conform to the shapes around us. Our

teaching and our authority become transparent in the face of the claim of
philia, a claim that demands that we let our language speak us even as we
speak it. (p. 529)

I take feminist work like Grumet's and Pagano's to be part of the critique
of critical pedagogy, since the views they hold as central are most often
ignored or on the periphery of work done by male radical educators.
Feminists such as Brennan (1989), Grumet (1988), Pagano (1988), and
Weiler (1988) have sought to increase our awareness of gender issues and
feminist approaches to curriculum, to contradict without totally rejecting
radical masculinist conceptions of epistemology. Other feminist critics have
taken a far stronger stance against critical pedagogy.

Carmen Luke (unpublished manuscript), whose work was mentioned
earlier, believes that the original failure of radical male educators to reflect
critically on the essentially masculinist assumptions of their own theorizing
makes problematic their entire project for curriculum. For example, the
attempt by critical pedagogues to give voice to women in "democratic"
classroom settings can be viewed as an add-on strategy of incorporation
which fails to deal with the more fundamental conditions that limit
genuine female citizenship. The radical male educator, in Luke's view, has
retained the private/public dichotomy at the core of liberalism and the
classical model of citizenship derived from the Greeks. In practice, female
work is frequently relegated to the private sphere while males have far
more opportunity to engage in the "public sphere."

Luke also finds a similar orientation on the part of reconstructionist
oriented progressives like Counts and Dewey. For Luke, these are
patriarchal liberals whose work has often been valorized in critical
pedagogy (e.g., Giroux and McLaren 1986, 216; Giroux 1988c, chaps. 1
and 2). Luke (unpublished manuscript) cites the following statement by
Dewey to document his masculinist orientation and clear-cut position
regarding the separation of public and private. "[W]hen men act, they act
in a common and public world" (Dewey 1916, 297). The failure by critical
pedagogues to acknowledge and critique the masculinist theorizing of
Greek philosophers, liberal progressives, and Marxists constitutes, for Luke
(unpublished manuscript), an instance of "dangerous memory," that is,
a conception of male individualism, power, and discourse obscured by
a rhetoric of individual and social empowerment.

According to Luke, critical pedagogy has overlooked the history of the
private/public split that has provided a ground for both liberal democratic
theory and division (along gender lines) of work and political involvement
in our society. A gender-blind valorization of male masterdiscourses has,
ironically, undermined the very effort by critical pedagogy to provide a
language of critique to challenge various forms of domination. Luke does

accept that it is important to encourage critical dialogue and give students the analytic tools to better understand their experiences and the forces acting on them. However, to engage in this approach to pedagogy within the framework of the current sociocultural matrix seems to assume that the development of critical praxis via education will somehow lead to the transformation of the structures and contradictions of our patriarchal society. For Luke, this is an unrealistic hope, since women and other marginalized groups are often too intimidated to participate in counter-hegemonic practices in male-dominated educational settings. This is a concern raised earlier by Lewis and Simon (1986) and in Ellsworth's (1989) more recent critique of critical pedagogy.

Luke (unpublished manuscript) also questions the authenticity of those "confessions" of marginalized students who do occasionally give voice to their views and feelings. There is a real danger, argues Luke, that critical pedagogues will valorize such examples as authentic and above criticism, regardless of the racism, sexism, homophobia, or other experiences that might structure these student expressions. As Luke argues:

> privileging experience as foundational to knowledge or as a transparent window to the "real" denies its situatedness in networks of discourses that constitute subjectivities in the first place, and that enable articulation of experience from discussing constituted subject positions. (p. 19)

Both teachers and students are implicated in discursive formations. This situation does not preclude an emancipatory pedagogy, but it does suggest that the attempt to employ critique and action at the classroom level without first criticizing the metanarratives (mostly male) that help maintain the current institution and discourses of schooling might entirely miss the point. Put another way, the attempts by male critical pedagogues to democratize classrooms and promote counterhegemonic practice is unlikely to have much impact on the very gender-structured divisions that have served to sustain liberal capitalism and its knowledge industries. Indeed, the system of liberal democracy has itself stimulated and absorbed various discourses and strategies for equality.

Critical pedagogy, Luke agrees, is a more responsible approach to schooling than dominant, conservative transmission models. But Luke laments the failure of critical pedagogues to clarify how they hope to translate their practice into democratic social change, given the current emphasis on an androgynous conception of citizenship located in a culture characterized by male domination. In the end, the discursive radicalism of critical pedagogy appears grounded in an idealist form of liberalism.

Luke (unpublished manuscript), like Grumet and Pagano, relies heavily on the work of Chodorow (1978). She also draws much of her argument from Hartsock's (1987) work. Luke (unpublished manuscript) claims that she has not taken an essentialist position regarding gender, and she denies that gender provides any justification for sexual division related to either child rearing or labor. Yet gender does suggest a set of boundary config- urations that are sexually differentiated, and these configurations might help shape different male and female orientations toward the self, the other, and life in general. Here, Luke relies on the work of Hartsock (1987) who claims that females face a series of boundary challenges (e.g., pregnancy, giving birth, coitus, menstruation) that preclude holding a view of rigid separation for the objective world (p. 167). Conversely, males appear to rely on a more egocentric and boundary-dependent conception of the self. By rejecting the female relational experience of life, males construct a self that seeks to dominate life and devalues the feminine aspects of life such as nature. Luke (unpublished manuscript) argues that the historical record of the human capacity for self-destruction is largely a male phenomenon.

Luke finds traces of this male orientation toward domination of life in the Critical Theory that permeates much of the scholarly work in critical pedagogy. While Critical Theory does seek to critique patriarchal relations, Luke believes this school of thought has failed to recognize its own masculinist orientation, for example, its valorization of a Western concep- tion of the rational self as universal. Thus, Critical Theory fails to account for the formation of human subjects who are not Western males. One manifestation of this phenomenon is Critical Theory's hostility to popular culture and mass culture in contrast to the privileging of male-oriented high culture. Luke argues that critical pedagogy has incorporated this orientation by idealizing and romanticizing human agency and cultural authenticity. A major goal of critical pedagogy is to develop student's literacy so as to reveal the distortions of mass culture. But this posits a false dichotomy that leaves no space for the genuine integration of mass and popular culture. Such uncritical valorization of popular culture amounts to what Wexler (1987) has called a "backward looking radical romanticism" (p. 184).

Feminist critiques have simultaneously stimulated and problematized the course of critical pedagogy. Feminists have had some success getting radical male educators to take women's issues seriously and to recognize gender as a major focus of domination along with class, race, ethnicity, sexual identity, and so forth. Indeed, feminists appear to have had a major influence on the incorporation of "difference" or "otherness" into the discourse of critical pedagogy. One conspicuous example is Michael Apple who has made gender a major focus of his analysis of domination and education (Apple and Weis 1983a, 1983b; Apple 1986b). Many other radical male educators have joined in this effort, and the evidence would suggest that there is a growing attention to gender issues and feminist scholarship on the part of male radical educators (e.g., Giroux 1988a, 1988b, 1988c; Lewis and Simon 1986; McCarthy 1988; McLaren and Hammer 1989; McLaren 1988c, 1988d; Pinar 1988a, 1988b; Wexler 1987). And yet Wexler (1987), Luke (unpublished manuscript), and Ellsworth (1989) still lament the failure of most radical male educators to make a serious commitment to the study and incorporation of feminist scholarship.

Feminist critics are correct to point out those instances of continued resistance and indifference to their scholarship on the part of radical male educators. A case in point, reexamination of my own earlier work on education indicates that I have given relatively little serious attention to feminist scholarship. Too often, radical male educators have assumed that the oppression of women could be addressed via some more general framework (e.g., class, communicative competence, etc.), and did not require an in-depth analysis of feminist scholarship. Consequently, much of the recent attention by male educators to gender and feminist theorizing often appears to be an add-on, a supplement to the core of critical pedagogic theory based on neo-Marxism, Critical Theory, and other elements. And even those radical male educators who have demonstrated a significant awareness of the importance of feminist scholarship are still capable of producing scholarship in which feminist theory appears as relatively marginal when judged in terms of the actual textual space devoted to such theory (e.g., Beyer and Apple 1988; Giroux and McLaren 1989; McLaren 1989).

Nevertheless, there are real signs of positive change, and we should also try to understand the dissemination of feminist thought in a wider historical context. For example, the present theoretical orientations of critical pedagogy (e.g., various forms of neo-Marxism and Critical Theory) were not accepted or incorporated overnight. As recently as 1980, one could participate in national professional conferences where it was obvious that very few members of the audience had ever heard of Critical Theory. Today references to the terminology and work of critical theorists has become relatively widespread, even in some mainstream journals. This dissemination of theory has not occurred without considerable resistance, nor has it led to any monological convergence of thought as the recent conflicts among radical educators makes clear. Furthermore, the scholarship of male theorists (e.g., Dewey, Counts, Habermas, Freud, Freire, Marx, and others) is, like feminist scholarship, susceptible to being distorted, reduced to a mere add-on to a more favored theory, or cited with only a superficial understanding of the work itself. We need to recall that all serious scholarship requires extensive study before its relation to current theory and practice is revealed. To accomplish this level of study one must turn away, at least temporarily, from his or her current practice. This turning toward something new is not a simple process. It requires both an intellectual and emotional investment. A change in theoretical orientation takes time and energy, and it is too reductionist to attribute the failure to incorporate feminist scholarship merely to a masculinist approach to thought. Dichotomous theories of male versus female modes of thought have been called into question by many feminist scholars (e.g., Nicholson 1990), and there are always numerous factors and contingencies that might help explain how and why new theoretical positions are incorporated, resisted, distorted, or ignored.

What is encouraging is the evidence of the rapidly increasing awareness by radical male educators of the importance of feminist theory. Giroux (1988c) has acknowledged that "no adequate understanding of contemporary social issues and problems can neglect the theoretical and political contributions of women" (pp. 91–92), and he cites an extensive list of feminist scholarship that has influenced his thinking (p. 234). Some feminists might wish that such scholarship was more thoroughly incorporated into Giroux's work, but he does seem to be making a serious attempt to understand feminist scholarship and how it informs curriculum theory. We can also note other recent examples of the serious exploration of feminist theory by radical male educators (e.g., McCarthy 1988; McLaren 1988c, 1988d; McLaren and Hammer 1989; Pinar 1988a, 1988b; Pinar, Reynolds, and Hsu, forthcoming; Wexler 1987). So while we must acknowledge that the incorporation of feminist scholarship by radical male educators has too often been belated and incomplete, there is good evidence that the influence of feminism will continue to grow and be a major source of critical curriculum theory.

Luke's (unpublished manuscript) argument that critical pedagogy has not adequately reflected on its intrinsically masculinist heritage and theory is questionable. Luke is correct to suggest that we should consider the gender-blindness of male theoreticians, since this might have had a negative impact on their theory, and her specific observations regarding the pervasive gender-blindness of orthodox Marxist theory are well taken. However, her arguments concerning Aristotle, Dewey, Marx, and Critical Theory are less convincing. Part of the problem stems from Luke's rather narrow view of the private/public dichotomy. While a distinction between private and public action has formed a focus of analysis in Greek political thought and much subsequent theorizing, the sort of practical reasoning (*phronesis*) discussed by Aristotle is not limited to the public sphere as narrowly conceived. While the encounter among relatively equal, male, white citizens in the polis was, for Aristotle, the paradigmatic locus of practical reasoning, such reasoning could never be restricted to the polis. We will consider this question in greater detail in Chapter 6. At this point, we should note that practical reasoning transcends public and private dichotomies, that is, the sort of reasoning required to be a competent citizen is the same as the reasoning we need to be competent family members, parents, friends, or even the solitary reader of texts (Gadamer 1975; Whitson and Stanley 1988, 1990). So while Greek thinkers might have assumed that males were innately superior practitioners of practical reasoning, even they could not restrict this competence to men only. Thus, Aristotle, despite his considerable sexism, remains an important theoretical source.

Luke's reading of Dewey is particularly distorted. Dewey was careful to describe democracy as a way of life, a form of thinking and human activity that could not be restricted to political institutions. Furthermore, he constantly argued against false dichotomies such as public versus private or society versus individual. Dewey, like most male theoreticians of his generation, wrote little that was explicitly focused on women. Nevertheless, his views could never be exclusively derived from or limited to male concerns. Certainly Luke is right to adopt a suspicious stance toward any theoretician whose gender-blindness might undermine his or her theorizing. But we also must guard against our own blindness to the genuine insights of those theoreticians who might also display some other behavior to which we might object. This issue has been raised most clearly in the recent controversy over the work of Heidigger and Paul DeMan. The point is that ideas have a semiotic importance that always exceeds the intentions or characteristics (e.g., gender, race, ethnicity) of authors.

Luke also neglects the substantial critique by male critical pedagogues of their own intellectual foundations. Apple's (Apple and Weis 1983) incorporation of gender into his analysis was not merely an acceptance of an element of feminist theory but also an acknowledgement of the limitations of the Marxist theory that informs so much of his work. In 1986, Lewis and Simon called our attention to the problems associated with conducting democratic classrooms and trying to give voice to marginalized student groups within the patriarchal environment of schooling. As this chapter should make clear, there is also substantial debate among male critical pedagogues regarding resistance theory, Critical Theory, and related topics. More recently, the challenge of postmodern and poststructuralist theorizing (including many feminist variants of this critique) has led to further critical self-reflection on the part of male critical educators (Burbules and Rice 1990; Giroux 1988a, 1988b, 1988c; McLaren 1988b, 1988c, 1988d, 1989; McLaren and Hammer 1989). In short, the very sort of critical self-examination called for by feminist educators has begun. As McLaren (1988d) has pointed out, it is part of the legacy of critical pedagogy to explore the "preconditions of its own categorizations and assumptions" (p. 73).

At this point, any critical educator (male or female) would have to be obtuse not to appreciate that the ancient Greeks, Marx, Freud, Heidigger,

Adorno, Lacan, DeMan, and many others have, at times, acted in ways we might find morally reprehensible or at least antithetical to a democratic way of life. Yet we have been able to draw on all these individuals to help construct democratic theory and critical approaches to education. For example, consider the feminist appropriation of Marx, Freud, and Lacan. The problem, I think, is that Luke's effort to alert us to a legitimate concern ultimately becomes an oversimplified rejection of important theoretical insights.

We should also explore further the question of male versus female modes of thought raised by Luke (unpublished manuscript), Grumet (1988), and Pagano (1988). As noted earlier, this line of explanation found in the work of Chodorow (1978), Dinnerstein (1977), and Gilligan (1982) has been criticized by many feminists as too reductionist or essentialist (e.g., see Fraser and Nicholson 1990; Bordo 1990; Butler 1990; Yeatman 1990). In part, the feminist reaction to essentialist positions has been shaped by the incorporation of postmodern and poststructuralist ideas into feminist discourse. We need to be careful not to underestimate the valid insights contained in Dinnerstein, Chodorow, and Gilligan's work. Even if we question the universalist assumptions of their theories, they nonetheless can help us better understand how the forces of domination work through gender and sexual categories and relations, especially in particular (as opposed to universal) settings (Bordo 1990). What must be guarded against is pushing such insights to the point where they impede our understanding. Pagano and Grumet seem to call for a dialogical understanding of male and female ways of knowing. These approaches to knowing are used as heuristics for analysis, and they are not the exclusive province of either gender. In fact, Pagano and Grumet argue that we all should combine the best elements and insights of these different ways of knowing and warn us against the potentially negative effects of each. Lasch (1984) has made a related argument from a somewhat different theoretical vantage point.

Luke (unpublished manuscript), in contrast, seems more concerned with establishing the boundaries between masculine and feminine modes of thought (an ironic position given her hostility toward dichotomies). The danger, of course, is that what starts out as a valuable insight into gender and the mechanics of oppression can turn into another monologue or metanarrative. Luke's critique of the public/private dichotomy and attempt to link it to Greek political theory, progressivism, and Critical Theory approaches this sort of monological critique.

Perhaps the strongest feminist reaction to critical pedagogy has been made by Elizabeth Ellsworth (1989), who, in a sweeping critique, describes critical pedagogy as an abstract and utopian approach to education that is overly dependent on rationalist assumptions. Given the serious questions Ellsworth raises and their relevance to issues to be explored in Chapter 5 and 6, we will consider her objections in some detail. Ellsworth employed the language, goals, and strategies of critical pedagogy in a graduate course she taught at the University of Wisconsin-Madison, *Curriculum and Instruction: 607, Media and Antiracist Pedagogy*. As a result of this experience, Ellsworth concluded that

> key assumptions, goals, and pedagogical practices fundamental to the literature on critical pedagogy—namely "empowerment", "student voice", "dialogue", and even the term "critical"—are repressive myths that perpetuate relations of domination. (p. 298)

In other words, the application of the techniques and goals of critical pedagogy "produced results that were not only unhelpful, but actually exacerbated the very conditions we were trying to work against, including Eurocentrism, racism, sexism, classism, and 'banking education' " (p. 298). To the extent these negative results occurred, the very discourse of critical pedagogy had become a vehicle of oppression.

Ellsworth believes that the negative effects of critical pedagogy can be traced to the failure of critical pedagogues "to launch any meaningful analysis of or program for reformulating the institutionalized power imbalances between themselves and their students, or of the essentially paternalistic project of education itself" (p. 306). Lacking an adequate analysis of these central concerns, critical pedagogy can only seek to meliorate or redress the negative effects of domination in classrooms. A variety of "student empowerment" strategies are employed within the framework of critical pedagogy, but they are directed at treating the symptoms of domination while failing to name or treat the disease. Thus, critical pedagogy functions to leave intact the essentially authoritarian teacher/student relationship.

Ellsworth criticizes several of the key teaching strategies posed by proponents of critical pedagogy. One such strategy is to reject education as inculcation by more powerful and knowledgeable teachers in favor of an approach based on reflective inquiry into issues and the application and analysis of various moral positions. This strategy rests on the assumption that students can be given the skills and dispositions to make them rational individuals capable of freely choosing moral positions in the manner supposedly modeled by their teachers. But the danger is that "in a classroom in which 'empowerment' is made dependent on rationalism, those perspectives that would question the political interests (sexism, racism, colonialism...) expressed and guaranteed by rationalism would be rejected as 'irrational' (biased, partial)" (p. 306).

A second strategy involves having teachers become more like their students by highlighting the teacher's need to learn about the student's reality and knowledge. This would also involve the teacher relearning the very objects of instruction as they are reexamined in terms of the student's perceptions. But the ultimate purpose of this approach is for the teacher "to devise more effective strategies for bringing the student 'up' to the teacher's level of understanding" (p. 306). The implied superiority of the teacher's knowledge and assumed (but undefined) progressiveness of this strategy remained untheorized and unproblematized.

A third classroom strategy advocated by some critical pedagogues is to acknowledge the inevitable "directiveness" and "authoritarianism" of education and "judge particular power imbalances between teacher and student to be tolerable or intolerable depending upon" whether or not they served emancipatory ends (p. 307). In other words, such a strategy would involve the strategic use of "emancipatory authority". This approach requires gaining the students trust by making available "the political and moral referents for authority [teachers] assume in teaching particular forms of knowledge, in taking stands against forms of oppression, and in treating students as if they ought to be concerned about social justice and political action" (Giroux and McLaren 1986, 226). From this vantage point, the purpose of empowerment becomes the criterion for judging the use or misuse of teacher authority.

Ellsworth (1989) argues that, unfortunately, critical pedagogues tend to define empowerment in terms of ahistorical and depoliticized abstractions. There are vague references to "human betterment," the expansion of social identities, human agency to act as part of a moral and political community, action to transform society, and other similar abstractions. For Ellsworth, this boiled down to a broad humanist plea to have students acquire a "capacity to act effectively" without providing a reason "to challenge any identifiable social or political position, institution, or group" (Ibid). The paternal essence of traditional education also remains unchallenged. Emancipatory authority assumed the possibility of an emancipated teacher, but Ellsworth questioned if this were possible when teachers remain unable totally to free themselves of their own learned forms of sexism, racism, classism, and other sorts of oppressive thought.

The conception of emancipatory authority also rested on a second assumption, that is, teachers can understand the object of study (e.g., racism) better than students. But Ellsworth argued that there are students who have had experiences that enable them to understand racism (or other forms of oppression) in ways the teacher may never fully grasp. From Ellsworth's perspective, our understanding of oppression and domination will always remain shaped and constrained by our personal biographies, and she contends that it is *impossible* for anyone to be free from the effects of "oppressive formations at this historical moment" (p. 308). There is also no way to eliminate the institutional effects that attach to teacher authority.

to teacher authority. So in practice, the teacher's institutional role will effectively weight their discourse differently from those of students. We need, therefore, to turn away from a critical pedagogy oriented towards utopian projects or emancipated teachers. These goals are both unattainable and undesirable, because they "are always predicated on the interests of those who are in a position to define utopian projects" (p. 308).

What was required, in Ellsworth's view, was a very different orientation to pedagogy that takes seriously the unequal power relations in classrooms and the consequent barriers to the authentic expression of student voice or dialogue. The critical educator must always be aware that she or he can never unproblematically "help" or "affiliate" with oppressed groups. Indeed, since critical pedagogues are always implicated in the very structures they allegedly seek to change, genuine expression of student voices might put these teachers at risk. We must also accept that there can be no voice that functions as the origin of knowledge or authority in the classroom. Since "all knowings are partial, . . .there are fundamental things each of us cannot know—a situation alleviated only in part by the pooling of partial, socially constructed knowledge in classrooms. . ." (p. 310).

Ellsworth believes her position to be in sharp contrast to what critical pedagogy had done by default, that is, produced a generic conception of the "critical teacher" rooted in the more general category of "generic human that underlies classical liberal thought" (p. 310). In fact, what critical pedagogues conceived as generic was no more than a particular conception of critical teacher based on a mythic norm. When we employed such normative conceptions, we tended to reduce gender, race, class, and other differences to mere variations or additions grafted on to the generic human. But in a true critical pedagogy, student voices would not be seen as additions to a norm but as concrete instances of "defiant speech" or "talking back" to present alternatives and opposition to the norm (p. 311). For example, feminist voices have helped to forge women's self-definitions in opposition to definitions posed by others to further the subordination of women. Nevertheless, we must also keep in mind that since all knowledge is partial, all student voices are only partial accounts or self-interpretations. Furthermore, an individual student voice will always be contradictory and filled with the traces of other voices (e.g., one might speak as a lower-class, black, lesbian, woman).

Another important issue that must be reexamined is the role of dialogue in critical pedagogy. Critical pedagogues would like to have classrooms function as approximations of the public sphere wherein students could develop the competence for democratic citizenship. This would entail: 1) giving students the equal opportunity to speak, 2) promoting a mutual respect for the rights of other students, 3) creating a sense of feeling safe to speak, 4) tolerating all ideas submitted for discussion, and 5) the rational critique of ideas in terms of fundamental judgments and moral principles. The outcome of dialogue is seen as an open question, but critical pedagogy assumes there should be a consensus regarding the emancipatory purpose of dialogue (p. 314).

Ellsworth claims, however, that the intrinsically asymmetrical conditions of classrooms precluded the sort of dialogue envisioned by critical pedagogy. Any attempt at consensus regarding the emancipatory purpose of dialogue ignores the complex dynamics of subordination present in all classrooms. Without this awareness, we tended to fall into a we/them dichotomy of victims verses oppressors. Ellsworth, drawing on the work of Martin and Mohatny (1986), argues "for creating new forms of collective struggle that do not depend upon repressions and violence needed by 'dialogue' based on and enforcing a harmony of interests. [Since]. . . 'unity'. . .is necessarily fragmentary, unstable, not given, but chosen and struggled for—but not on the basis of 'sameness' " (p. 315).

The conventional view of dialogue expressed in the discourse of critical pedagogy assumes the existence of "rationalized, individualized subjects capable of agreeing on universalizable 'fundamental moral principles' and 'quality of human life' that become self-evident when subjects cease to be self-interested and particularistic about group rights" (Ellsworth 1989, 316). Yet under present conditions, the power relations among and between students and teachers of different race, class, and gender are unequal and unjust. Individuals in such circumstances are generally not capable of acting in a fully rational or disinterested manner. Each person normally represented multiple social positions that are likely both conscious and unconscious. Neither were fundamental moral and political principles given, absolute, or universalizable. The determination and application of basic principles could only be established by some prior intersubjective process via the reflection and interpretation of subjects.

Ellsworth noted how her students found various informal ways to establish smaller affinity groups outside the classroom to discuss material interests and respond to specific needs. She interpreted this phenomenon as a necessary response to counter the ways in which "current historical configurations of oppressions were reproduced in [her] class" (p. 317). The focus of her class gradually shifted from attempting to produce a dialogue among "equal" individuals to "building a coalition among multiple, shifting, intersecting, and sometimes contradictory groups carrying unequal weights of legitimacy within the culture and the classroom" (p. 317). In this context Ellsworth cites the observation of Lugones and Spelman (1983) that political or theoretical self-interest is neither sufficient nor appropriate to provide the motivation to follow others into their worlds. Only friendship is adequate because the task is so difficult. "[I]t requires that you be willing to devote a great part of your

life to it and that you be willing to suffer alienation and self-disruption...
[w]hatever the benefits you may accrue...they are not worth your while"
(p. 576, as quoted in Ellsworth 1989, 327).

Ellsworth (1989) wants to move toward a pedagogy of the unknowable. Since every individual subject is shaped by conscious and unconscious reaction to "multiple, intersecting, and contradictory subject positions," no one could ever fully know even their own personal experiences. And even student affinity groups that work together to fight oppression could never be certain that their efforts would not have negative consequences for other affinity groups, or even their own. Any affinity group can only be formed on the basis of its own perceived self-interest and the exclusion of other voices (pp. 318–19). These phenomena should not be seen as either failures or a problem to be resolved.

> Realizing that there are partial narratives that some social groups or cultures have and others can never know, but that are necessary to human survival, is a condition to embrace and use as an opportunity to build a kind of social and educational interdependency that recognizes differences as "different strengths" and as "forces for change." (p. 319)

We must develop a pedagogy that moves beyond the mere toleration of differences to a conception of differences as what Andre Lorde calls "a fund of necessary polarities between which our creativity can spark like a dialect" (Lourde 1984, 112, as cited in Ellsworth 1989, 319). When we use this conception of difference we can better understand the importance of interdependency.

Ellsworth (1989) has come to see the unknown and unknowable as much less frightening than political or educational projects that claim legitimacy on the basis of the kind of knowledge claims she believes underlie current approaches to critical pedagogy. Ellsworth refers here to the claim that we can achieve an understanding of objects, nature, and others at a level never granted the individual knower (p. 321). This sort of knowledge is not possible in classrooms where a multiplicity of partial, contradictory, and irreducible knowledges, shaped by social relations in and outside the classroom, is the usual state of affairs. These partial knowledges cannot be known or make sense in terms of any master discourse. Furthermore, any attempt to combine the partial knowledges present in a classroom could only result in the construction of yet another form of partial knowing. We must accept that any political project taken up in classrooms "will already, at the moment of its definition, lack knowledge necessary to answer broader questions of human survival and social justice" (p. 321). Ellsworth draws on the work of Trinh Minh-ha (1986/87) to suggest a pedagogical approach to cope with the unknowable. Such a new pedagogy might take many forms, but it should be directed toward supporting teachers and students in what Minh-ha sees as a continual "moving about" as captured in the following quote concerning an "Inappropriated Other"

> who moves about with always at least two/four gestures; that of affirming "I am like you" while pointing insistently to the difference; and that of reminding "I am different" while unsettling every definition of otherness arrived at. (Minh-ha T.T. 1986, 1987, 9, as quoted in Ellsworth 1989, 322)

Within this framework, a subject's identity is conceived as "nonessentialized" and emerging from one's biographical experience. But this is only a necessary starting point; it does not require a particular outcome. This pedagogical orientation employs identity as "a vehicle for multiplying and making more complex the subject positions possible, visible, and legitimate at any given historical moment, requiring disruptive changes in the way social technologies of gender, race, ability, and so on define 'Otherness' and use it as a vehicle for subordination" (Ellsworth 1989, 322). From Ellsworth's perspective, any search for a general, coherent narrative was counterproductive. What would be more relevant is a "persistent critique" of all received narratives or a priori approaches to critique such as class, race, and gender. This persistent and open form of critique was different from those postliberal or post-Marxist discourses that construct "repressive unities," in effect, undervaluing the "profoundly heterogeneous networks of power/desire/interest" (Ibid.). The sort of critique advocated by Ellsworth would certainly make the task of education more complex, necessitating a constant readjustment in strategies to cope with the continually changing conditions of resistance. One's alliance with oppressed groups did not create a social position exempt from either critique or the potential to become implicated in the process of domination. In the end, we were all someone else's Other, since we all experience some dissonance from dominant cultural norms. Obviously, some groups suffered far more from the forces of oppression than others, but Ellsworth was seeking to avoid "oppressive oversimplification" by insisting that domination be understood and resisted contextually (p. 323).

Contextual resistance of domination requires a clear understanding that our ability to unsettle differences and unclear positions was dependent on the others with whom we interact. In other words, a teacher's moving about between privileged subject and inappropriate/d Other "cannot be predicted, prescribed, or understood beforehand by any theoretical framework or methodological practice" (p. 323). Here, Ellsworth is describing a pedagogy of the unknowable that must be contextual/historical and social in structure. It was a pedagogy antithetical to the discursive positions of critical pedagogy that assumes a prior and superior insight regarding the origins of what we can know and what action we should take (p. 322).

Ellsworth's approach to communication across differences in teaching is summarized in the following quote.

> If you can talk to me in ways that show you understand that your knowledge of me, the world, and the right thing to do will always be partial, interested, and potentially oppressive to others, and if I can do the same, then we can work together on shaping and reshaping alliances for constructing circumstances in which students of difference can thrive. (p. 324)

The questions Ellsworth raises, by and large, are important and troubling. Ellsworth's work is much more than a feminist critique, because it draws on postmodern and poststructuralist theory employed to support feminism. Many of the postmodern or poststructuralist grounds for Ellsworth's critique of critical pedagogy have been greeted with concern and skepticism by other feminists (e.g., Benhabib 1990; Bordo 1990; Hartsock 1990; Di Stefano 1990; Harding 1990). For some of these writers, postmodernism and poststructuralism come dangerously close to the abandonment of theory. We will deal more specifically with these issues in the following chapter. For now, we will concentrate on other related issues.

We should acknowledge that Ellsworth accurately describes several real obstacles to the sort of critical classroom dialogue advocated by critical pedagogy. These obstacles include the institutional authority of teachers, asymmetrical teacher/student and student/student relations, the unknowable dimensions of otherness, as well as the tacit assumptions and personal histories of those involved. Like Luke's views discussed earlier, Ellsworth is also concerned that the conception of rational dialogue espoused in critical pedagogy will tend to exclude personal or relational factors. And she rejects attempts by those critical pedagogues who attempt to distinguish between "authority" and "authoritarianism" in an effort to legitimize the emancipatory authority of teachers. Ellsworth argues that critical pedagogues have failed either to acknowledge these limitations or to construct an adequate theoretical analysis of the key concepts and relationships (especially teacher/student relations) required for their project.

Not surprisingly, some critical pedagogues see relatively little merit in Ellsworth's critique. McLaren (1988d) contends that Ellsworth's attempt to describe critical pedagogy amounts to a caricature that both misrepresents the movement and undermines her arguments. He agrees with Ellsworth (and by implication Luke) regarding the need "to ascertain in which ways the language of critical theory may be part of the oppressive unity of that which it attempts to liberate" (p. 72). But McLaren claims that Ellsworth either fails to understand or acknowledge that critical self-reflection *is* a central part of critical pedagogy's discourse. He also recognized that there were elements of critical pedagogy still linked to failed modernist discourse that contain confusing and contradictory commentary on the role and importance of difference. The cure for eliminating such distorted discourse is more critical self-reflection and a rejection of any monological approach to pedagogy "in which moral authority and theoretical assurance are arrived at unproblematically without regard to the repressed narratives and suffering of the historically disenfranchised" (p. 73).

But this pragmatic approach does not preclude, indeed it requires, the formation of a utopian vision to help link current forms of difference in the quest for solidarity and collective agency. Critical pedagogy is oriented toward building solidarity, where possible, while preserving "the specificity of difference" (p. 74). McLaren sees this as consistent with Cornel West's (1989) view of "prophetic pragmatism." As McLaren (1988d) explains, "empowerment of the self without regard to the transformation of those social structures which shape the very lineaments of the self is not empowerment at all but a sojourn into a version of humanistic therapy where catharsis is coextensive with liberation" (p. 76). Giroux (1988a) has made a similar point, accusing Ellsworth of holding an extreme view regarding the importance of student differences. Giroux believes that Ellsworth's view of difference precludes exploring the possibility of identifying interests we might hold in common (despite our differences) or the capacity to act in solidarity toward the realization of a more democratic sociocultural order consistent with such human interests (p. 177).

Ellsworth, like Luke, has described critical pedagogy too narrowly and thus underestimated the extent to which various critical pedagogues have anticipated her concerns and begun to address them. Another difficulty is that Ellsworth appears to be making a greater claim than her argument allows, and it would have been helpful if she had made some explicit caveats. For example, we must recall that her conclusions are primarily drawn on the basis of her experiences over one semester in one graduate-level course as these experiences related to her understanding of and attempts to employ critical pedagogy in her classroom. In contrast, critical pedagogy is an approach to schooling at all levels. Ellsworth never addresses questions of teacher authority as it might relate to elementary or secondary schools. Beyond this, her experience, however rich and well-documented, is very limited. Although her research is in the autobiographical and case-study genre, she makes the sort of empirical claims that her limited data were never meant to support. Had she merely qualified her claims, I believe it would have made her arguments more plausible. As it is, there is the risk that some will simply reject those valid claims she does make based on their reaction to the more extreme aspects of her rhetoric.

Of course we should try to understand the feminist critique of critical pedagogy in the context of the wider debate among radical academics, and radical educators in particular. The disputes among radical male theoreticians has a long history, and in this chapter we have discussed some of the serious debates among such radical educators. These disputes can be constructive to the extent they pose problems in a way that stimulates reflection and theoretical reconstruction. I would argue that the critiques of critical pedagogy made by Ellsworth and Luke do provide such an opportunity. If we do not overreact to the elements of the arguments that seem exaggerated or incorrect, we will acknowledge that both authors raise concerns shared by both radical male and other feminist educators.

The response to Ellsworth's critique by Burbules and Rice (1990) is a case in point. They chose to focus on those elements in Ellsworth's critique that they regard as legitimate concerns. For example, Burbules and Rice agree with Ellsworth that a teacher's authority is always connected to institutional and historical contexts that determine most of the status and privileges teachers receive regardless of whether or not they merit these advantages. This is a prevailing situation that cannot be overcome merely by good intentions alone. I also agree with the observation by Burbules and Rice that there is no way to eliminate teacher authority by constructing more egalitarian or democratic classrooms environments. Nevertheless, teacher authority is not intrinsically antithetical to democratic schooling. Seeking information from those better informed and/or skilled is a constant condition and necessity of daily existence. Ellsworth is right to urge us not to take teacher authority for granted. Yet, at appropriate times, it will be necessary to assume the value of teacher authority, because education is not possible without some level of this authority.

Nevertheless, the acceptable level of teacher authority *is* something to be reexamined and adjusted over time. Burbules and Rice urge that we consider several factors in this process, including: (1) our knowledge and attitude toward the "others" learning, (2) understanding the students' perspective and interests, (3) the changing nature of teacher-student relations which are never static, and (4) that authority cannot be attached to only one participant in a dialogue and might shift as topics in a dialogue change. Burbules and Rice also emphasize the importance of listening, a skill that can mediate the authority relation, convey respect for the "other," and encourage the expression of marginal student voices. Of course listening alone is never sufficient, and we must also seek to alter environmental constraints on dialogue in education. The irony is that, when properly conceived, teacher authority will undermine itself. In other words, the goal of teacher authority in an emancipatory context is to have students move beyond it, even to reject it. In this way, we can acknowledge legitimate teacher authority in teaching contexts without reifying it.

Dialogue is also central to the educational process. Indeed, it is difficult to conceive of education without dialogue. Ellsworth comes dangerously close to espousing a form of radical perspectivism that would preclude genuine dialogue. Again, she is correct to emphasize that difference and otherness always contain dimensions we can never know. Thus, there will always be an element of the unknowable in pedagogy. This is a real constraint but not an in-principle argument for radical incommensurability. Paradoxically, arguments for incommensurability, like those for relativism, undermine their own premises. But more importantly, the competence to engage in dialogical reasoning is basic to our human being-in-the-world (Whitson and Stanley 1990).

Burbules and Rice (1990) describe the possibility of two kinds of communication in education. One type leads to a convergence of understanding, while the other involves divergent communication across differences that does not lead to a narrowing of understanding, but the opening or construction of new perspectives and meanings. We cannot be certain in advance as to which direction discourse might lead. But even if the attempt to build argument via dialogue should fail, it also holds out the opportunity for further divergent dialogue (akin to Bakhtin's [1981] heteroglossia) and the communication of new meanings. Education requires both forms of communication, because convergence makes dialogue possible and divergence makes it worthwhile. And we need to develop the pragmatic competence to identify and work within and across each mode.

Yet even if we are able to construct arguments to support the necessity and possibility of educational dialogue, a problem remains. Even if dialogue is possible in principle, to what extent is that possibility consistent with the projects of social reconstructionism and critical pedagogy? Each of these projects has envisioned education as the means to transform society for the better. But constructing a conception of a "better" society to orient social transformation would seem to require some adequate level of convergent communication. Do the constraints of dialogue across difference preclude this possibility? I do not think so, but this is one of the challenges to critical pedagogy posed by Ellsworth, Luke, and others (e.g., Cherryholmes 1988).

SUMMARY

We have seen that there is a strong relationship between social reconstructionist theory and the more recent development of critical pedagogy, although the latter movement appears to have developed, for the most part, independently of the former. Only recently have some critical pedagogues called our attention to the strong connections between the two educational reform movements. Critical pedagogy has also made significant advances beyond the initial critique and theoretical position taken by the reconstructionists. But as was the case with reconstructionism, critical pedagogy has provoked considerable criticism from mainstream and other critical educators. Indeed, the fragmentation and conflict among radical educators remains a serious problem that, at times, undermines the movement's potential. Conversely, much of the critical reaction has stimulated and expanded the theoretical base of critical pedgogy.

At present, we have at least two major challenges to critical pedagogy. First, there are those who posit a different set of goals or values as the purpose of education. This is most typical of the conservative or liberal critique of critical pedagogy. However, this is also an issue between certain critical pedagogues. Second, is the thesis or view that difference and otherness function to preclude the sort of dialogue and teacher authority required by critical pedagogy. This is an essential part of the critique raised by Ellsworth and Luke. Such arguments are often linked to postmodern or poststructuralist theory that, although dialogue is possible, there is no way to universalize or provide a ground for the outcome of any dialogue beyond the framework in which it was originally structured. The last critique contests the very possibility of the first. We will consider these and related issues in the next chapter as we turn to an examination of the impact of postmodernism and poststructuralism on curriculum theory.

5

NEOPRAGMATISM, POSTSTRUCTURALISM, AND CRITICAL PEDAGOGY

Recent developments in postmodern and poststructuralist thought have had a significant impact on the human sciences, and, not surprisingly, curriculum theory has been drawn into the debates generated by this new discourse. Most significantly, postmodernism and poststructuralism have contributed to the continuing deconstruction of mainstream (neopositivist) conceptions of social science, philosophy, and, of course, the related mainstream discourse of curriculum theory. One important result of this critique has been to heighten what Richard Bernstein (1983) calls the "Cartesian anxiety" or the fear that either we have objective foundations for truth or we must fall into the abyss of relativism, skepticism, and nihilism.

There is some confusion regarding the meaning of postmodernism and poststructuralism. This is understandable given the great volume of writing about these movements and the complex and even contradictory positions associated with each term. The problem is confounded by the tendency of many writers to employ the terms as synonymous. While both terms point to many similar ideas, they are not isomorphic. There are numerous studies of postmodernism or poststructuralism (e.g., Arac 1986; Culler 1982; Derrida 1976; Descombs 1980; Dreyfus and Rabinow 1983; Eagleton 1986; Huyssen 1984; Rabinow 1984; Kaplan 1988; Lyotard 1984; Norris 1985, 1987; Poster 1988; Rorty 1979; Sarup 1989), and there will be no attempt to engage in a detailed analysis of either concept here. However, I will present a brief sketch of some key assumptions prior to analyzing the relations between poststructuralism, critical pedagogy, and reconstructionism.

Postmodernism is the more global of the two terms and also the more difficult to define. Some of the best exemplars of postmodern theorizing are found in the work of Baudrillard (1981, 1983a, 1983b), Lyotard (1984), and Rorty (1979, 1982, 1985). Although the prefix "post" indicates a break with a prior period or way of thinking, some have questioned whether the case can be made for any clear break with modernism (Habermas 1987;

Kaplan 1988; Poster 1989). In fact, Lyotard (1984), perhaps the most prominent proponent of postmodernism, holds that we should not understand the postmodern as chronologically subsequent to modernism. Rather postmodernism is part of the modern era, "not. . .at its end but in the nascent state" (p. 79). Lyotard used the term modern to refer to any philosophical or scientific approach "that legitimates itself with reference to a metadiscourse" (p. xxiii). Metadiscourses are those that claim to be able to critique related (but subordinate) discourses by appeal to some kind of "grand narrative." Capitalism, Marxism, positivism, scientism, structuralism, transcendentalism, as well as other forms of philosophy and theology, have all been employed as metanarratives. Lyotard defines postmodernism as an "incredulity toward metanarratives" (p. xxiv). Hence, postmodernism reflects a wider interpretive movement to reject or deconstruct claims that some objective foundation or ground exists for making definitive interpretations regarding human behavior, cultures, and societies.

While Lyotard's analysis provides a sense of postmodernism, the term remains problematic because of the ambiguity regarding its definition. For example, postmodernism has now come to form a significant part of feminist theory (Nicholson 1990). It is also frequently used in conjunction with poststructuralism, although, as I will argue below, there are good reasons for trying to keep a distinction between the two terms. It often appears that postmodernism is employed as a general label for a movement that includes elements of feminist thought, poststructuralism, antireductionist forms of pluralism, certain approaches to neopragmatism (e.g., Rorty 1979), and various media and cultural studies.

Some appear to see in postmodernism a distinctive perspective or theoretical orientation (e.g., Lyotard 1984; Rorty 1979, 1982, 1985). But an examination of this position raises more questions than it answers. In fact it is difficult to determine distinct contributions of postmodern theory that were not already present in other theoretical perspectives such as poststructuralism, neopragmatism, or philosophical hermeneutics. Perhaps postmodernism is better understood as a description of the kind of universe in which contemporary critical discourse takes place, that is, the condition of our contemporary world (Whitson forthcoming). As we shall examine below, the ambiguity of postmodern theory has created some special problems for attmepts to develop critical approaches to curriculum theory.

Poststructuralism is often described as part of the larger postmodern framework, but it has a more concrete focus. It is best described as that school of thought that has emerged as a critique of the structuralist theory so influential in the 1950s and 1960s. Poststructuralism takes structuralism seriously without embracing its more transcendental or foundationalist claims. Like Whitson (forthcoming), I would argue that poststructuralism is directly relevant, indeed necessary, to the development of a critical pedagogy focused on counterhegemonic praxis. This position will be developed in more detail as we proceed. Although it is a more focused concept, poststructuralism, like postmodernism, remains a general term that describes the work of a number of writers with quite distinct perspectives (e.g., Barthes 1972, 1975, 1976; Derrida 1976, 1988; Deleuze 1986; Descombs 1980; Eagleton 1986; Foucault 1972, 1973a, 1973b, 1975, 1979, 1980a, 1980b, 1980c; and Lacan 1977a, 1977b). Furthermore, any attempt to define poststructuralism runs the risk of distorting it, since poststructuralism is more a way of thinking about human existence than a formulaic philosophy or methodology reducible to any set of propositions. Still, we can highlight some of the important issues and points raised in the poststructuralist critique.

Jonathan Culler (1982) has explained the difference between structuralism and poststructuralism in the following terms.

> Structuralists take linguistics as a model and attempt to develop "grammars" —systematic inventories of elements and their possibilities of combination— that would account for the form and meaning of literary works; poststructuralists investigate the way in which this project is subverted by the workings of the texts themselves. (p. 22)

Although there are great differences between structuralists, positivists, phenomenologists, and certain hermeneuticists (e.g., Dilthy, Betti, and E. D. Hirsch), what they have all had in common was the assumption that systematic, objective knowledge was possible. For structuralists, stable textual meaning could be determined by finding the code that explained how the various elements of a text (or text analogue such as a painting, wedding, sporting event, or schooling, etc.) were related to each other to create meaning. Such codes normally included transcendental signifiers whereby, as Eagleton (1983) explains, "certain meanings are elevated by social ideologies to a privileged position or made the centers around which other meanings are forced to turn" (p. 131). In our society, terms such as democracy, freedom, family, and so forth have served this function of signs which give meaning to all other signs. The poststructuralists view all claims for transcendental meaning as fictions. It might be that such fictions are necessary for day-to-day existence, but no signifier can be defined as the origin of the meaning of all the others "because for this meaning to have been possible other signs must already have existed" (p. 131). So while structuralists and others have sought to defend the possibility of objective, systematic knowledge "post-structuralists claim to know only the impossibility of this knowledge" (Culler 1982, 22).

It was the structuralists who helped develop the conception of human experience as textural whereby human activity could be read or interpreted much as a form of writing. But the poststructuralists have challenged the ontological integrity of the very grammars of signification that structuralists found inscribed in texts. For poststructuralists, these grammars are at least fictitious and often "purposeful deceptions that need to be perceived as inherently hegemonic" (Gunn 1987, 42). But some critics of poststructuralism have argued that when carried to its logical conclusion, poststructuralist deconstruction becomes a "hermeneutics of suspicion to the point of converting disbelief into the only operative intellectual category and playful cynicism into the only viable stance" (p. 42). Indeed, the discourse of poststructuralism can be read as claiming "that we are the prisoners of our own discourse, unable to raise reasonably certain truth claims because such claims are merely relative to our language" (Eagleton 1983, 144).

We should emphasize that the perceived threat of postmodern or poststructuralist theory is widely held by theorists from across the political spectrum. Bruner (1986) discusses the hostility to deconstruction on the part of humanist George Steiner as well as the linguist Tzvetan Todorov. While Bruner ultimately rejects their "solutions," he agrees that "deconstructionist know nothingness" holds a potential threat to "critical humanism" (pp. 151–60).

One can see the potential for poststructuralism to undermine and threaten the projects that argue for a critical pedagogy (including social reconstructionism) based on emancipation and social justice. A case in point, Ellsworth's (1989) critique of critical pedagogy discussed in Chapter 4 is strongly influenced by elements of poststructuralism. Like Ellsworth, I believe that poststructuralism and postmodernism pose some troubling questions that challenge much of the theory of critical pedagogy. However, I do not share her pessimism regarding the possibility of reconciling critical pedagogy with a pedagogy of the unknowable as it relates to difference and otherness, nor do I accept her case that most current theories of critical pedagogy should be understood as repressive myths. On the other hand, the theories of critical pedagogy do need to be reshaped or reconstructed to account for the insights of poststructuralist thought (including feminist poststructuralism), and such efforts are in progress (Cherryholmes 1988; Giroux 1988a, 1988b, 1988c; McLaren 1986, 1988c, 1988d; McLaren and Hammer 1989; Whitson 1988; Stanley and Whitson 1990; Whitson 1991, forthcoming).

In this chapter we will first examine some of the critical reaction to poststructuralism and postmodernism by both conservative and radical critics. I believe it is helpful to understand some of the similar concerns held by critics on the right and left regarding what each side sees as a threat to its respective political and cultural projects. Like the curious alignment between certain feminists and reactionary religious fundamentalists in opposition to pornography, some elements of the right and left share a mutual fear of what they see as an assault by poststructuralists on rationality itself.

Following our brief examination of the critical reaction to postmodernism and poststructuralism, we will reexamine the poststructuralist position from an admittedly partial analysis of neopragmatism as it relates to the work of Jacques Derrida. While Derrida is only one among several prominent poststructuralists, certainly he is a central figure in this movement. To the extent his views can be reconciled with critical pedagogy, the negative reaction to poststructuralism by educators on the left is diminished. I also hope to illustrate how poststructuralism and critical neopragmatism can contribute to the development of critical pedagogy. I will leave it to others to grapple in detail with the right's fear of poststructuralism.

THE RIGHT/CONSERVATIVE CRITIQUE OF POSTMODERNISM/POSTSTRUCTURALISM

It is not surprising that conservative critics would reject the postmodern/poststructural critique with its antifoundational stance and decentering of the subject. One sample of the conservative reaction is presented in *The Intercollegiate Review* published in the fall of 1987. In this issue, Shaw (1987) argues for a restoration of Matthew Arnold's conception of the humanities as "the best that is known and thought in the world" (p. 6). Shaw views French poststructuralist thought (as well as feminism and Marxism) as part of "an antihumanist attack that displaces the Protagorian view of the individual as the center of scholarly interest and the measure of all subliminal things" (p. 6). He did not seem to realize the potential irony of this point, since the Protagorean version of relativism is usually denounced as the most radical and untenable form—and a form other critics claim is reflected in postmodernism and poststructuralism. Shaw criticizes some of Foucault's antihumanist statements from *The Order of Things* (1973b) and argues that, like Foucault, Derrida's avowed purpose is to do battle with humanism (p. 8). According to Shaw, the poststructuralists seek to reduce humanism to whatever consensus human communities produce regarding knowledge. In other words, poststructuralism sought to make cultural relativism the "new" standard for the humanities. The cost of this intellectual move has been to trivialize our classical tradition including the values of bravery, loyalty, patriotism, justice, truth, freedom, virtue, and beauty (p. 9).

Shaw recognizes that the classical tradition includes a historical record of racism and sexism, but he argues that the traditional view of the humanities represents the best knowledge in terms of what has "been redeemed from the ancient record" (p. 9). He concludes that the defender of the traditional conception of the humanities recognizes "the precedence of the past—its having already thought our thoughts," and he is skeptical regarding radical "departures from social and cultural norms. In politics, such a person will tend to be anti-utopian. . ." (p. 14). Shaw believes there is something about the past that is more appropriate than our evaluation or deconstruction of it. Put another way, over time, "the past begins to measure *us*" and in this way functions as "a kind of superego or restraining influence" (p. 14). These benefits were threatened when the natural human impulse to interpret is "infected" with the ideology of opposition manifest in philosophical approaches like poststructuralism.

In a related argument, R. V. Young (1987) has taken issue with the recent critique of constitutional interpretation by antifoundationalist literary critics influenced by poststructuralism (p. 50). For example, Young comments on the work of Stanley Fish.

> In arguing that meaning is created by interpretive communities, wielding cultural norms and discursive rules, Fish overlooks the contrary and more significant fact that interpretive communities are themselves created in part by works of literature, since literature is a constituent of culture. The very texts subject to interpretation are one of the constraints upon any interpreter. (p. 55)

Indeed, without giving any explanation of human nature that was prior to the various ways it was manifested in concrete cultural situations, Fish could not explain the existence of human interpretive communities or "how any disagreement could ever arise once the interpretive communities are in place" (p. 56). Thus, texts must be understood as constituting human communities, and in cases such as the Constitution, its authority was "prior to the community which interprets it. . ." (p. 55). According to Young, this did not suggest that the truth of texts was transparent, but that the quest for the truth of a text was a rational quest even if it would always elude the interpreter's grasp (p. 56).

More recently, education professor Lawrence Stott (1990), in a critical response to some of the recent postmodern influence on educational theory, makes the following claims:

> Post-modernist thought has no moral grounding, preferring to stand on a shifting abyss. Little wonder then that its philosophizing is reduced to probing and aping the art and science of politics. The main tools of politics have always been fine talk, promise and deception, conscious or unconscious. (pp. 84–85)

According to Stott, schools do and should support and legitimize capitalism because it is the "best thing" that has happened in human history as well as our best hope for eliminating poverty. In contrast, the left (including postmodernists) only offers empty promises (pp. 84–85).

The critical comments of Shaw, Young, and Stott can be understood as part of a wider conservative critique of radical influences in educational thought (e.g. D'Souza 1990; Taylor 1991; Kimball 1990; Lehman 1990; Paglia 1991, and others). These conservative critics charge that leftist academics have gained a dangerous level of influence in our educational system. As a result, they have instituted a radical agenda for curriculum emphasizing a radically particularistic version of multiculturalism, a preoccupation with difference, and a new form of "left McCarthyism" that violates academic freedom by insisting on a "politically correct" ideology. The conservative critics see left critical theories, especially forms of Marxism, feminism, poststructuralism, and postmodernism, as the major sources of this new radical curriculum movement. For these conservatives, the most dangerous ideas posed by these new leftists theories are the rejection of our Western traditions, the denial of the possibility (and thus the value of seeking) truth or objectivity, the consequent decline in educational standards, and the rise of relativism.

It is difficult to predict what impact this evolving conservative critique will have. Currently, it has received wide attention and media support. Indeed, several moderate and liberal scholars have given these critics a sympathetic hearing (e.g., Lehman 1990; Searle 1990; Schlesigner 1991; Woodward 1991; Genovese 1991).

In my view, this new conservative criticism raises some valid concerns but is largely a vacuous, distorted, and groundless attack (Berube 1991; Robbins 1991a, 1991b). In Chapter 4, I tried to demonstrate the relevance of neo-Marxist and feminist thought to curriculum theory. Throughout this Chapter and Chapter 6, I will attempt to present an argument for the value of poststructuralism and neopragmatism for curriculum reform.

THE LEFT/RADICAL CRITIQUE OF POSTMODERNISM/POSTSTRUCTURALISM

The left has mounted its own parallel critique of the new discourses of postmodernism and poststructuralism, and we will consider this critique in greater detail, given its relevance to the focus of this study. A number of neo-Marxists (including some in critical pedagogy) have expressed concern that postmodernism and poststructuralism promote the growth of relativism, nihilism, and the deconstruction of emancipatory political and cultural projects. For many neo-Marxists, "the task is not only to strike out against this counter-offensive against the principles of historical materialism, but equally to understand why it now occupies a privileged position in theoretical debate" (Montag 1988, 88). For instance, curriculum theorist James Sears (1988) recently charged that poststructuralism was ahistorical and apolitical, because it functioned to deconstruct "all claims to absolute knowledge, meaning, or values" (p. 12). Sears pointed to Paul de Man's early links to Nazism and Derrida's defence of de Man as illustrations of the moral and political bankruptcy of poststructuralism. The deconstruction espoused by these scholars "highlights the dubiousness of intellectual activity which is divorced from ethical and moral roots. Such activity encouraged political disengagement and fosters nihilistic thinking" (p. 14). Sears fears that "a new orthodoxy is emerging in curriculum theory, one that reflects a narcissistic and nihilistic trend within the...field" (pp. 20–21).

The neo-Marxist Sarup (1984, 1989) has expressed some similar sentiments regarding the danger of poststructuralism. For instance, Sarup believes that Derrida's deconstructionism with "its emphasis on the undecidability of meaning leads to a depoliticizing relativism" (1984, 153). In addition, Sarup maintains that Foucault's poststructuralist rejection of "essential" Marxist concepts has helped support the neoconservative development of the "New Philosophers" in France. Still, Sarup agreed that the poststructuralist theorists have provided *methods* which, although frequently appropriated by the right, are also useful to the left. For in fact, "there is no theory that belongs to only one side; in the context of class struggle developments should, if possible, be utilized by the left or they will be used against it" (p. 67). Nevertheless, Sarup (1989) concludes,

> For poststructuralists, unity and universality are inherently oppressive and any move which promotes their disintegration is to be approved. It is assumed that once the aspiration to universality is abandoned, what will be left is a harmonious plurality of unmediated perspectives. But this sort of Nietzschean pluralism or perspectivism is fundamentally inconsistent because, in fact, the right to difference can only be upheld by universal principles. (p. 166)

Others like Sultan (1989) agree that recent developments in postmodern and poststructuralist thought have provided a useful critique of the neo-Marxist tendency to hold an essentialist conception of the Enlightenment tradition. This critique has helped to expose the theoretical economism of much neo-Marxism and its tendency to undertheorize subjectivity and desire. While recognizing the value of these insights, Sultan believed that the postmodern (and by implication the poststructuralist/feminist) critique had gone too far, "throwing the baby out with the bath water" (p. 19). Postmodern and poststructuralist theory were too reductionist, because "to treat curriculum and education as a 'text' even metaphorically, is to grossly ignore the specificities involved in producing" texts as well as to obscure their historicity (p. 20). Instead, we need a pragmatic attitude toward theory and practice, and the most promising available is the Critical Theory of Jürgen Habermas.

Sultan has been strongly influenced by Habermas's (1987) critique of poststructuralism or what Habermas has called "neostructuralism." Habermas interpreted the work of the poststructuralists like Foucault and Derrida as an assault on rationality itself, because they had abandoned the intellectual's primary purpose to seek norms or standards of critical judgment. For Habermas, poststructuralism amounts to a postanalytic relativism derived from an overreliance on the anti-Enlightenment stance of Nietzsche and Heidegger, and he accuses poststructuralists like Derrida and Foucault of being de facto conservatives.

The charge that poststructuralist theory is a variant of neoconservatism is among the most frequently made criticisms of this movement. Peter Dews (1986, 1987), for example, argues that what he sees as a poststructuralist rejection of the Enlightenment conception of rationality and grounded values has had essentially the same political impact as conservative political theory, that is, the preservation of the status quo. Thus, poststructuralism is viewed by some as an escape into theory wherein radical intellectuals might satisfy their professional status without posing a serious threat to current social and cultural forms of domination (Sarup 1984, 1989; Scholes 1985, 1988, 1989; West 1988, 1989; Lentricchia 1984, 1988). The interrelated impact of theories that decenter the human subject and interpret social reality as textual can lead to a detachment from corporal existence and the actual suffering of oppressed individuals and groups in concrete historical contexts (Megill 1985; Yudice 1989).

Montag (1988) has reminded us of the dangers involved in oversimplifying the debate over postmodernism and poststructuralism. For example, Perry Anderson's (1984) critique of Lacan is described by Montag as a superficial analysis which does not even acknowledge that much of Lacan's work has not yet been published (Montag 1988, 92–93). More important is the almost unreflective description by many scholars of Marxism as a totalizing critique (a point frequently reinforced by postmodern theorists). Montag rejects this contention even though he realizes that many Marxists have argued that they have provided a totalizing critique. He cites Marx's quip that "one does not judge an individual by what he [sic] thinks about himself."

> Theory exists everywhere in a practical state. Marxism, whatever the conceptualizations it has offered of its own practice, has never functioned as a metanarrative. In its practical existence, it speaks of nothing other than a struggle for which there is no outside and which is never structured according to the order of a logic or a law. Political practice acts within a conjuncture in order to act upon it, caught or "entangled" (Lenin) in the very relationship of forces it attempts to modify. (p. 96)

We must also be alert to a danger inherent in the very concept of postmodernism. "In its totalizing, transcendental pretensions, this concept precisely forecloses progress in thought by denying the possibility that fissures, disjunctions, breaks in contemporary social reality are symptoms of an impending crisis" (Montag 1988, 102). This dimension of postmodern thought claims to demonstrate the end of all crises, narratives, resistance, and the potential for revolutionary transformation. Kellner (1988) has made a similar point in a critique of what he considers Lyotard's de facto treatment of postmodernism as a metanarrative.

The feminist reaction to postmodernism and poststructuralism has been mixed. Some feminists have been among those most receptive to postmodern theory (Butler 1990; Ellsworth 1989; Nicholson 1989; Fraser and Nicholson 1990; Flax 1990; Kristeva 1980; Lather 1989a, 1989b; Young 1990). However, other feminists are very critical of certain aspects of postmodern theory and worry that it might pose a threat to feminist projects. Like other critics of postmodernism, certain feminists are concerned that the postmodern emphasis on the incommensurability of discursive claims and the view that validity criteria are limited to local contexts is breeding a new form of relativism (Benhabib 1990). There is a tendency on the part of many feminists to blend together postmodern and poststructuralist theory.

Sandra Harding (1990) is a feminist who sees much of value in postmodern theory, but she fears that in the rush to incorporate postmodern ideas we risk abandoning the valuable methods and insights of feminist empiricism and feminist standpoint theory. Both these epistemological orientations support a view of scientific knowledge as cumulative and the idea that we can determine that some arguments are more true than others. Harding does not claim we can return to a traditional Cartesian view of objectivity, but she is concerned that postmodernism might lead to a new form of "interpretivism" that negates the real gains of feminist epistemologies.

Like Harding, Yeatman (1990) and Bordo (1990) recognize the value of the postmodern critique of the normative modernist position, but they also fear that the extreme postmodern endorsement of particularity and difference poses a danger of relativism. Some earlier instances of feminist theorizing (e.g., Chodorow, Firestone, Gilligan) made claims that can be criticized for being too reductionist or essentialist, and postmodernism has helped enrich feminist theory with a more balanced view. Certainly "gender forms only one axis of a complex, heterogeneous construction, constantly interpenetrating, in historically specific ways, with multiple other axes of identity" (Bordo 1990, 139). But there seems to be a dangerous suggestion in postmodern theory that we can move beyond such insights to a new privileged position which legislates correct intellectual work and determines who has gone astray (Ibid.). In other words, elements of postmodern theory posit an "in principle," a priori attack on gender as an essentialist or totalizing concept. Yet, even Chodorow's work, though flawed, can help us better understand the forces of domination. At the very least, we stand on the shoulders of scholars like Chodorow. While we can no longer sustain an objective totalizing discourse, this does not mean that all totalizing discourses have been equal in terms of their capacity to expose power relations and the mechanisms of subordination (p. 141). There is no escaping the fact that "in our present culture, our activities *are* coded as 'male' or 'female' and will function within the prevailing system of power relations" (p. 152). Ironically, the use of general categories of social identity, like gender, have provided our most effective recent strategies for deconstructing liberal humanist pretensions to neutrality. Bordo asks why we should abandon such critique a priori. Instead

> we need to reserve *practical* spaces for both generalist critique (suitable when gross points need to be made) and attention to complexity and nuance. We need to be pragmatic, not theoretically pure, if we are to struggle effectively with the inclination of institutions to preserve and defend themselves against deep change. (p. 153)

Many feminists also wonder why postmodern theory has come about at this particular historical juncture. As Bordo (1990) reminds us, the postmodern critique of feminist gender theory emerged barely a decade after these theories were first posed. Compared to the history of masculine totalizing theories, how dangerous could feminist gender theories be? Bordo wonders to what extent the timing of the postmodern critique actually serves to help maintain forces of domination.

This curious convergence of postmodern critique and the popularity of feminist theory has also aroused the suspicions of other feminists (e.g., Brown 1987; Christian 1987; Harding 1990; Hartsock 1987a, 1987b, 1990; Mascia-Lees, Sharpe, and Cohen 1989). Hartsock (1987a), for example, has asked why is it that at the very moment when so many marginal groups have begun to challenge their subordination and claim an identity that demands empowerment, a new postmodern theory has emerged that makes the human subject problematic and questions the very possibility of theorizing to ground critique and social change (p. 196). Kaplan (1987) suggests the possibility that postmodern discourse "has been constructed by male theorists partly to mitigate the increasing dominance of feminist theory in intellectual discourse" (p. 150).

One possible answer to such concerns is that the current postmodern despair regarding the possibility of truth is no more than a reversal of Western theoretical arrogance. In other words, because white males are unable to define truth, then such truth does not exist (Mascia-Lees, Sharpe, and Cohen 1989, 15). And Christine DiStefano (1990) argues that post-modern theory is more relevant to males who, having the historical tradition of "their" Enlightenment to fall back on, are in a better position than females to accommodate arguments for a decentered self and the inability to establish objective truth claims. For women, the unstable and fragmented politics of postmodernism appears to weaken the force of the feminist critique developed during this century. Susan Bordo (1990) argues that a similar situation arose during the 1920s and 1930s when professional women turned against the earlier activist feminist arguments based on gender differences. This earlier "post-feminist" orientation urged a focus on being human and adopting a unisexual orientation toward rationality and objectivism as opposed to gender consciousness. But when living in "a culture that is *in fact* constructed by gender duality,...one *cannot* simply be human" anymore than "we can 'just be people' in a racist culture" (p. 152). Bordo worries that we are entering a new postfeminist era wherein feminist fragmentation will undermine the transformative potential of feminism (p. 153). And she reminds us that before postmodern critics such as Rorty helped expose the illusions of epistemological objectivity and neutral science, the liberation movements of the 1960s and 1970s had already made the same point by claiming the legitimacy of marginal cultures and exposing the partiality of dominant perspectives (p. 137).

Yet Bordo (1990) does accept that postmodern theory has provided valuable insights and a necessary modification in the more essentialist variants of feminist theorizing. What Bordo appears to be questioning are those elements of postmodern theory that argue against projects for sociocultural transformation beyond the most local and particular contexts. She does not deny the postmodern claims regarding the instability of constructs like gender but does claim such social categories can be sufficiently stable to provide a basis for critique in certain contexts. But as Butler (1990) argues, we need to be sensitive to those instances where the very categories (like gender) we employ for emancipation might also function to help maintain our domination.

Iris Young (1990) makes a similar argument regarding the concept of community. Her point is that community as an ideal can actually work to diminish our respect for others with whom we disagree. Indeed, "[r]acism, ethnic chauvinism, and class devaluation,...grow partly from a desire for community..." (p. 311). That is, the desire for homogeneity and common understanding entails that we identify those differences that are external to our community. Instead of community, Young posits "the unoppressive city" as a more relevant political ideal (p. 317). Her arguments are interesting and persuasive, even if she has posed an overly restrictive definition of community for the purpose of her analysis. What is most relevant to our discussion is her use of Derrida's poststructuralist theory as a means to uncover the instability of a concept central to radical theorizing, including critical pedagogy wherein community is generally held to be a central concept. It is also of interest to note that this is a specific example of how poststructuralist theory (in this case Derrida's) is discussed as if it were one instance of a larger body of postmodern theory.

Whereas even the most severe feminist critics of postmodernism acknowledge its contributions to feminist thought, others (e.g., Flax 1990; Haraway, 1990; Fraser and Nicholson 1990) argue for the need to construct a postmodern feminism. For these feminists, postmodernism does not preclude "large historical narratives" or "analyses of societal macrostructures" (Fraser and Nicholson 1990, 34). It does require that we abandon unitary or universal views of gender and other social constructs "with plural and complexly constructed conceptions of social identity" (pp. 34–35). Such a postmodern-feminist theory would be pragmatic and subject to ongoing reconstruction in the face of new knowledge. A postmodern feminism could also provide an argument for forming alliances across differences. Actually, the emergence of feminism is implicitly postmodern, and a postmodern-feminist theory "would be the counterpart of a broader, richer, more complex, and multilayered feminist solidarity, the sort of solidarity which is essential for overcoming the oppression of women" (p. 35).

In many respects, the combination of both critique and incorporation of postmodern and poststructuralist thought on the part of feminists is mirrored in the reaction of many critical pedagogues to postmodern and poststructuralist theory. What we observe in both cases is a fundamental tension between an appreciation of the arguments for rejecting metanarratives and foundationalist theory and the conflicting perception that we continue to require a way to ground and conduct critique for sociocultural transformation.

Giroux's views on poststructuralist and postmodern theory are of particular interest, given his prominent role in critical pedagogy and the effort he has made to use elements of these theories (1988a, 1988b, 1988c). Giroux (1988a, 1988b) argues that postmodernism has made a number of important contributions to the project of critical pedagogy. Nevertheless, he is concerned that "postmodernism is too suspicious of the modernist notion of public life and of the struggle for equality and liberty that has been an essential aspect of the liberal democratic discourse" (1988b, 25). Giroux is particularly concerned with those poststructuralist theorists (he tends to see postmodernism as informed by poststructuralism) who have overemphasized the decentering and "death" of the subject in a way that "undermines the possibility of those who have been excluded from the centers of power to name and experience themselves as individual and collective agents" (p. 24).

Giroux's critique of postmodernism and poststructuralism must be understood against the background of his arguments for building a moral theory to orient critical pedagogy. He has been critical of neo-Marxists and others on the left for failing to build an adequate moral theory to ground an emancipatory educational and political project (1988c, 6–7). Giroux believes the left has been unduly concerned with reforms leading to material needs while the right has focused more on moral well-being. An emphasis on morality is essential to the left's project if it seeks to move from a language of critique to include a "language of possibility, one that combines a strategy of opposition with a strategy for constructing a new social order" (p. 31).

In Giroux's (1988c) estimation, the left had, in general, "retreated from a discourse of hope, conceded the moral high ground, and embraced a view of schooling that is fundamentally incapable of defining a notion of the public good" (p. 38). As noted in Chapter 4, Giroux has argued for a conception of "provisional morality" that was oriented by "a history of emancipatory struggles that enabled us to understand the consequences of taking ethical positions on injustice and examples of what principles have to be defended and fought against in the interest of freedom and life" (p. 40). This is a frankly partisan interpretation of history viewed from what Walter Benjamin called the perspective of its victims.

While the radical left has failed to devote adequate attention to the theoretical dimensions of morality, Giroux (1988c) argues that conservative and liberal approaches to moral theory are also inadequate. The right posits an essentialist view of morality that rests on an unproblematic view of history and culture. This analysis endorses an approach to education that rationalizes the transmission of traditional American values and forms of knowledge (pp. 42–43). But the prevailing liberal theory of morality is also unsatisfactory in Giroux's view, because it displays an oversimplified and naive view of the value of reason and scientific progress. Liberals promote an abstract view of morality that depends on procedural justice and a conception of the "individual" as a right-bearing subject. As a consequence, the human subject is reified and abstracted from history and community (pp. 55–56). In this sense, liberal theory forms a morality designed for a society of strangers. Prominent examples of this liberal moral orientation can be found in the work of Kohlberg and Habermas (p. 57). Giroux prefers Horkheimer's view of ethics which includes a consideration of human happiness and the good life, both of which are rooted in the analysis of historical and material conditions that enhance or limit human potential (pp. 57–58).

As troubling as the failures of the left, right, and liberals to articulate a viable moral theory were, Giroux (1988c) seemed at least equally disturbed by some recent developments in postmodernism, poststructuralism, and neopragmatism. This collective assault on foundationalism had not only further decentered the unified subject that had been essential to conservative, liberal, and radical theory but has also "resulted in a one-sided methodological infatuation with deconstructing not simply particular truths, but the very notion of truth itself as an epistemological category" (p. 61). This theoretical tendency exacerbated the current flight from ethics and politics. Giroux acknowledged that postmodernism, poststructuralism, and neopragmatism have all made positive contributions to the critique of dominant culture and ideologies. But in the effort to critique the correspondence theory of truth, positivist hyperrationality, and the conception of a unified subject, these philosophical positions have also deconstructed "any firm moral, ethical, or political project upon which to justify [the] undoing of the text, subject, truth, and other such terrains which have been the traditional constructions of meaning and agency" (p. 62).

Giroux, often combining postmodernism, poststructuralism, and neopragmatism, understands these philosophical positions as displaying a fundamentally anti-utopian character that is in opposition "to any project designed to foster critique and hope in the service of an ethics and political philosophy linked to the construction of a radical democracy" (p. 62). This dispute regarding the value of a utopian perspective seems to be a major difference between the right and left critique of postmodernism and poststructuralism. Richard Rorty's neopragmatism is described by Giroux as illustrative of the worst anti-utopian impulse of the postmodern trend. According to Giroux, Rorty's position amounts to a "sweeping rejection of any attempt to ground one's judgments" (p. 63). Moreover, from Rorty's perspective, "the intellectual is reduced to simply being a somewhat privileged member of the community in the service of conversation, a member without a politics, a sense of vision, or a conscience" (p. 64). This position is an instance of an extreme form of cultural relativism wherein truth is determined by the conventions of the local community.

Giroux is further distressed that even some radical educators who recognize the importance of a critical moral discourse (e.g., Beyer and Wood 1986) have taken a "Rortyian turn in arguing that a moral discourse is dependent on the interpretive community of which it is a part" (Giroux 1988c, 67). Giroux rejects such interpretations and maintains that "the grounds of an ethical discourse are not to be found in their social interpretive construction but in the question of how they affect the meaning and quality of life" (p. 67). He does not make clear how interpretations regarding "the meaning and quality of life" are qualitatively different from "social interpretive constructions" to ground ethical discourse.

Giroux argues that critical pedagogy must resist the flight from ethics and politics. Even if we grasp that competing discourses are oriented by real and conflicting moral interests, we must go beyond merely presenting students with different positions and letting them chose "the moral discourse that suits their own lives and experiences" (p. 67). Instead

> a critical educator can demonstrate his/her moral courage through a content that gives real meaning to ethical action while allowing students to read, debate, and align themselves with moral discourses brought to bear on the issues that become a legitimate object of discussion. Although a teacher cannot demand a student not be a racist, he/she can certainly subject such a position to a critique that reveals it as an act of political and moral irresponsibility related to wider social and historical social practices. (p. 67)

Those who hold that critical educators have no right to impose their positions on students misrepresent critical pedagogy and argue from a flawed theoretical position that contributes to the flight from ethics and politics while reinforcing the status quo (p. 68). We must understand that

> educators have a moral and ethical responsibility to develop a view of radical authority that legitimates forms of critical pedagogy aimed at both interpreting reality and transforming it. . . . Developing an oppositional language needs to be judged in the context of a theoretical project that provides teachers, students, and others with the possibility for alternative readings of their own experiences and the nature of the larger social reality. (pp. 68–69)

But in no way does an appeal to a theoretically "correct" view give teachers the right to impose knowledge in any way that serves to silence a student's critical competence. This argument is, according to Giroux, consistent with Freire's view that teachers have an obligation to make their positions clear to students but not to impose a given position on them (p. 69).

Giroux (1988c) does not, however, join in what he calls the "totalizing" critiques of postmodernism made by those like Perry Anderson (1984) and Fredric Jameson (1983, 1984a, 1984b), since there are several "oppositional elements in postmodern philosophy that constitute important critical interventions against the dominant cultural ideologies of late capitalism" (Giroux 1988c, 61). Giroux also acknowledges in footnotes that some of the recent work by Foucault, Deleuze, Guattari, Donzelot, and feminists such as Luce Irigaray, Julia Kristeva, and Teresa de Lauretis have made significant contributions to social critique and begun to deal with the question of the political project (pp. 228–29). For example, Giroux claims he shares the views of Gandal (1986) and Rajchman (1986–1987) that some of Foucault's latter work made a contribution to a theory of ethics. He does not elaborate this connection in any detail.

In his most recent work, Giroux (1988a, 1988b) has been more specific regarding the contributions postmodernism makes to the critique of modernism in terms of shifting conceptions of power, knowledge, subjectivity, progress, and history. Postmodern criticism can best be understood as offering "a combination of reactionary and progressive possibilities" (Giroux 1988b, 6). For critical pedagogy, therefore, it is a matter of making progressive appropriations of postmodern theory (p. 14). For example, in the process of rejecting the liberal, humanist view of a unified, rational subject, postmodernism has posed "a faith in forms of social transformation that understand the historical, structural, and ideological limits that shape the possibility for self-reflection and action" (Giroux 1988a, 164).

For Giroux (1988a), a progressive appropriation of postmodern theory would not entail the rejection of the insights of modernism but a combination of the best insights of both theoretical orientations. We need to combine the modernist emphasis on the capacity of individuals to use critical reason to address the issue of public life with a critical postmodernist concern with how we might experience agency in a world constituted in differences unsupported by transcendent phenomena or metaphysical guarantees. In that way, critical pedagogy can reconstitute itself in terms that are both transformative and emancipatory. (p. 164).

This combination of modern and postmodern theory would serve as a corrective to those variants of critical pedagogy that are unduly influenced by modernism and overemphasize technique and procedure (e.g., Shor 1979). For Giroux (1988a), this overly modernist approach to critical pedagogy comes too close to "the liberal-progressive tradition in which teaching is reduced to getting students to merely express or assess their own experience" (p. 164). Such pedagogical strategies amount to a "flight from authority" and an overly narrow conception of political action that excludes a utopian dimension. Giroux urges that we move instead to what he calls a "border pedagogy of postmodern resistance" (p. 165). This pedagogic blend of modern and postmodern theory

> presupposes not merely an acknowledgment of the shifting borders that both undermine and reterritorialize different configurations of power and knowledge, it also links the notion of pedagogy to a more substantive struggle for a democratic society. It is a pedagogy that attempts to link an emancipatory notion of modernism with a postmodernism of resistance (p. 165).

A border pedagogy would encourage students to be sensitive to the multiple, nonsynchronous relations between one's identity, social position, and other possible cultural constructions. By employing the insights of postmodernism, students would be in a better position to reject master narratives that impede their understanding of oppression and emancipation. But Giroux cautions that often the language of postmodern theory "runs the risk of undercutting its own political possibilities by ignoring how a language of difference can be articulated with critical modernist concerns for developing a discourse of public life" (p. 169). Giroux cites the work of Chantal Mouffe (1988) to argue that, while it is necessary to challenge the often pretentious modernist domination of intellectual discourse rooted in the progressive potential of rationality, the postmodern critique of modernism does not require that we reject the emancipatory values of modernism, only that we reconsider these values in multiple contexts and in terms of an indeterminacy that opens them to being defined in unpredictable ways (Giroux 1988a, 170). In this way, post-modernism can serve to reintroduce an element of radical democracy to counter the foundationalist tendencies of modernism. In other words, educators need to construct "a critical politics of difference not outside but within a tradition of radical democracy" (Ibid.).

Within the frame of the postmodern critique, Giroux argues, we would understand the concept of counter-memory so central to critical pedagogy "not as an essentialist and closed narrative, but as part of a utopian project that recognizes" the open, heterogeneous, and indeterminate nature of a democratic tradition (Ibid.). Counter-memory can play a key role in this process by questioning current modes of truth and historical interpreta- tions that create the potential for changing the present by creating new ways to understand and reinterpret it. A point Giroux has insisted on of late, along with Alcoff (1988) and others, is that the left cannot be content with a movement based solely on critique, it must also hold out an alternative vision of a better society to motivate political action (Giroux 1988a, 171–72).

Giroux (1988a) seeks to differentiate counter-memory as remembrance from the concept of tradition which he defines as ideological and pedagogical practices that "refuse to interrogate public forms and which deny difference as a fundamental referent for a democratic society" (p. 172). Conversely, remembrance is concerned with specific struggles over history and power. Remembrance as a form of counter-memory seeks to present what has not been presentable, a reinstatement of silenced voices to function as a subversive challenge to the forces of domination. Border pedagogy linked to a form of counter-memory can, in Giroux's view, provide the ethical and epistemological basis for a political solidarity within difference and located in the more general struggle for the expansion and revitalization of public life. This approach simultaneously rejects any monolithic tradition that seeks unreflective acceptance. "Instead, counter- memory attempts to recover communities of memory and narratives of struggle that provide a sense of location, place, and identity to various dominant and subordinate groups" (p. 173). This does not amount to a liberal celebration of pluralism for its own sake but a pedagogy and political practice that helps enable teachers and students to challenge oppression by giving them a sense of how they have been oppressed, their possible complicity with domination, and the ways they might transform such sociocultural arrangements (p. 173).

As noted in the previous chapter, Giroux rejects what he sees as Ellsworth's (1988, 1989) notion that differences among students are merely antagonistic and that separatism is the most viable political option. In the end, according to Giroux (1988a), Ellsworth's position amounts to a "crippling form of political disengagement [and] ignores the necessity of exploring differences for the specific irreducible interests they represent, . . . and for the pedagogical possibilities. . .to work with other groups as part of a collective attempt at defining a radical language of democratic public life" (p. 177). Giroux acknowledges the tension within critical pedagogy (a tension he believes Ellsworth ignores) between ideological correctness and pedagogical error. While teachers might not be able to speak inclusively as the "Other," they are able to "work *with* diverse others to deepen their understanding of the traditions, histories, knowledges, and politics that they bring to schools" (p. 178). This pedagogical approach involves more than a clarification of differences. It also involves working to reveal the potential solidarities that exist in terms of the forms of repression and struggle experienced by subordinate groups. Giroux acknowledges that the modernist faith in rationality or human agency is severely challenged by the postmodern critique, but this makes the need for human agency all the more urgent. The postmodern illumination of the loss of certainty is not a cause for despair or acquiescence in nihilism. We can still snatch hope "from the weakening grasp of modernity" and identify "historically privileged groups" who are committed to social change consistent with the goals of radical democracy and human survival (p. 179).

In a related argument, McLaren and Hammer (1989) reject the view of those (e.g., Sarup 1989) who contend that "poststructuralist/postmodernist theories. . .are *necessarily* antagonistic to the project of self and social emancipation" (p. 31). They agree, for example, that there exists an oppositional form of postmodernism that can help deconstruct forms of domination. On the other hand, there are reactionary forms of postmodernism that do function to undermine resistance. The problem remains, however, that "even the postmodernism of resistance fails to incorporate a language of possibility or the capacity for utopian thinking" (p. 58). While acknowledging the limited emancipatory potential of postmodernism and poststructuralism, McLaren (1988d) seems more concerned with the "authoritarian servility, pronounced anti-utopianism, and incipient nihilism" promoted by such theories (p. 77). It is often necessary to deconstruct representations, but it is quite another thing "to reinscribe them in a language that takes seriously the discourse of democracy and emancipation" (McLaren and Hammer 1989, 58).

For McLaren and Hammer (1989), the central task of critical educators in the postmodern era is "knowing how to live contingently and provisionally without the certainty of knowing the truth, yet...with the courage to take a stand on issues of human suffering, domination, and oppression" (p. 32). Such is the new configuration of critical human agency. One danger is that, in the process of deconstructing grand theories of modernism, we will become mired in "a new postmodernist relativism, where the question 'How can we eliminate suffering?' collapses into the question, 'What is suffering?' " (p. 33). In contrast, critical pedagogy refuses to abandon either utopian thought or the focus on social transformation consistent with human emancipation.

McLaren and Hammer (1989) accept the postmodern and poststructuralist critique of the modernist view of the "self" as having an objective essence derived from reflection. But this does not mean that the self must be reduced to a mere interpellation of discourse (p. 49). McLaren and Hammer argue that human beings *are self-conscious rather than self-constituting.* In other words, as humans we are, in part, constituted by self-consciousness but also by conditions external to our consciousness, that is, by both what we are aware of and what we repress. Certainly our self-awareness is distorted, more or less, by ideology and those elements we have repressed. "But we are nevertheless self-conscious enough to recognize our own constitution outside of the exigencies of our own volition" and our awareness of "the constitution of our self is what makes liberation possible" (p. 49). It is a goal of critical pedagogy to make students more aware of the process of human self-formation. Students need to acquire a sense of their interests and real needs, and this is only possible via the mediating knowledge of those social conditions that generate such needs. Helping to promote this knowledge is an important purpose of critical pedagogy. Thus, critical pedagogy should remain focused on a language of possibility connected to a conception of real empowerment. The ground for a pedagogical praxis is to achieve solidarity with the oppressed in their struggle to overcome their suffering.

There is an apparent optimism, on McLaren and Hammer's (1989) part, regarding the human capacity to discern "real" needs and "genuine" wants. Their utopian orientation is based on the assumption that lacking any idea of what we want society to become, "we will never know if, in our struggle for human freedom, those conditions have been met" (p. 53). The existence of radical otherness does not preclude a pedagogy for emancipation, because this pedagogy is focused on helping students construct something new from their multiple subjectivities (p. 54). Teachers as transformative intellectuals convey critical knowledge and values to help enable "differentiated human capacities to be realized through the construction of social forms that inhibit the crippling distortions of social and moral regulation that deny individuals from speaking out of their own histories, traditions, voices, and personal experiences" (p. 55). We must acknowledge that our students are "always already" shaped by gender, race, class, and other forces, but this does not preclude their capacity to acquire a critical voice. McLaren and Hammer claim that "while it may be true that there is no privileged vantage point to subjectivity from which we can escape our own constitution in external technologies of power, it does not follow that we should submit ourselves without a fight to the processes which have made us who we are" (p. 56).

We can certainly agree with the arguments by Giroux, Hammer, McLaren, and others that postmodernism does not entail a rejection of modernist insights. Even Lyotard, as noted earlier, acknowledged that postmodernism should not be understood as a clear break with modernism but as modernism in its nacent phase. That postmodernism does not involve a simplistic rejection of modernism is a point also emphasized by Laclau (1988) and Montag (1988). But, as Whitson (forthcoming) notes, because modernism developed as an emancipatory rejection of premodern ecclesiastical authority, the current critique of totalizing discourses can be seen as a reassertion of the modernist tradition. Whitson argues that it remains unclear just what postmodern theory itself actually adds to counterhegemonic thought and practice beyond the insights already available in modernist theory. On the other hand, I would agree with Whitson's contention that the poststructuralist conception of textuality does provide a necessary element for a counterhegemonic approach to pedagogy. We will explore this point in more detail in the next section.

The reaction to postmodernism and poststructuralism by radical educators also reflects a tension that can be traced back (at least) to the social reconstructionist critique of the 1930s. Here again is the fear of a relativism that could threaten a pedagogy for sociocultural transformation toward a truly democratic society and culture. The reconstructionists could not deny the philosophical insights and methodological value of pragmatism. Yet they were skeptical of what they understood as pragmatism's instrumentalism, relativism, and complacency in the face of mass social problems and suffering. The emergence of postmodern and poststructuralist theory has fragmented meaning, decentered and deconstructed the modernist conception of the human subject, problematized rationality, and emphasized the centrality of difference and alterity. Thus, these new theoretical developments have posed serious constraints on the radical educator's ability to construct utopian conceptions to orient praxis. There is no simple solution to this problem and it remains as a central tension within critical pedagogy. The reaction to postmodern and poststructuralist theory also helps to illuminate the wide range of views and internal conflicts within what we have loosely termed critical pedagogy.

It is interesting to observe that questions related to the interpretation and application of pragmatism remain at the center of the debate over postmodernism and poststructuralism. For example, Derrida's poststructuralism incorporates the work of C. S. Peirce, and Rorty's postmodern neopragmatism involves a significant reinterpretation of Dewey's pragmatic philosophy. Habermas, a leading critic of postmodern and poststructuralist theory, utilizes the ideas of both Peirce and Dewey in his theorizing. And elements of pragmatic theory remain prominent in the discourse of critical pedagogy (e.g., Brennen 1989; Cherryholmes 1988; Giroux 1988a, 1988b, 1988c; McLaren 1988c, 1988d; Stanley 1989; Sultan 1989; Wexler 1987; Whitson and Stanley 1988, 1990). What remains unclear in the debate within critical pedagogy is the relationship (or tension) between utopian thought, values, and pragmatic theory. In other words, while the postmodern and poststructuralist critique has led many radical educators to accept the problematic and contingent nature of all values—including those of radical democracy—there remains an inclination on the part of critical educators to employ such contingent values (e.g., emancipation, freedom, empowerment, democracy, justice, solidarity, etc.) as the basis of a utopian view to orient sociocultural transformation. Of course this characterization oversimplifies the situation, since many critical educators also stress the importance of developing student competence to analyze problems critically and make value decisions. What remains ambiguous is whether or not contingent values should remain as the primary ground for utopian thought in critical pedagogy. One could posit an alternative conception derived from pragmatic theory in which a student's critical competence is conceived as a primary human interest that is prior to yet necessary for the realization of democratic (or other) values. I believe that many critical educators are reluctant to move to a position that gives primacy to critical competence, because they fear that this amounts to a retreat from ethics or morality and further strengthens the conservative effort to control the moral agenda in the debate over educational reform. As we continue this discussion, we will return to this issue that has troubled radical educational theory throughout this century. In the next section, we examine the poststructuralist theory of Jacques Derrida as it relates to neopragmatism. I am hopeful that this analysis will help illuminate the extent to which poststructuralism can provide a basis for a new approach to critical pedagogy beyond the more limited contributions recognized by its critics.

POSTSTRUCTURALISM AND POSTMODERNISM RECONSIDERED

It might be useful to consider how such a negative and fearful appraisal of poststructuralism and postmodernism has developed. No doubt there are numerous reasons, but two stand out and are mutually supportive.

First is the widespread concern Bernstein (1983) has called the "Cartesian anxiety," the anxiety or fear that either we maintain grounds for objective knowledge or we will drift into the abyss of relativism or nihilism. As noted earlier in this chapter, variations of this Cartesian anxiety seem to permeate much of the reaction to the emergence of poststructuralism and postmodernism (e.g., Arac 1986; Bernstein 1983; Habermas 1987; Nicholson 1990; Norris 1985, 1987; Rabinow and Sullivan 1987; Sarup 1984, 1989). In other words, Bernstein (1983) has called our attention to a theoretical tension that pervades our culture and shapes our response to new theoretical developments.

A second reason for the negative reaction to poststructuralism and postmodernism lies in the nature of the theoretical texts themselves. Derrida (1979) makes the point, in commenting on Nietzsche's appropriation as a proto-Nazi ideologist, that this critique of Nietzsche cannot be dismissed as a mere misreading or distortion of his texts. In part, Nietzsche's texts were capable of such an interpretation (although it can also be argued that it is neither a necessary nor the best interpretation of his work). So too the texts of Baudrillard, Deluze, Derrida, Foucault, Lyotard, Rorty, and others can be read as supporting a form of radical relativism or nihilism and thereby radically undermining the grounds for any emancipatory project. Indeed, it is the alleged propensity of postmodernism and poststructuralism to destroy the basis for emancipatory social action that forms the core of the reaction against such theorizing (e.g., Arac 1986; Habermas 1987; Sarup 1984, 1989).

Nevertheless, this negative reading of postmodernism and poststructuralism is (like the reading of Nietzsche as a proto-Nazi) neither necessary nor the preferred reading of these texts. More specifically, I would argue in consort with the position of Whitson (forthcoming) that while postmodernism does contain some nihilistic elements, the poststructuralist theory of those such as Derrida and Foucault is not "intrinsically vulnerable" to the charge of being nihilistic or functioning to undermine critical praxis. In fact, the reverse is true, that is, critical counterhegemonic praxis requires the insights of poststructuralist theory.

In the present study, I have attempted to locate the common elements, goals, and methods of poststructuralism, Critical Theory, and neopragmatism as they contribute to the construction of a counterhegemonic critical pedagogy. I have chosen here to concentrate primarily on the work of Derrida as it contrasts with the variant of postmodern neopragmatism espoused by Rorty. We have noted earlier some of the critical reaction to Rorty's work, and Derrida is among the most frequently criticized of the poststructuralists. While Derrida's work is absolutely central to the poststructuralist critique, much of the argument presented here might also be applied to the work of Foucault, Deluze, and other poststructuralists.

Finally, there is no single thing as *the* poststructuralist position, thus we must always respond to particular arguments. It is hoped that this approach to analyzing poststructuralism will help illuminate its radical and emancipatory potential.

In some respects, and despite the conservative claims for the need to ground basic values, it can be argued that nihilist assumptions are deeply entrenched in our culture. For example, our historical focus on individualism, political choice, the market economy, instrumentalism, and scientism all promote a view that reduces truth to procedural outcomes or market forces (Bell 1977). Lasch (1984) has criticized our cultural overemphasis on the value of choice and adherence to a distorted form of radical pluralism whereby many have concluded that

> no one has a right to "impose" his [sic] own preference on anyone else. They appear to assume that moral values can no longer be taught or transmitted through example and persuasion but are always "imposed" on unwilling victims. Any attempt to win someone to a point of view different from his [sic] own becomes an intolerable interference with his [sic] freedom of choice. (p. 36)

This nihilistic tendency might appear to conflict with conservative (and any other) attempts to develop a curriculum for cultural transmission by denying the ground for any such activity. However, in practice our cultural support for radical pluralism can help reify the conservative status quo in two ways. First, it serves conservative interests by helping to undermine arguments for the need to transform society. Second, it actually helps transmit conservative values and institutions by naturalizing what is by describing it as the outcome of individual free choice.[1]

While the postmodern arguments of critics like Feyerabend (1978) and Rorty (1980, 1982) holds a radical critical potential that might undermine the conservative commitment to individualism, pluralism, and choice, their theories also tend to degenerate into a critique without any grounds for emancipation. For example, Feyerabend (1978) has argued that in an "objective" sense, "there is not much to choose between anti-semitism and humanitarianism" and that relativism "gives an adequate account of the situation which thus emerges" (pp. 8–9). Rorty (1980) did accept the values of pragmatism which involved a willingness to discuss issues with others, yet he held out no guarantee for the success of such discussions. This was a reasonable position, but Rorty has also claimed that he did "not even know what 'success' would mean" beyond the mere "continuance" of the conversation (p. 734). At best, since pragmatic values were

---

1. I am indebted to discussions with William F. Pinar for helping to clarify Lasch's relevance to this issue (also see Pinar 1988c).

only justified within the limits of a specific community and culture and we had no external means to guide their application beyond these cultural boundaries, we could only argue that we should continue the conversation for our own edification. For Rorty, this was sufficient, and we should cease trying to aspire to something more. In other words, we must stop trying to gain some privileged vantage point for analysis. A similar position was presented by Lyotard (1984) who has helped shape our current sense of postmodernism by denying our ability to construct any metanarratives to explain our situation.[2] Yet Lyotard, like Foucault, seems more committed than Rorty to the importance of critique and resistance, although such efforts must always be local and limited by our inability to ground them in any larger narrative justification.[3]

Bernstein (1983), who shares Rorty's rejection of claims for any totalizing critiques or the possibility of objective knowledge, has also issued a pertinent caution by noting that those who espoused an extreme version of this line of thought often failed "to see how easily a playful relativism that seems so innocent in 'civilized' conversation can turn into its opposite in the practical realm—how the restless *esprit* of unrestrained negativity can become a potent force for unrestrained destruction" (p. 200). In fact, Rorty has constructed a relatively narrow reading of pragmatism which limits the value of his approach to neopragmatism. I believe his position understates Dewey's legacy, but his neglect of Peirce is the most serious limitation in his interpretation of pragmatism (Rochberg-Halton 1986). Peirce, like Dewey, understood truth to be what is validated by the community of inquirers, that is, warranted assertability. But for Peirce, while the development of human knowledge was an open social process, it should always be oriented toward human betterment and truth (Haskell 1984a). In other words, the quest for human knowledge always had a social purpose beyond mere edification.

Rorty (1980) describes Derrida, along with Dewey, Gadamer, and the latter Wittgenstein, as an "edifying" philosopher or one of those who "are reactive and offer satires, parodies [and] aphorisms" rather than arguments (p. 369). Of course, Rorty realized that edifying philosophers did offer arguments, but he maintained that it was not necessary to do so. Perhaps this position (like Feyerabend's) was only meant to be taken as a satire or read ironically, since Rorty must present an argument to explicate it. In any case, Rorty's reading of Derrida is much too limited, because Derrida insists on argumentation as central to philosophy (Culler 1982; Norris 1985,

---

2. Although, as Montag (1988) and others have observed, this assertion amounts to a new and self-contradictory metanarrative.

3. Rorty's (1989) more recent work has shifted focus somewhat and he now also sees solidarity as a major purpose of human critical dialogue.

1987; Derrida 1988). Furthermore, while Derrida's deconstruction has much in common with Rorty's view of neopragmatism, there are important distinctions between the two theoretical positions.

As Culler (1982) has explained, deconstruction, like pragmatism, "sees representations as signs that refer to other signs, which refer to still other signs, and depicts enquiry as a process in which propositions are adduced to support other propositions and what is said to 'ground' a proposition proves to be itself part of a general text" (p. 153). But there were also two important differences between Derrida's deconstruction and Rorty's neopragmatism. First, Rorty's pragmatic conception of truth was problematic, because it appealed to consensus and convention. This approach tended to rely on norms as a foundation, for example, Rorty's (1980) appeal to "agreement among sane and rational men [sic]" as to what would constitute their truth (p. 337). Such determinations depend on exclusions of Others, especially those considered to be marginal or irrational, as well as the nonserious. In short, it was a consensus sustained by the exclusion of the different and marginal in society. But deconstruction is focused on what has been excluded and cannot accept a view of truth limited to what is demonstrable within a given system or community. Instead Derrida

> tries to keep alive the possibility that the eccentricity of women, poets, prophets, and madmen might yield truths about the system to which they are marginal—truths contradicting the consensus and not demonstrable within a framework yet developed. (Culler 1982, 154)

The second problem with Rorty's neopragmatism related to the process of reflective inquiry. Rorty argued that there was no human effort that could enable us to stand outside the framework in which we conducted inquiry. Deconstruction was also skeptical regarding the possible solution of epistemological problems or our capacity to conduct critique outside the logocentric limits of Western thought. Still, deconstruction "repudiates the complacency to which pragmatism may lead and makes reflection upon one's own procedures and institutional frameworks a necessary task" (p. 134). As Culler argues

> even if in principle we cannot get outside conceptual frameworks to criticize and evaluate the practice of self-reflexivity, the attempt to theorize one's practice, works to produce change. . . . Theoretical inquiry does not lead to new foundations—in this sense the pragmatists are right. But they are wrong to reject it on these grounds, for it does lead to changes in assumptions, institutions, and practices. (p. 154)

Deconstruction has rejected claims to ground epistemology in any authoritative foundation, since "the critical project depends on resisting the notion that truth is only what can be demonstrated within an accepted framework" (p. 154). We must come to understand the duplicitous or double reference of truth as "what can be demonstrated within an accepted framework and what simply is the case, whether or not anyone could believe it or validate it" (p. 154). This paradoxical position was evident in the argument between pragmatists and those seeking to defend the correspondence theory of truth. The latter argued that objective truth must exist on the grounds that without it we have no rational way to interpret human behavior or develop policy. Contrast this with the pragmatist's (objective) claim that relativism must be accepted as an essential characteristic of human society; that is, truth *is* relative. Deconstruction does not offer a better theory of truth, rather it helps to reveal those aporias that arise in various attempts to tell the truth (p. 135).

For Derrida (1976), meaning was never fixed apart from its location in a text or spoken statement. Thus, meaning was *always* determined in relation to other texts in which the signifiers in question had already been employed. Each time we used a signifier its meaning contained the *trace(s)* of prior uses. Transcendental signifiers were not possible since the meaning of *any* concept was always referred to previous use of the concept in prior discourses. Consequently, there was no fixed meaning as meaning itself was always deferred. Like Foucault, Derrida's work decentered the human subject. Both argued that discourse shaped the individual in the sense that the speaker or writer became an effect of the organization and use of his or her language. For both writers, one could resist, subvert, or deconstruct aspects of the systems they confronted. However, with a decentered subject and no fixed ground for meaning it was not possible to construct a *single* interpretation of the social text that possessed an absolute claim to truth.

Regarding charges that his philosophy was apolitical or conservative, Derrida (1982) argued that deconstruction could not be reduced to a method and separated from the political-institutional problematic; it must always question the structures and conditions of discourse. Thus, deconstruction often took a radical position but not one reflecting an established program, since genuine critique might lead to possibilities we could never calculate in advance. Derrida argued that this did not inevitably lead to a conservative complacency, because we must constantly struggle on two fronts, that is, "the critique of current institutions and the deconstruction of philosophical opposition—while nevertheless contesting the distinction between the two" (p. 159). So while Derrida (1988) recognized that certain of his writings or practices did reflect a conservative stance, he simultaneously worked to call into question the very traditions that supported conservative positions. Consequently, deconstruction was never intrinsically conservative. In fact, it was more relevant to speak of deconstructions rather than a univocal conception of deconstructionism, since no single, inclusive explanation of this mode of thought existed or could exist.

Nevertheless, deconstruction does involve *destabilization* of meaning as a principle theme. Derrida has argued that destabilization cannot be reduced to negativity since it "is required for 'progress' as well. The 'de' in *de*construction signifies not the demolition of what is constructing itself, but rather what remains to be thought beyond the constructivist or deconstructionist scheme..." (1988, 147). But deconstructionism must not be read as leading to a fundamental indeterminacy regarding meaning. Derrida insisted he has not used the term indeterminacy, but has spoken of "undecidability" which is a very different concept. This argument over undecidability raises an issue central to the debate over critical curriculum theory.

The point is that "undecidability is always a *determinate* oscillation between possibilities (for example, of meaning, but also of facts). These possibilities are themselves highly *determined* in strictly *defined* situations (for example, discursive—syntactical or rhetorical—but also political, ethical, etc.). They are *pragmatically* determined" (p. 148). Derrida used undecidability rather than indeterminacy, because he was interested in relations or differences of force and "everything that allows, precisely, determinations in given situations to be stabilized through a decision of writing...which also includes political action..." and other elements of experience (p. 148). In short, indecision could not exist "were it not between *determined* (semantic, ethical, political) poles, which are upon occasion terribly necessary and always irreplaceably singular" (p. 148). Therefore, deconstruction, whether in semantics, ethics, or politics, should not lead to an extreme form of relativism or to any form of indeterminacy of meaning.

Put another way, for structures of undecidability to exist—including decision and responsibility structures—"there must be a certain play, *différence*, nonidentity" (p. 149). This condition did not amount to indetermination but to the *"différance* or nonidentity with oneself in the very process of determination" (p. 149). Consequently, we should not confound *différance* with indeterminacy since it is the former that "makes determinacy possible and necessary." This was *not* because *différance* is in itself equivalent to "indetermancy." First, *différance* is "in *itself* nothing outside of different determinations; second, and consequently, it never comes to a full stop anywhere, absolutely..., and is neither negativity nor nothingness (as indeterminacy would be). Insofar as it is always determined, undecidability is also not negative in itself" (p. 149). We should recall that Derrida (1976) coined *différance* as a neologism to help convey the sense in which the meaning of terms is derived from their differences with other terms but such meaning is also simultaneously deferred to prior uses of the term in previous textual situation. Thus, *différance* incorporates both the meanings of to differ and to defer.

This analysis of undecidability is relevant to Derrida's (1988) conception of power or force which he understood as "differences of power or force" that are equally qualitative and quantitative (p. 149). So like Nietzsche, Derrida believed we must start "from difference in order to accede to force and not vice versa" (p. 149). This vantage point opened us to a paradox: "the ostensibly greater force can also be the 'lesser' (. . .which supposed the essential possibility of an inversion of meaning, . . .a mutation of meaning not limited to the semantics of discourse or the dictionary but which also 'produces' itself as history)" (p. 149). Such paradoxes, tropes, and ruses must always be taken into account as we analyzed things such as power, force, and repression.

Derrida has never argued that concepts such as truth, reference, and stable interpretive contexts must be put radically into question if by this one means contesting "that there *are* and that there *should be* truth, reference, and stable contexts of interpretation" (p. 150). Instead, he has done something quite different, that is to pose questions

> that I hope are radical concerning the possibility of these things, of these values, of these norms, of this stability (which by essence is always provisional and finite). This questioning and. . .discourse. . .evidently no longer belong simply, or homogeneously to the order of truth, of reference, of contextuality. But they do not destroy it or contradict it. They are themselves neither false, nontrue, nor self-reflexive (identical to themselves and transparent), nor context-eternal or metacontextual. Their "truth" is not of the same order as the truth they question, but in pragmatically determined situations in which this "truth" is set forth they must submit (in large measure. . .) to the norms of the context that requires one to prove, to demonstrate, to proceed correctly, to conform to the rules of language and to a great number of other social, ethical, political-institutional rules, etc. (pp. 150–151)

It is always necessary to account for the stability of interpretive contexts and those norms which depend on them (p. 151). However, such an accounting did not require a conservative move in an effort to maintain such instances of contextual stability at all costs. Also, the attempt to account for contextual stability was itself accomplished within a frame that defined the essence of interpretive contexts as provisional and finite, and this required that we grasp the "historicity" and "nonnaturalness of ethics, of politics, of institutionality, etc." (p. 151). To recall this might be radically to interrogate the stability of interpretive contexts. But given that "there is no stability that is absolute, eternal, intangible, natural," instability is implied in the definition of stability. In other words "stability is not an immutability; it is by definition always destabilizable" (p. 151).

Nevertheless, our praxis requires that we consider certain contexts as relatively stable, for example, the practice of critique involved in writing about a particular situation or issue. In such contexts it was reasonable to expect that we act in accordance with certain norms, and Derrida (1988) has taken several of his critics (e.g., Searle and Habermas) to task for not conducting their practice in this manner (pp. 151, 157–59). The fact that Derrida could point to such failures by critics to read him correctly or to respect the rules of grammar, morality, or pragmatic argument confirmed his view that contexts were only relatively stable. The connections between words, concepts, and objects, truth and reference, could never be guaranteed in any absolute way by some metacontext or metadiscourse. However stable, complex, and overdetermined it may appear

> there is a context and one that is only relatively *firm*, neither absolutely solid...nor entirely closed..., without being purely and simply identical to itself. In it there is a margin of play, of difference, an opening; in it there is "supplementarity"...or "paragonality." (p. 151)

Contrary to the allegations of his critics, Derrida (1988) claimed that he has never believed in or spoken of "complete freeplay or undecidability" (p. 115). There was never completeness regarding undecidability, that is, the issue could not be reduced to an either/or choice "between pure realization of self-presence and complete freeplay or undecidability" (p. 115). This was a critical point in terms of decisions involving ethical-political responsibility. Indeed, for Derrida, undecidability was a necessary condition for such decisions.

> A decision can only come into being in a space that exceeds the calculable program that would destroy all responsibility by transforming it into a programmable effect of determinate causes. There can be no moral or political responsibility without this trial and this passage by way of the undecidable. Even if a decision seems to take only a second and not to be preceded by any deliberation, it is structured by this *experience and experiment of the undecidable.* (p. 116)

Regarding the question of the repressive nature of law, legal institutions, and political powers, Derrida (1988) pointed to the need "to distinguish very carefully if we are not to succumb to the facile solutions and ideological consensus of the *doxai* of right or left" (p. 132). The police and law were not inherently repressive "even in [their] negative, restrictive, or prohibitive prescriptions" (p. 132). Nevertheless, although the police need not be "politically suspect a priori," they were never a politically neutral or apolitical phenomenon. And we must always seek to distinguish, via a process that "is never neutral," those forms of unjust brutality that violated the very laws to which they appealed (p. 133).

On a related point, Derrida denies that he has ever considered "laws, constitutions, the declaration of the rights of man, grammar, or the penal code to be the same as novels" (p. 134). He only wants us to recall that such phenomena are not "natural realities." In other words, "they depend upon the same structural power that allows novelesque fictions or mendacious inventions and the like to take place" (p. 134). It is in this sense that the study of literature could better enable us to understand law, rights, and political power.

For Derrida (1988), political evaluation was always "formulated in a given context, starting from given forces or interests, against another manner of determining the context and of imposing this determination" (p. 135). This process was not apparent in all cases and never only or always discursive in nature.

> It often dissimulates itself, articulates itself or translates itself through mediations that are numerous, differentiated, potential, equivocal, difficult to decipher. It often depends upon codes that are still poorly apprehended, allowing therefore for different possible implementations, given the mobility of contexts that are constantly being reframed. (p. 135)

There is a politics of language, education, ethnic relations, etc., that impinged on all social institutions, practices, and styles. But we must be very careful regarding what conclusions we drew from such propositions. A basic constraint was that no political critique could be possible except in terms of another contextual determination that was as political as the focus of the political critique itself. Consequently, critique could never be a neutral practice as it always took place within a context that had deep and potentially unlimited boundaries. Deconstruction's project has involved taking "this limitless context into account." A major source of the criticism directed at Derrida was provoked by his statement "there is nothing outside the text." What this meant, says Derrida, was that "there is nothing outside context" (p. 136). Derrida believed that both forms say exactly the same thing. While the latter form would have been less shocking, he was not certain that it would have contributed more to our understanding of the issue. There are several important clarifications derived from Derrida's argument for the unavoidable centrality of context.

First, his use of context should not be reduced to a form of radical relativism, characterized by skepticism, empiricism, or nihilism. This was, in part, because an extreme form of relativism is self-contradictory. But more importantly, the "deconstructive" way of thinking "was neither a philosophical position nor a critique of finite contexts, which it analyzes without claiming any absolute overview" (p. 137). Yet, since deconstruction itself was unavoidably "rooted in a given context, . . . it does not renounce (it neither can nor ought to do so) the 'values' that are dominant in this context," for instance truth (p. 137).

Furthermore, Derrida's conception of "text" was never confined merely to books. Text was not something self-contained. Derrida's use of text did not

> suspend reference to history, to the world, to reality, to being, and especially not to the other, since to say of history, of the world, of reality, that they always appear in an experience, hence in a movement of interpretation which contextualizes them according to a network of differences and hence of referral to the other, is surely to recall that alterity (difference) is irreducible. *Différance* is a reference and vice versa. (p. 137)

There was also a paradox that further complicated our attempts to engage in critique. When our conception of text "accommodates reference as difference and inscribes *différance* in presence, this concept of text or of context no longer opposes writing to erasure. The text is not a presence, any more than 'remains'. . .are the same as permanence" (p. 137). Unavoidably, deconstruction's "concept of writing or of trace perturbs every logic of opposition, every dialectic. It de-limits what it limits" (p. 137). We could never, therefore, secure a finite context or "essential nontotalization." Given these constraints, the violence inherent in any attempt to limit context "can always communicate, by virtue of the erasure just mentioned, with a certain 'weakness,' even with an essential nonviolence" (p. 137). This is a conceptually difficult, dangerous, and unstable relationship, but one in which political responsibilities jell. "That will seem surprising or disagreeable only to those for whom things are always clear, easily decipherable, calculable and programmable: in a word, if one wanted to be polemical, to the irresponsible" (p. 137).

In an interesting analysis of Derrida's work, David Wood (1987) has argued that deconstruction takes "the very idea of a concept as the expression of a desire to restrict a term, a sign, to a particular way of operating in a text, one which, together with other concepts, will give to that text a coherent and grounded meaning" (p. 179). Of course, deconstruction must use concepts in the sense "that not every semantic expectation can be disappointed at the same time. . ." (p. 180). Still, no term has any permanent immunity to a deconstructive treatment. Thus, "deconstruction is effective in displaying the workings of texts that legitimate political oppression" (p. 180). Deconstruction, therefore, complimented Foucault's work by providing a "logic" of theoretical textuality, "a capacity for a more vigilant reading," and a competence for intervention lacking in mere analysis of discourse (p. 180).

Deconstruction's capacity for a more vigilant reading holds great potential for new interpretations but does so without allegiance to any pregiven programmatic objectives beyond seeking better readings or interpretations. As Norris (1987) puts its, for Derrida

> There is always the possibility of some radically new reading that would utterly change—for better or worse—the way that...writings impinge on our social and political practices. But this is not to license a relativist euphoria, a free-for-all approach that would brook no constraints upon the "freeplay" of interpretative discourse. For it is still possible to perceive and deconstruct the various forms of angled misreading which make up this history of ideological claims-to-power. (p. 205)

As noted above, Derrida has neither maintained that there was nothing outside the text nor that some form of pure textuality existed outside the concerns of ethical or political life. He has only argued that there is no privileged vantage point outside the text to which one might appeal for a correct reading. Nonetheless, the quest for better interpretations was Derrida's project, even if this process were consigned to a sort of radical hermeneutics. To do otherwise, to reject reason, was to give up all hope of any informed rational critique and settle for a weak consensus theory of truth specified by the effect of performative utterances as determined within a given community according to its standards, and Derrida finds this approach unacceptable (Norris 1987, 159). In this respect, Derrida has, in practice, sought to blend modern and poststructuralist thought contrary to the claims of various critics (e.g., Habermas 1987; Giroux 1988b).

Another major criticism of Derrida's work is that he has denied the existence of the human subject necessary for agency, resistance, and emancipation. This is an important concern of those critical pedagogues skeptical of poststructuralist theory. Yet, Derrida does not deny the reality of the human subject. Rather he questions a conception of the subject as existing prior to language, experiences, and capable of immediate self-knowledge (Wood 1987, 182). This critique of the subject was a threat to political and moral agency only for those who insisted on a neo-Kantian view of morality requiring "a self that prescribes rules for itself, and hence escapes deterministic insertion in the world of mere causes" (Ibid.). But deconstruction held that the insights of conscience were linguistic and intrinsically social. From this view, a purely personal conscience was not possible. Furthermore, consequences were another important considera-tion in terms of decisions based on conscience, and the importance of consequences served to undermine the basis for conscience in immediacy as the conclusive form of legitimation.

For those who claimed that deconstruction offered no basis for ethics, Wood (1987) points to Derrida's sustained engagement with the question of ethics in his discussion of Levinas in "Violence and Metaphysics" (Derrida 1978a). Levinas considered ethics to be the root of philosophy and believed the fundamental ethical moment occurred in face-to-face relations. A face-to-face engagement constituted an asymmetrical relation involving the infinite otherness of another subject who could never be reduced to a mere object, be totalized, or be completely captured (Wood 1987, 180). Levinas did not ground his conception of ethics on sympathy or what "others have in common, but upon difference, the otherness of the others" (Ibid.). The basis of ethical theory rested on the assumption "that the other is/has a face, a face which put into words means the prohibition of murder" (pp. 180–81).

Consequently, those who claim deconstruction has no ethics should read Derrida's comments on Levinas and consider the possibility of an ethics of difference as a component of deconstruction. Wood understood that this conception of ethics

> is not without its difficulties, but the claim that the basis of ethics is not the alter ego, the other like me, but the other as he or she resists my attempts at ecological projection surely opens up new avenues in ethics. While there is little doubting the success of liberal political reform in the last two centuries, it may be that the overcoming of discrimination by reference to the underlying sameness of the two groups in question is a fragile success, and allows for the subsequent emergence of difference that would justify further exclusions. An ethics of difference, however, would be premised on a non-assimilative respect for difference. (p. 181)

Wood (1987) also believes, that to a large extent, the critique of deconstruction "has been the object of a fantastic desire, that something that explicitly marks out its distance (however problematically) from philosophy should none the less fulfill the traditional philosophical role of providing a reassuring foundation for life, meaning, action, and so on" (p. 184). In this context, Wood's "fantastic desire" appears to be similar to Bernstein's (1983) "Cartesian anxiety." Yet as we have seen, deconstruction can never be reduced to a rejection of truth or even the claim that no one truth could exist. Nevertheless, that the arguments for deconstruction are susceptible to such an analysis heightened its capacity to disappoint (Wood 1987, 184). This pain of disappointment is analogous to Caputo's (1987) discussion of human concern when confronted with the reality of "cold hermeneutics" and brings to mind Hegel's caution that "philosophy should beware of the wish to be edifying" (Wood 1987, 185). As Wood has reminded us, "the ultimate justification for philosophy may be that it makes familiar things strange" (p. 186). Certainly deconstruction does accomplish this purpose.

Beyond making the familiar appear strange, Derrida's scholarship and practice have also been directed toward critique and political action. Still, although he understood the importance of critical praxis, Derrida has reminded "us that the rhetoric of directness, of immediacy, of 'action' can be as cruelly misleading in political intervention as it is in philosophy" (Wood 1987, 191). And fundamental to a critical, emancipatory project was the "uncovering of relations, principles, concepts, etc., that we ordinarily take for granted" (p. 193). What must be resisted first were the effects of everyday life that led to the loss or forgetting of questions. And deconstruction helped accomplish this purpose as well.

As Norris (1987) has pointed out, Derrida (unlike Rorty) was more influenced by Peirce than James or Dewey. Rorty was put off by Peirce's belief "that every intellectual discipline requires some ultimate cognitive faith, some idea...of 'truth at the end of enquiry' " (p. 160). Derrida accepted this insight but disagreed with Peirce's view that we cannot "demand a reason for reasonableness itself." For Derrida, reason was derived from "a highly specific historical formation which cannot be appealed to as some kind of ultimate ground" (p. 160). Nevertheless, he acknowledges that there is no way of "thinking back beyond the origins of this 'false' enlightenment" (p. 160). We need instead to question the principle of reason without "giving way to an irrationalism devoid of critical force" (p. 161). Since it is reason that "has shaped every aspect of Western experience and...set the main terms for debate," we must realize "that this experience can only be grasped by a critique that upholds the values of enlightened reason, even while seeking to diagnose their present repressive or distorting effects" (p. 157). Again, this illustrates Derrida's understanding of the need to unite modernist and poststructuralist theory.

Norris has used Derrida's views on nuclear criticism to illustrate the application of deconstruction to the analysis of social policy. Commenting on the obsolete knowledge of "experts" and their lack of competence to make nuclear policy, Derrida (1984a) noted that

> The dividing line between *doxa* and *episteme* starts to blur as soon as there is no longer any such thing as an absolutely legitimizable competence for a phenomenon which is no longer strictly techno-scientific but techno-militaro-politico-diplomatic through and through, and which brings into play the *doxa* or incompetence even in its calculations. (p. 24)

In such cases, deconstruction could help reveal the rhetorical (or performative) nature of the arguments used to defend policy. This was critical, since such statements were actually fictions with no ground in the logic or facts of nuclear confrontation. Thus, for Derrida, the complexities of nuclear strategy could "never do without a sophistry of belief and the rhetorical simulation of a text" (p. 24).

One might ask why proponents of deconstruction thought it offered any level of competence beyond that contained in the enlightened critique posed by proponents of Critical Theory like Habermas. Indeed, Habermas (1987) has argued that deconstruction is a new form of irrationalism incapable of confronting essential philosophical or political questions. Norris (1987) believes that deconstruction's claim to a special "competence" was illustrated by Derrida's argument that the very threat of war and nuclear holocaust existed "because deterrence" has neither 'original meaning' nor measure" (p. 166). Deconstruction offered a way to analyze "the 'logic' of alogical transgression and the effects of 'rhetorical escalation' as against the 'measure' of enlightened reason" (p. 167). Nevertheless, Norris also believed that Derrida's recent writing "shows distinct signs of convergence with the project of a critical theorist like Habermas." Both supported "an idea of communicative competence which allows for specific *distortions* in present day discourse, but which also holds out the possibility of grasping and transcending these irrational blocks" (p. 169). To do otherwise, to succumb to an "unprincipled pragmatism which renounces the very possibility of reasoned critique" was, in effect, to deprive thought of any capacity to "engage with social and political realities on other than passively conformist terms" (p. 169). In this sense, poststructionalist analysis was not a rejection of the reconstructionist or neo-Marxist faith in critique. Rather it was a far more complex and qualified endorsement of critical reason, but an endorsement nonetheless.

CRITICAL PRAGMATISM, POSTSTRUCTURALISM, AND CURRICULUM

Bernstein (1985) has argued that by 1945 pragmatism was a largely discredited philosophical tradition and an unlikely candidate for revival. Yet such a revival has occurred, and some variant of pragmatism should form an important part of the challenge to the technical and instrumentalist mode that dominates current curriculum discourse and practice. Cherryholmes (1988) suggests a variety of ways pragmatism, in concert with poststructuralism, might improve curriculum theory, research, and schooling. He maintains that it is necessary to distinguish between "critical" and "vulgar" forms of pragmatism, since the latter functions as a counterproductive influence that thwarts critique and helps sustain the status quo. Cherryholmes employs Rochberg-Halton's (1986) conception of vulgar pragmatism as "pure utility or expediency" (p. 4). Pragmatism in its vulgar form took too literally William James's dictum that the truth or conception of something was to be determined in terms of its practical effects. One negative consequence of this form of pragmatism is a tendency to accept existing practices and institutions as natural or normal. In other words, what we consider "true and valued is what works in terms of what exists" (Cherryholmes 1988, 178). This amounted to another variant of instrumentalism, that is, an unreflective and dangerous orientation that missed the necessary sense of crisis regarding the need to reevaluate the "very criteria of what is to count as a solution" (Ibid.). In this way, vulgar pragmatism promotes "local ideologies as global and past ideologies as present and future" (p. 179).

Critical pragmatism draws on a different tradition, one that harmonizes with many of the critical dimensions of postmodernism and poststructuralism. Cherryholmes (1988) relies primarily on Rorty for his conception of critical pragmatism, and this choice creates certain problems with his analysis as we shall see. For Cherryholmes, "critical pragmatism continually involves making epistemological, ethical, and aesthetic choices. . .and translating them into discourses—practices" (p. 179). Decisions, therefore, were made within the context or frameworks of our communities as no universal standard exists to produce definitive, objective decisions. In this sense, Cherryholmes understood the Rortian conception of pragmatism as consistent with Bernstein's (1983) position that in the final analysis all philosophical concepts must "be understood as relative to a specific conceptual scheme, theoretical framework, paradigm, form of life, society, or culture" (p. 8). Thus, Cherryholmes accepted that Rorty's (1985) pragmatism was ethnocentric but not relativist, because it defined "truth" as an instance of "well-justified beliefs." We should point out, however, that Bernstein's (1983) analysis of Rorty, while sympathetic, is more critical than Cherryholmes' of the possible nihilistic tendencies in Rorty's work.

Cherryholmes (1988) recognizes that there has been considerable criticism of Rorty's position, such as Putnam's (1983) argument that Rorty's ethnocentrism amounted to a form of cultural relativism which became cultural imperialism. But as Cherryholmes (1988) points out, Putnam (1983) himself acknowledged that ethical decisions could only be understood when evaluated in terms of an inherited tradition which was itself subject to critique and reinterpretation. And this, in Cherryholmes' (1988) view, is the fundamental assumption of the critical pragmatic tradition favored by Rorty. To be nonrelative, a discourse or practice would "require a nondeconstructive grounding idea or concept" (p. 184). Therefore, the charge of relativism levied against either critical pragmatism or poststructuralism (and by inference postmodernism) was an empty charge since it applied to *all* forms of thought (p. 184). Patti Lather (1989a, 1989b) has developed a similar argument from a feminist perspective. I agree with this last point, and it is one that Margolis (1986) has raised in a critique of Bernstein's (1983) objectivism/relativism dichotomy.

However, there is reason to argue that Cherryholmes' distinction between vulgar and critical pragmatism is too limited. We also need to distinguish between the critical pragmatism espoused by Rorty and another form of critical pragmatism that might be grounded in the work of Peirce, Dewey, and Habermas (e.g., see Bernstein 1983; Rochberg-Halton 1986; Margolis 1986; Gunn 1987; Haskell 1984a). This latter form of critical pragmatism appears to have more in common with the poststructuralism Cherryholmes (1988) described as reinforcing the critical pragmatic project (p. 151).

Cherryholmes (1988) describes several links between poststructuralism and critical pragmatism. For both, "meaning is subject to continual reinterpretation," and the educational and social discourses and practices we conduct are derived substantially from the effects of power and the way it is exercised (p. 151). Consequently, our social choices and actions "are pragmatic responses to the situations in which. . .we find ourselves" (p. 151). Given these conditions, the poststructural critique provides a valuable, and potentially radical, new dimension to the pragmatic process of decision making.

In his analysis, Cherryholmes distinguishes between judgment and critique. He links the former to vulgar pragmatism which makes choices by applying given standards or criteria. Critique (employed in critical pragmatism) involves treating our "criteria and standards as themselves problematic" (p. 151). What Cherryholmes does not discuss is that critical pragmatism can also degenerate into the distopian critique made by Rorty which calls into question any quest for an emancipatory project beyond those that are local and bounded by a given community's norms. The problems generated by the complacency of this line of thought were explored in the previous section and in the discussion of Giroux's critique of Rorty in Chapter 4. Somehow, Cherryholmes (1988) has missed this contradiction logged in the heart of his project. He quotes with approval Rorty's view that we can offer no form of argumentation, regardless of how rigorous, that is not merely "in obedience to our own conventions" (p. 177). This position simply cannot stand in harmony with Habermas' view, or with Derrida, who acknowledges the inevitability of arguing from a framework, but draws very different conclusions than Rorty.

Yet I think Cherryholmes is still right to argue that poststructuralism and critical pragmatism are mutually reinforcing. At times, he seems to present poststructuralism merely as a method, and such a conception is too limited as illustrated earlier. But on other occasions, Cherryholmes does appear to grasp poststructuralism and pragmatism as bound up with our being-in-the-world. In this sense, he (leaving aside his rather generous reading of Rorty) presents a view that can harmonize with (but could also be enriched by) Bernstein's (1983) and Caputo's (1987) positions on neopragmatism and philosophical hermeneutics.

Bernstein (1983) and Caputo (1987) understand philosophical hermeneutics as fundamental to what it means to be human. This is captured in the Aristotelian concept of *phronesis* or practical judgment. *Phronesis* is a fundamental human competence essential to a democratic culture but also prior to *techne* and *episteme*. But as Habermas, Derrida, and Foucault have argued (in different ways), the polis is often corrupt. This is a critical point since "*phronesis* presupposes the existence of *nomoi* (funded laws) in the polis or community" (Bernstein 1983, 157). Otherwise *phronesis* itself is capable of degenerating into mere cleverness. Yet our present cultural condition is one of "great confusion and uncertainty" regarding norms, and as Caputo (1987) argues, "*Phronesis* functions only within an existing framework, an established paradigm" (p. 217). A divided polis does not provide these conditions.

It is true, as Bernstein (1983) contends, that the capacity of *phronesis* to survive in some form under the most hostile conditions is truly remarkable. Nevertheless, we need the sort of critique that could help us understand how and why we have lost our sense of community and to suggest an emancipatory project of reconstruction to reclaim and build the sort of community wherein *phronesis* can flourish. This is why debates between critical thinkers like Habermas and Derrida can be so tragic since they both enrich our understanding of and quest for an emancipatory project (e.g. see Wood 1987). We will discuss *phronesis* in greater detail in chapter 6.

CONCLUSION

The main purpose of this chapter was to make a case for the relevance of poststructuralism and neopragmatism to the development of critical pedagogy. In this process, I have argued that the critique of poststructuralism as a form of antirationalism or nihilism in unfounded. Far from being nihilistic, poststructuralism provides a way for humans to understand the "textuality" of the social world in which we live and to act to change that world. In this sense, poststructuralism is not merely a method at the disposal of any political movement (a nihilistic position) but a way of understanding the human condition that is essential to counterhegemonic praxis (Whitson forthcoming).

In developing this argument, I have tried to make two important distinctions, that is, between postmodernism and poststructuralism, and between relativism and nihilism. This first distinction is problematic since some key poststructuralist theorists, for example, Derrida and Foucault, are also seen (properly so, I think) as participants in the discourse of postmodernism. Nevertheless, we can describe a form of postmodernist thought that is not informed by specifically poststructuralist principles. As Whitson (forthcoming) argues, this form of postmodernism does not provide either the language of possibility or the capacity to form utopian visions that critical pedagogues like Apple, Aronowitz, Giroux, McLaren, and others see as essential to a critical approach to education. The problem is that by confounding postmodernism and poststructuralism, critics, including many critical pedagogues, have extended the charges of nihilism or antirationalism to poststructuralists like Derrida and Foucault. This involves more than the misreading of poststructuralism; such misinterpretations serve to deny to critical pedagogy an essential element of counterhegemonic praxis. In short, I agree with Whitson (forthcoming), Cherryholmes (1988), Norris (1985, 1987), Wood (1987), and others that poststructuralism is not vulnerable to the criticisms that might apply to certain postmodern discourses uninformed by poststructuralist principles.

The distinction between postmodernism and poststructuralism relates directly to the second distinction noted above, between relativism and nihilism. Relativism is the background or condition under which we seek knowledge in the human sciences and in our daily practical existence. Relativism, as we have observed, *does not* imply that all human knowledge claims are equal or that we have no effective way or basis for discriminating among various knowledge claims. I have argued here that the relative nature of truth is only a serious problem for those who insist on the possibility of and need for an objective (in the sense of certain) foundation for human knowledge Conversely, nihilism is an intellectual position that would permit all forms of life in principle. Put another way, nihilism denies the human competence to make discriminating judgments regarding the preference for particular forms of life over others, (e.g., equality over racism or sexism).

In the next chapter we will examine some possible conclusions of this study and suggest a direction critical pedagogy might take in the coming decades. Specifically, I will reconsider the relevance of social reconstructionism to critical pedagogy and how my conclusions on this issue relate to recent developments in poststructuralism, Critical Theory, neopragmatism, and philosophical hermeneutics.

6

CURRICULUM, RECONSTRUCTION, AND POSSIBILITY

Throughout this century, curriculum has been seen as a vehicle for some form of social reconstruction. This is a theme supported by most mainstream educators as well as those on the right or left. In other words, representatives of each of these positions (and the variants within each) have tended to view schooling as one of the major institutions for shaping human behavior and dispositions, including an individual's conception of a preferred social order. Certainly there have been exceptions, such as educators who believe schooling should be neutral. Traces of the neutrality position are evident on the part of those neoconservatives who hold an unproblematic view of the tradition or canon they wish to transmit or in the preoccupation of certain liberals with methodology and process, such as generic approaches to teaching critical thinking (e.g., Beyer 1987). Others like Arons (1983) argue more directly for teaching our children at home to help eliminate the political nature of schooling.[1] Nevertheless, as the prior chapters have tried to make clear, the avowed political nature of schooling has been accepted by most educators at all points on the political spectrum. There is also considerable evidence that the public supports the political dimension of schooling, especially as it pertains to areas such as character development, values, our political culture, and economic heritage (Stanley 1985a).

Acknowledging the widespread support for the politicization of schooling does not resolve the inquiry that motivated this study, that is, to what extent is the social reconstructionist approach to curriculum still relevant to critical pedagogy in the current postmodern era? That mainstream educators and those on the right have become more open about the political nature of schooling only confirms the earlier diagnosis of Counts, Brameld, and other reconstructionists regarding the political nature of schooling. While various educators have questioned the influence of

---

1. See Whitson (1988) for a good explanation of the weakness of this argument and the real danger it poses to democratic society.

reconstructionist ideas since the 1940s (e.g., Stanley 1981b, 1985a; Giroux 1988c), this study takes a more optimistic position. If we do not take an overly restrictive view of reconstructionism, it is evident that there has been a widespread incorporation by liberal and radical educators of many elements of reconstructionist curriculum theory (see Chapters 3 and 4).

Nevertheless, social reconstructionism per se remains a minority view among mainstream curriculum theorists or practioners. In addition, most of those who appear sympathetic to reconstructionist ideas have only supported certain portions of the reconstructionist rationale. Often such support appears to be informed by little or no knowledge of the original reconstructionist position and history. What we have then are persistent but incomplete and even contradictory traces of the reconstructionist program. For example, there are elements on the political right that would use the schools to help transform society in ways antithetical to the democratic focus of reconstructionism. There are of course some critical pedagogues (e.g., Giroux 1988c) who have embraced a good deal of the reconstructionist rational, but these remain notable exceptions. So the evidence for resisting, rejecting, or ignoring reconstructionist curriculum theory is still considerable. In a sense, this is one aspect of the wider historical reaction to most forms of radical thought in our culture and society. But the question remains, if we accept the need for a radical curriculum theory, to what extent does the social reconstructionist legacy contribute to this project? Seeking to answer this question, we also need to consider the direction critical pedagogy might take in the final decade of this century.

The recent neoconservative resurgence adds a sense of urgency to the examination of such questions. As Giroux, McLaren, and others have argued, it is important to restore counter-memories to document and explain the deep roots of human resistance to various forms of domination. This is an important point, but it still begs the question as to what should count as relevant countermemory, and specific to our concerns, to what extent is reconstructionism a valuable instance of such counter-memories? I believe we can answer the latter question in the affirmative, but to do so will require a rather significant reinterpretation of reconstructionism to make it relevant to present historical conditions. With regard to a reinterpretation of reconstructionism, there are at least four major problems that must be addressed. First, we need to reconsider the argument for socio-cultural transformation as the goal of social reconstruction. Second, the reconstructionist view of ideology, while more open than orthodox Marxist explanations, still remains rooted in a framework of false consciousness. Third, we need to consider the implication for counterhegemonic praxis posed by poststructuralist theory. Finally, there is the reconstructionist attempt to deal with what Bernstein (1983) has more recently

recently referred to as the false dichotomy of objectivism versus relationism. The reconstructionists attempted to address this issue by combining pragmatism and a radical critique of society oriented by a utopian vision of a preferred social order. This effort was never entirely successful, but it posed one approach to construct a curriculum based on a form of critical pragmatism. In many respects, critical pedagogy reflects a continuation of this theoretical tension. Following the analysis of these issues, I will conclude with some suggestions regarding the direction critical pedagogy might take in the future.

THE TRANSFORMATION/TRANSMISSION DICHOTOMY

It is doubtful that anyone literally believes in education solely for sociocultural transformation, since it is inevitable that some things will always be transmitted in the process of curriculum construction and schooling. But such a limited critique of the transformation/transmission dichotomy does not capture the complex nature of this issue. For the reconstructionists (and many contemporary critical pedagogues), transformation is clearly the privileged term in this binary opposition. Transmission is associated with domination, transformation with emancipation. But as Cherryholmes (1988) illustrates, even the opposition emancipation/domination deconstructs upon closer examination. Because those who currently hold a disproportionate share of wealth and power are unlikely to give up these advantages voluntarily, they will have to be pressured or coerced into relinquishing their privileged position. In other words, at some point the success of an emancipatory project is likely to involve some domination in the name of emancipation. When this happens, it is no longer simply a case of emancipation versus domination but one form of domination (emancipatory?) verses another (oppressive?). We cannot avoid this dilemma merely by arguing that any confusion between emancipation and domination is more a semantic paradox than real; that emancipatory domination is not really domination in any meaningful sense but rather a strategic move to further emancipatory practice. This line of reasoning will only persuade the converted. Unless we are prepared to insist that all powerful groups operate only on the basis of pure self-interest, we must acknowledge that such groups are often motivated (at least in part) by what they understand as valid arguments to legitimate their power.

So the notion of emancipation versus domination often turns on an argument for the authority to establish a preferred social order. For example, many conservatives argue for a meritocracy on the basis that this *is* the best possible form of sociopolitical organization to enable individual development. We have considered arguments against a meritocracy throughout this study, and admittedly, some might use arguments for meritocracy as cynical rationalizations of the status quo. Nevertheless, it also seems clear that the meritocratic theory is often an honest, well-motivated position for many conservatives and some liberals as well. In these instances, to coerce sincere advocates of a meritocracy to support some more egalitarian system is asking them to work against their own ethical convictions and perceived interests. From a conservative's vantage point, this would appear as a form of domination.

We can understand the relation between transformation and transmission in a similar way, although I think it is even more complex. Every curriculum theory must operate with some social vision in mind, some conception of the kind of individual and society schooling might help produce. Again, unless we would conceive of schooling to produce a social order that has never been conceived or realized in any way, all curriculum (including a reconstructionist approach) will involve attempts to transmit some present or past ideas and practices. Consequently, every curriculum represents what Raymond Williams called a "selective tradition"; that is, of all the possible available knowledge, one particular set or combination will be selected and privileged. The nature of the selected knowledge changes over time, but some selected set of knowledge emerges in every cultural and historical juncture.

Many critical pedagogues argue that a critical curriculum theory would entail measuring a social order against its own best claims (e.g., the civil rights movement would be an example of our society struggling to live up to its ideals). This phenomenon is captured in Terry Eagleton's (1983) observation that "Like all the best radical positions, . . . mine is a thoroughly traditionalist one" (p. 206). Eagleton speaks of drawing on deep historical roots and "returning to the ancient paths" we have abandoned. In this sense, the radical/reactionary opposition deconstructs as well. Both radical and conservative educators would use schools to help transform societies that are not presently like these educators (whether radical or conservative) think such societies ought to be. So when reconstructionists speak of education for sociocultural transformation, they do so because they believe that in some significant ways the present social order is not sufficient in the current historical context. None of these observations can be used as arguments against the often very pressing need for social transformation. Rather my intent is to problematize the simplistic opposition of transformation/transmission by calling attention to the often unacknowledged conservative impulse in radical reform.

A sensitivity to the complexities of transformation versus transmission is also relevant to conservative educators. Those committed to transmission must determine their version of the "selective tradition." We can never transmit *all* cultural possibilities (even those favored by dominant groups) via schooling, and, consequently, we must always exclude far more than we can ever transmit. The process of selection requires interpretation and there is no way to ensure that succeeding generations or even the present generation will maintain a consensus regarding what to transmit. Furthermore, there will always be unconscious influences on the selection process. As the selective tradition inevitably changes, the result is a form of sociocultural transformation. While this form of transformation is unlikely to reflect radical concerns, it is transformative nonetheless. Furthermore, there is no way to stabilize or predict the future direction or effect of this admittedly conservative approach to schooling. Of course, the same can be said of the outcome of radical attempts to construct and direct the course of curriculum. In practice, curriculum in modern societies will always be a dynamic semiotic process characterized by change, conflict, and surplus meaning—a process with an undetermined outcome.

Another major problem confronting simplistic accounts of transformation/transmission is the dialogical nature of all cultural systems. Too often, the reconstructionist account of culture was couched in a we/they framework. This generally involved a somewhat monological concept of culture; in other words, a preferred culture would be supported by reconstructionists in opposition to the dysfunctional dominant culture. In contrast, conservatives would seek to maintain (or resurrect) some variant of a dominant culture perceived as unproblematic and by implication, monological. But developments in cultural theory and discourse theory have effectively deconstructed such claims by either the right or left. For one thing, there is no single dominant *or* oppositional culture to transmit. The so-called dominant culture is really a plurality of cultures, each with its own internal conflicts (Apple 1986a, b; 1988a, b; Williams 1977; 1981). And as Jameson (1979) and Brenkman (1979) and others have pointed out, even the most jaded forms of dominant culture hold a utopian potential. Thus, the most flagrant attempts to impose a dominant cultural position hold the potential to deconstruct their own arguments. As the explanations of hegemony discussed in Chapters 4 and 5 demonstrate, domination is never complete, because it is continually resisted by counterhegemonic cultural practices and undermined by its own internal contradictions.

But a similar problem faces counterhegemonic cultural resistance, that is, the countercultural sources of opposition upon which social reconstruction or critical pedagogy tries to build its case. First, there are a multiplicity of popular cultures that form part of the resistance to the varieties of dominant cultures. Furthermore, subcultures or popular cultures cannot be understood as repositories of the "truth" (Hebdige 1979, 238). In other words, while popular cultures or subcultures help reveal forms of domination and document the reality and capacity of resistance, they do not necessarily offer any clear guide to a preferred social order.

Often they are byproducts of domination reflecting many of its dysfunctional features such as racism, sexism, and homophobia. Some of the lyrics of punk rock, heavy metal, and rap music offer examples of such characteristics. None of these analyses should be understood as arguments against reconstructionism or other approaches to critical pedagogy. Rather it is hoped that an exploration of these issues will help illuminate the unstable and dynamic context in which curriculum theory must always proceed.

THE ROLE OF IDEOLOGY

It was Brameld (1956) who presented the most developed reconstructionist position on ideology. Brameld was also the reconstructionist most influenced by orthodox Marxism. Consequently, it is not surprising that he was inclined to understand ideology in terms of the concept of false consciousness. Yet Brameld's views could never be reduced merely to Marxist orthodoxy, and his conception of ideology was no exception. Brameld saw ideology as encompassing the complex of ideas, beliefs, and practices that "more or less accurately" express a culture or some important portion of it (p. 87). Ideology is not intrinsically invidious and "may take the form of the sincere effort of an age to depict itself" (p. 87). In general, however, ideologies do function to help rationalize cultural arrangements and practices. As such, ideologies amount to "a kind of verbal and sometimes pictorial superstructure laid over the supporting structure of real institutions and practices" (p. 87).

Brameld (1956) argued that all ideologies were formed in a historical context and passed through three phases: emergence, maturity, and decline. Although an ideology might present a reasonably accurate view of the culture and society it represented, this was not normally the case. In the early stages of sociocultural development or change, ideology might point ahead to future meanings or needs and hold a valuable utopian potential. At the most mature point of sociocultural development, the consonance between the ideology and sociocultural reality was the closest. Eventually, however, as sociocultural change continues, ideology begins to perpetrate "an image which...resembles the actual culture less and less" (p. 87). These phases of ideological development described by Brameld were derived, in part, from the anthropological theory of cultural lag which held that change in social practice tends to outpace ideological change.

Dominant groups often employed ideology as one means of securing their power in the face of social change, but Brameld, anticipating the views of many contemporary cultural theorists, believed that even the most reactionary ideologies usually contained some trace of a utopian vision.

Utopia, for Brameld, referred to a projected image for cultural change designed to promote the real interests of the majority. On the other hand, while all utopias had at least some ideological component, even the utopian vision of reconstructionism "if ever carried out, would also eventually become ideological. . ." in the degenerate sense of no longer accurately representing sociocultural reality (p. 89). The reconstructionists believed that an accurate assessment of our culture required that educators should seek to penetrate those degenerate forms of ideology that rationalized the current exploitive system and to act to change society along the lines of a utopian vision "geared to the satisfaction of the maximum number of wants of the maximum number of people [and] the expansion of freedom" (p. 91).

Thus, Brameld's variant of social reconstruction understood ideology as having both positive and negative functions, and this position was an improvement over the narrower orthodox Marxist view of ideology as false consciousness. In other words, ideology might represent false consciousness for reconstructionists but it might also function as a utopian projection or a more or less accurate description of a sociocultural context. Brameld's position regarding the positive and negative functions of ideology is similar to some of the recent work of Giroux (1988a, 1988b, 1988c), Douglass Kellner (1978), James Donald and Stuart Hall (1986), and Peter McLaren (1988c).

McLaren (1988c) cites the work of Gibson Winter to help illustrate the multiple functions of ideology in the current era. Winter (1981) maintains that ideology

> may be primarily oriented to preserving and legitimating the established powers in a society. It may also face primarily toward the future and project a utopian model for a more just society. In either case, ideology draws upon the symbolic powers that generate a peoples identity whether to legitimate powers that be or to authorize proposals for transformation. (Winter 1981, 97, cited in McLaren 1988c, 167–68)

And Winter's point is further elaborated in the work of Kellner (1978) who argues that ideology "commonly refers both to those ideas, images, and theories that mystify social reality and block social change, and to those programs of social reconstruction that mobilize people for social activism" (cited in McLaren 1988c, 167). This conception of ideology is also central to Giroux's approach to critical pedagogy. For Giroux (1983b), ideology works on and through individuals to gain their support for the dominant order, but it can also serve the interest of emancipatory social transformation (p. 145).

McLaren (1988c) describes the connection between the work of James Donald and Stuart Hall and the conception of ideology developed by

Giroux. Donald and Hall (1986) conceived ideology as "frameworks" people used to give meaning to or make sense of their social world. These frameworks can function in positive or negative ways. A framework was positive to the extent it provided the concepts, images, and ideas necessary to make some sense of the world and to act in it. In fact, without such frameworks meaning would not be possible (pp. ix–1). On the other hand, our frameworks also worked to limit our perceptions. In this latter sense, frameworks functioned in a negative way since they were inevitably selective and organized our understanding by the exclusion of other possible ways of knowing. Therefore, the positions on ideology taken by Donald and Hall as well as Giroux were duplicitous in the sense of being more complex than simplistic characterizations of ideology as either positive or negative. This was so because, for these critics, any instance of ideology might simultaneously be implicated in *both* positive and negative social functions. Ultimately, there was no way to form a utopian conception of ideology without the exclusion of other views. Therefore, all ideological concepts were, at best, partial, incomplete, and potentially negative, since we can never be certain of the future consequences of exclusion (McLaren 1988c).

In addition to the limitations on the concept of ideology described above, individuals and groups tended to hold multiple frameworks by which they sought to make sense of their world. These various frameworks might conflict with each other or even contain internal contradictions. As a set of meanings and ideas, ideologies could be either coherent or contradictory; they could function within the spheres of both consciousness and unconsciousness; and finally, they could exist at the level of critical discourse as well as within the sphere of taken-for-granted lived experience and practical behavior (Giroux 1983a, 143).

That ideology is able to function at an unconscious level is a particularly important point and derives, in part, from the work of Althusser (1969, 1971a). Althusser (1969) held that, despite conventional interpretation, ideology had very little to do with consciousness. In practice, ideology

is profoundly unconscious, even when it presents itself in a reflected form. Ideology is indeed a system of representations, but in the majority of cases these representations have nothing to do with "consciousness": they are usually images and occasionally concepts, but it is above all as structures that they impose on the vast majority of men [sic], not via their "consciousness." They are perceived-accepted-suffered cultural objects and they act functionally on one in a process that escapes them. Men [sic] "live" their ideologies as the Cartesian "saw" the moon at two hundred paces away: not at all as a form of consciousness, but as an object of their "world"—as their world itself. (p. 223, cited in Giroux 1983b, 264)

Of course Althusser's (like Bourdieu's) view of ideology was too limiting for any approach to critical pedagogy that involved genuine resistance. If ideology were merely imposed on unwitting subjects at an unconscious level, resistance in any meaningful sense would be impossible. Furthermore, the view of ideology's capacity to perform a positive function and provide utopian potential would be inconceivable without subjects who acted consciously and intentionally. Nevertheless, the arguments made for an unconscious dimension of ideology by Althusser, Bourdieu, and others, although overstated, were not without merit. Consequently, the analysis and application of ideology in critical pedagogy must be understood as an extremely complex process wherein our grasp of ideology was always limited by its own internal contradictions, our incomplete knowledge of what has been excluded in the construction of ideologies, and those aspects of ideologies that functioned below our level of consciousness.

While Brameld's conception of reconstructionism did account for both the positive and negative dimensions of ideology, it was a more limited understanding than the more recent views summarized by critical pedagogues like Apple, Giroux, McLaren, and others. This is not surprising, given the historical context in which reconstructionism emerged and reacted. The reconstructionists simply did not have access to the concepts and modes of analysis upon which contemporary critical educators can draw. One difficulty was the strong, scientific orientation of the leading reconstructionists that was linked to some form of a correspondence theory of truth. Brameld (1956) was well aware of the important role played by the irrational, prehension, and mythology in human affairs, but he believed these elements tended to come into play more in the utopian or early phase of ideological development. Eventually, however, cultural formations (new or old) must be tested "scientifically." Brameld and the other reconstructionists relied on the explanatory and critical power of the social sciences to help solve human problems. While the reconstructionist position was complex and occasionally contradictory, one can discern a pervasive tendency to assume some privileged, objective (scientific) vantage point whereby culture might be evaluated and improved along relatively linear, progressive lines.

The critique of a correspondence theory of truth was addressed in Chapters 4 and 5 and has been discussed in more detail elsewhere (e.g., Habermas 1971, 1973a, 1973b, 1979; Bernstein 1976, 1983; Culler 1982; Gadamer 1975; Rabinow and Sullivan 1987). In brief, it is no longer taken for granted that there is any possible clear equivalence between our ideas about reality and some "objective" reality that existed prior to our thinking about it. If one accepted only a positivistic version of the correspondence theory of truth, then it would make sense to think of ideology as false consciousness, at least in those instances where it did not accurately represent a reality that could be known. This seemed to be the position taken by Brameld and other reconstructionists who often discussed ideology as a distorted description of reality that served to obscure how the current social order served the interests of a dominant few at the expense of the interests of the masses. A reconstructionist curriculum was designed to clear up such distortion via careful critique. But how does one make a claim for false (as opposed to true) consciousness once the correspondence theory of truth is called into question?

As Habermas (1979) and others have pointed out, one's experience and perceptions are never equal to the statements we make about them. Thus, we cannot test hypothesis against reality in any simple sense. Since observations can only be reported symbolically, statements cannot be tested by direct access to experience but only in dialogue with other statements. For Habermas (1973b) then, truth claims can only be justified discussively, by argumentative corroboration. Nothing absolute or objective could anchor such a discourse. At best, according to Habermas, we might try to ensure that discourse remained open to new information, was free from distortion, and contained no asymmetries in term of privileged speakers. While this was clearly an idealization, the fact that we could conceive of such an ideal condition for communication formed the backdrop for attempting to establish communities wherein intersubjectivity could occur. If we did not think this was possible, then there would be no point in trying to communicate in the first place. Such a consensus theory of truth was employed to help choose among conflicting interpretations.

Brameld (1956) has described something similar to Habermas' ideal speech situation in terms of his (Brameld's) consensual validation process to establish the truth required to orient social change. But Brameld simultaneously appears to cling to a correspondence theory of truth similar to Popper's (1968, 1976) whereby one could regulate criticism via some more objective conception of truth. Like Popper, Brameld (1956) accepted that all truth was tentative in the sense of being falsifiable. He also seemed to accept the pragmatic view of truth as contingent upon the historical standards and criteria of the group making a decision. For Brameld then, there were no "timeless truths," but his standards for testing truth appeared to assume that we could get a good view of an external reality, including an objective conception of real human interests (p. 353). And if truth was always tentative, it was because our methods were never totally sufficient or accurate, and new, better knowledge might always be found to cause us to change our views. Thus, Brameld's consensual validation was more akin to some combination of neopositivist scientific method and democratic pluralism than to Habermas' conception of communicative competence.

In contrast, the poststructuralists have understood ideology as derived from the process of discursive formations. For Foucault (1972), discourse was constituted by "a body of anonymous, historical rules" which, in any time and place, defined "the conditions of operation of the enunciative function." Such rules governed what was said and not said, who could and could not speak, and what counted as evidence and truth. Truth was, therefore, a thing of this world, and every society has its regime of truth as illustrated and produced by its discursive rules and practices. This was especially evident in the process of education wherein the rules of discourse were taught and the various "societies of discourse" (e.g., the disciplines) are transmitted. Thus "every educational system functioned as a political means of maintaining or modifying the appropriation of discourses, with the knowledge and power they bring with them" (p. 46).

Any discourse produces meaning via a system of signs that are mainly understood in terms of how they relate to each other rather than to some objective reality. And since the system of signification is always rooted in history and culture, it remains in a state of flux. Thus, language always mediates our understanding of the world in terms of the particular and evolving discursive alignments in which we find ourselves. Consequently, we can never know the truth of the world in any direct objective way. In Foucault's view, rather than ask epistemological questions, we should focus on how discourses are produced and the effects they have in producing conformity and in determining which groups are relegated to the margins of society.

Viewed from this perspective, ideology did not so much function to distort reality but to produce and rationalize a regime or form of truth. In some respects, this was an even more difficult position to deal with than the orthodox Marxist view of ideology as false consciousness. Indeed, even if ideologies are produced by discursive practices that could represent different views of reality, that did not mean such representations were necessarily false. Ideology, as Althusser (1971a) or Laclau (1983) described it, could not be reduced to a set of ideas about reality but also involved practices that produced human subjectivity. In other words, ideologies involved practices that were lived and actually served to form the real behavior of human subjects. Thus, ideology was always an essential component of any culture. It had a positive dimension in that it formed subjects and could serve to realize certain elements of cultural fulfillment. Of course, it could function negatively as part of the process of domination of one group over others, as well as by forming a viewpoint via the exclusion of certain kinds of knowledge. But ideology could also be what human agents did when they sought to understand a world in which knowledge was both contradictory and undecidable. So ideology (as Brameld had argued) could contain a utopian dimension oriented toward a future in which we might construct a society that better realized human interests. Indeed, without some form of ideology we could neither make sense of the world nor construct the vision of a preferred future.

Such arguments should not obscure the real dangers posed by the negative functions of ideology (McLaren 1988a). Ideology can be used to legitimate domination and even conceal its existence. It can also function to exacerbate social contradictions and differences and to divide groups who might otherwise act together to resist domination. Finally, to the extent ideology becomes taken for granted, that is, separated from its historical origins and read as natural and given, reification results and limits the potential of human agency to resist domination (pp. 168–69).

This dual potential of ideology is consistent with Foucault's (1979, 1980b) position regarding the inseparability of power and knowledge. Knowledge does not merely reflect the relations of power; "it is immanent" in power relations. While power produces knowledge, it is also the case that there can be "no power relation without the correlative constitution of a field of knowledge, nor any knowledge that does not presuppose and constitute at the same time power relations" (p. 27). Consequently, truth cannot exist external to power nor in opposition to it. Power is not an object to be taken or shared. It is integral to the total complex of human relations, an ubiquitous phenomenon that "is not an institution, nor a structure, nor a possession. It is a name we give to a complex strategic situation in a particular society" (Foucault 1979, 93).

In the same sense then, ideology could be considered both the mediator of our experiences as well as the outcome of such experiences. Viewed this way, ideologies functioned to both limit and enable the projects of critical pedagogy. It might seem that in each of the modern thories described above we have come full circle back to Brameld's notion of ideology as having positive or negative functions, but this is only partly true. Brameld did not fully appreciate the problems with the correspondence theory of truth. Since human knowledge is socially constructed, we all hold a sort of "false consciousness," that is, an incomplete and/or distorted view of sociocultural reality. So there is no way to get "truth" right in some definitive way. We might say that *all* human consciousness is "false" in this sense. Brameld's thought also developed at a time before there was wide understanding of how ideology (or what Foucault calls discourse) could operate on and through the individual's body and how it was embodied in the very structures and practices of our lives. For all the social reconstructionists, ideology (whether positive or negative) was largely conceived as a system of ideas or a worldview that purported to describe, more or less accurately, some present or potential reality.

We must be cautious, however, not to reduce the ideology critique to an oversimplified debate between positivist proponents of a correspondence theory of truth and more critical proponents of a consensus theory of truth. The correspondence versus consensus theory of truth is both an unproductive and false dichotomy.[2] We might not be able to know reality in a direct objective way, but we are always trying to understand it. After all, what is the consensus in the consensus theory of truth about if not some agreement concerning how things are or should be in reality. We may never know if we have gotten it right, but that does not argue against trying to get a better understanding of "reality." Indeed the capacity to interpret and form an understanding of reality is part of what it means to be human (Gadamer 1975). The relationship between the correspondence and consensus theory of truth might be better understood by examining the work of C. S. Peirce (Parmentier 1985; Haskell 1984a; Culler 1982; and Whitson 1988, 1991, forthcoming). For Peirce, the community of human inquirers was striving to understand reality within the constraints and limitations of language and dialogue. The closest we might come to "truth" was the last best effort of the community of inquirers projected into the future (Parmentier 1985; Haskell 1984a). While humans might never fully understand reality, it was the quest for such knowledge that oriented human inquiry. Derrida made a related point (discussed in Chapter 5) when he criticized the pragmatic conception of truth (one based on consensus), because it denied that truth was *also* what is true regardless of what anyone thinks or concludes (Culler 1982).

McLaren (1988c) has pointed to some other ways to consider ideology. In his view, we could better understand schooling by looking at ideology as ritual performance. Rituals are at the heart of culture, constituting the "major symbolic networks, cultural contexts, and ideational domains through which attempts are made to regulate social life and keep it from slipping into" a state of indeterminacy (p. 171). Rituals functioned as generative forces that could be employed to adjudicate conflicts or as part of the structure of social control. Linked to symbols and metaphors, rituals served literally to "put us in our place" in the social order.

Ideology could have great power, McLaren believed, when it operated on and through the subject's body by being "inscribed in the geography of desire through ritual" (p. 171). In this way, ideology could not be limited to a property of an external text but must be understood "*as a process of production* in which pleasure and pain is produced by individuals in gestural engagement with their surroundings" (p. 171). Ideology, therefore was "performatively constituted" by human subjects and became "discourse given sentence" (p. 172). In other words

---

2. The author wishes to recognize James A. Whitson for helping to clarify this insight (e.g., Whitson, 1988, 1991, and personal correspondence with the author).

> Ideology cannot be theorized in purely cognitive terms so that false beliefs constitute inadequate information or distorted communication. Ideology is fundamentally related to the politics of pleasures and the body. Ideology, in this perspective, lies in the motional world; it "thematizes" its milieu through mindful bodily gesture. As a form of ideology, ritual has a tendency to become self-effacing since it often assumes the second nature of habits. That is, it completes its work by disguising its own activity. (McLaren 1988c, 172)

This situation posed a major problem for critical pedagogy, since ideology as ritual codes were among the most arbitrary and authoritarian socio-cultural forms which served to block reading or interpretation threatening to the status quo while distracting us with other inconsequential concerns.

Yet as McLaren (1986, 1988c) found in his own research, the ideological power of ritual did not foreclose resistance, because various subcultures (in this instance student street-corner subculture) provide counter-hegemonic rituals that served to undermine the rationality of domination and oppression, a point also recognized by Barths, Hebdige, Willis, and others. And in McLaren's (1988c) view, this sort of resistance held a utopian potential as students attempted to "ritually construct a transitional world that could erase the past and deconstruct present psychosocial adaptations in order to forge new self-presentation of greater potency" (p. 175). McLaren makes an important point, one that gives us an even better understanding of the earlier work of various resistance theorists.

I would, however, point out one limitation regarding the critical force of McLaren's analyses. Citing the work of Lawrence Grossberg (1986), McLaren appears to accept the cognitive/affective dichotomy as real and relevant to his position. He believes we should not limit our conception of ideology to an analysis of sign production within various discursive alignments in given historical contexts. We must also "give consideration to the affective power invested in particular ideologies and the body's sensuous relationship to the popular and everyday" (McLaren 1988c, 175). While I certainly agree that these are critical considerations, we cannot separate them from sign production and consumption as they are all of a piece. The production and interpretation of meaning is always simultaneously cognitive and affective. In other words, we do have feelings about meaning, whether produced or interpreted, which are inseparable from our cognitive activity in the process of semiosis. McLaren quite properly calls our attention to the affective aspect of human behavior, but if affect has been neglected, it is not because it is something separate from cognition. Indeed, it is the separation of cognition or affect that has often led to the neglect of the latter dimension.

POSTSTRUCTURALISM AND
COUNTERHEGEMONIC PRAXIS

In Chapter 5, I tried to make three related points regarding the import of poststructuralism: (1) poststructuralism is neither nihilistic nor antithetical to the purposes of critical pedagogy, (2) poststructuralism enhances our understanding of our sociocultural environment and how it is constructed, and (3) finally, the insights of poststructuralism are essential to the counterhegemonic praxis at the core of critical pedagogy. We need to say more about the importance of poststructuralism to reconstructionism and more recent projects for critical educational programs.

Central to the poststructuralist analysis is Derrida's (1976, 1978, 1988) concept of unbounded "textuality." In poststructuralist thought, textuality refers to the material nature of our human existence as manifested in our institutions, discursive practices, and power arrangements as each of these operate in the textual context of diverse and dynamic structural systems of signs and codes (Whitson forthcoming). By employing poststructuralist insights, critical pedagogy is in a far better position to uncover those intrinsic structural dimensions of education that function as forms of domination. But unlike structuralists (e.g., Lévi-Strauss), poststructuralists do not understand such structural networks as fixed grounds by which we can account for human behavior. As Whitson (1991, forthcoming) makes clear, the poststructuralist conception of textuality understands the structures of human agency as no less important than the more general deterministic structures (e.g., language) within which agency is exercised. More importantly, poststructuralism reveals how the apparent opposition between human agency and social structures is, in fact, part of the wider hegemonic ideology that limits our knowledge of the essential interweaving and interdependency of agency and structure within the textuality of our existence.

It is this sort of poststructuralist understanding that is absolutely essential to the counterhegemonic praxis espoused by both social reconstructionism and critical pedagogy. In this regard, Whitson (forthcoming) has called our attention to a frequently neglected dimension of Gramsci's concept of hegemony. We noted in Chapter 4 how hegemony refers to the way domination is maintained via a mixture of power and ideology. This mixture of coercion and ideology is never complete, and this leaves a space for opposition and resistance. But Whitson maintains that this explanation tends to neglect how hegemony also functions to achieve domination by incorporating elements of opposition within the wider hegemonic order. To the extent this occurs, apparent forms of opposition actually work to support rather than contest the dominant order (e.g., Willis 1981; Wexler and Whitson 1982; Whitson 1991, forthcoming).

It is essential to any critical approach to education that we understand how domination functions not merely by coercion and exclusion, but also by incorporating the opposition of various groups within the sociocultural matrix in ways that either render opposition harmless or actually use it to further the aims of hegemony. As Whitson (forthcoming) makes clear, an effective counterhegemonic approach to education must be post-structural, since such practice requires an understanding of both the structural nature of hegemony and how we might challenge these structural arrangements. It is in this area where we can see the value of poststructuralist as opposed to postmodern critique. While educators drawing on postmodern theory do help us identify the suppression of marginalized voices and why such voice should be included in curriculum discourse, poststructural theory enables us to deconstruct the very oppositions on which hegemonic arguments favoring mainstream versus marginal, academic versus nonacademic, high culture versus low culture, etc., depend. These are the sort of false dichotomies that form the central structure of the recent conservative critique of education (Shor 1986; Ellsworth 1989; Giroux 1988c; Whitson 1988, 1991, forthcoming). Consequently, it is necessary for any reconceptualized form of reconstructionism or critical pedagogy to be grounded in a poststructural counterhegemonic praxis.

CRITICAL PEDAGOGY, RECONSTRUCTIONISM, AND RELATIVISM

As noted in Chapter 5, one might wish Bernstein (1983) had not described relativism as an opposite term in a binary relation with objectivism, since all the alternatives that he offers to replace either/or thinking amount to de facto forms of relativism (Margolis 1986). As I have argued in Chapter 5, we need to distinguish between relativism and nihilism. While relativism is a fundamental dimension of human knowledge, nihilism, with its anything-is-permissible orientation, must be rejected as antithetical to human interests (Whitson forthcoming). Nevertheless, I believe that Bernstein (1983) has identified a central theoretical tension and was correct to reject the false dichotomy suggested by objectivism versus relativism as well as the either/or mode of thinking upon which such dichotomies rest. It is clear that either/or thinking permeates the mainstream discourse of educational reform and a good deal of critical pedagogic discourse as well (Whitson 1988, 1991, forthcoming). And as discussed in Chapters 4 and 5, more recent work by critical educators of various kinds has mounted a critique of this epistemological orientation (e.g., Brennan 1989; Ellsworth 1989; Giroux 1988a, 1988b, 1988c; Lather

1989a; McLaren 1988c, 1988d; McLaren and Hammer 1989; Pinar 1988a, 1988c; Wexler 1987; Whitson 1988, 1991, forthcoming; Whitson and Stanley 1990).

It would be both impossible and impractical to abandon all dichotomies in our analysis of education (e.g., gender, race, and class have dichotomous elements). But we need to discard the false dichotomies of positivist discourse—such as fact/value, cognitive/affective, and society/individual—and to view other dichotomies in a dialogical way, thereby precluding the assumption that things *must* be either this or that. What seems more appropriate is a pedagogy of neither/nor in the sense Merlu Ponty used these terms (Descombs 1980). Rejecting the false choices of objectivism or nihilism does not imply settling for something in between, that is, something located on a point along a continuum between the two. Rather, we must attempt to unthink the either/or dichotomy and to reconceive a form of knowledge that is neither objective nor nihilistic.

Nevertheless, as I have tried to demonstrate throughout this study, a fear of relativism as well as a confusion of relativism and nihilism pervade mainstream educational thought, the discourse of social reconstructionism, and more recent critical approaches to education, including critical pedagogy. The concerns expressed by radical educators regarding relativism and nihilism were described in some detail in Chapters 3, 4, and 5. A particular focus of this concern is expressed in the arguments for retaining key democratic values as a basis for social criticism and social transformation.

Analysis of the debate over core values is critical to our understanding of reconstructionism and more recent attempts to construct a critical pedagogy. There have been two interrelated but different purposes at the heart of the radical critique of education. First, there is the purpose of student empowerment which includes the competence to engage in various forms of sociocultural praxis, including social criticism. A second purpose is to enable students to construct a utopian vision of a preferred social order to orient their critical praxis. For the most part, such utopian visions have been built around core democratic principles or values. Both of these purposes were central to the reconstructionist program of Rugg, Counts, and Brameld. For the reconstructionists, the identification of key democratic values was seen as relatively unproblematic. In other words, we could establish relatively stable value hierarchies or sets of preferred values to guide the process of social transformation toward a better society. On the other hand, the reconstructionist position was also strongly influenced by pragmatic theory, and this influence caused an essential instability or tension between their utopian vision (grounded on preferred values) and pragmatic claims regarding the tentative nature of human knowledge. As we have seen, this was a tension the reconstructionists were never able to resolve.

We have also seen that the concern with identifying key democratic values as a basis for educational praxis remains at the heart of the discourse on critical pedagogy. For the purpose of the present argument, consider some of the following examples. In a recent critique of orthodox Marxist conceptions of ideology, McLaren (1988c) argues that

> it makes more pedagogical sense to ascertain the ways in which social relations and social practices represent various degrees of an emancipatory dominating logic. This should not be undertaken by employing empirical criteria but by advocating a set core of ethical principles....What really matters is *the political project around which the concept of ideology can be put into practice.* (p. 176)

McLaren is less concerned with testing for the incontrovertible truth of an idea than the extent to which an "idea can be linked to a praxis of emancipation" (p. 176). Praxis itself cannot serve as the criterion for theoretical truth, nor can philosophy or science. It is politics "which seems the more appropriate site for understanding the rules of justice and social transformation" (p. 176).

It seems that much of the work of Apple, Beyer, Giroux, and other critical educators rests on a similar set of assumptions. These critical educators are committed to an educational project that promotes critical democracy, individual freedom, and social justice by constructing a public sphere wherein citizens have the competence to engage in critical praxis for sociocultural betterment (e.g., Beyer and Apple 1988; Fine 1989; Giroux 1986, 1988a, 1988b, 1988c; Giroux and McLaren 1986; Giroux and Simon 1988; Liston and Zeichner 1987; Shor 1986). Some more specific representative comments should help illustrate this values orientation. For example, Beyer and Apple (1988) "self-consciously" align their educational program with Marcus Raskin's view of "the common good." This program opposes any "inhuman" acts employed to improve society and insists that all social programs must be judged in terms of their contributions toward enhancing equity, sharing, human dignity, security, freedom, and caring (p. 7). Another example of the link between critical pedagogy and certain value claims is evident in the conclusions of a recent book by Giroux (1988c).

> At stake here is the willingness of educators...to struggle collectively as transformative intellectuals...who have a social vision and commitment to make public school democratic public spheres, where all children,...can learn what it means to be able to participate fully in a society that affirms and sustains the principles of equality, freedom, and social justice. (p. 215)

Claims similar to these have been made throughout much of my own work (e.g., Stanley, 1981a, 1981b, 1981c, 1985a, 1985b, 1987, Stanley and Nelson 1986) which has reflected a social reconstructionist position. We also find the following observations in one of Giroux's most recent essays. For Giroux (forthcoming), pedagogy must be based on a political project and view of authority that seeks to promote student empowerment as well as the construction of a society better suited to extending the principle of "liberty, equality, justice, and freedom" in the widest manner possible.

In a separate but related argument, the philosopher Thomas McCarthy (1989–90) has summarized what he believes is at stake in the recent poststructuralist critique. In a specific criticism of Derrida's deconstructionist theory, McCarthy agreed that it was "necessary to interrogate and revise received notions of liberty, equality, justice, rights, and the like. . ." (p. 157). But he cautioned that to "disassemble without reassembling," that is, deconstruction sans reconstruction, "may be to rob excluded, marginalized, and oppressed groups of an important recourse." And McCarthy goes on to argue:

> It is sheer romanticism to suppose that uprooting and destablizing universalist structures will of itself lead to letting the others be in respect and freedom rather than to intolerant and aggressive particularism, a war of all against all in which the fittest survive and the most powerful dominate. Enlarging the social space in which otherness can be, establishing and maintaining a multifarious and spacious pluralism, seem, on the contrary, to require that we inculcate universalistic principles of tolerance and respect, and stabilize institutions that secure rights and impose limits. Otherwise, how is the tolerance of difference to be combined with the requirements of living *together* and *common* norms? (p. 158)

But we must proceed carefully and question where we get the authority for the universal principles McCarthy would have us inculcate, or, for that matter, the social reconstructionist or critical pedagogy programs to inculcate democracy. McCarthy seems to be saying (at least in part) that such universal principles are justified in terms of their potential effect. But as Derrida and Foucault might argue, we cannot know in advance what the effects of our policies will be; they could make things worse. Anything and everything can be dangerous. Such views should not be taken as an argument for inaction as I tried to explain in the discussion of Derrida in Chapter 5. Rather, McCarthy's (1989–90) critique of Derrida on this point is too harsh. Following Habermas, McCarthy is often critical of scholars like Derrida and Foucault for failing to answer a question they have never explicitly raised (Rajchman 1988). As John Rajchman explains with regard to the work of Derrida and Foucault,

> Their question is not that of an anxiety or uncertainty about the possibility of rational normative justification which it would be the sole business of philosophy to overcome. It is more a matter of *injecting* a little anxiety or uncertainty into forms of action, thought or expertise that operate unques-

tionably with routine self-evidence. It is concerned with a sort of "skepticism" about what is taken for granted in ways we go about things. (p. 172)

As explained in the last section of Chapter 5, the use of relativism as a negative characterization of a theoretical position only makes sense if we assume the possibility of objective knowledge (Bernstein 1983; Cherryholmes 1988; Gadamer 1975; Lather 1989a, 1989b; Whitson forthcoming). Once we acknowledge the pragmatic principle that all knowledge is contingent and formed in terms of a framework, then relativism is understood as a characteristic of all knowledge. In terms of values, McCarthy's liberal argument for the strategic importance of universal principles, while well-intentioned, only confuses the issue. Values like human dignity, justice, and equality are embedded in our history and culture. Giroux, Habermas, McCarthy, McLaren, and others are correct to argue that we neither can nor should abandon this modernist legacy. The poststructuralist critique, as Cherryholmes (1988) points out, does not reject the core values of modernism but does deny we can use them as "fixed standards against which evaluations and judgments are made" (p. 172). In other words, such values can have no transcendental or universal status. More and more, critical educators have come to accept this point as the recent work of Cherryholmes (1988), Burbules and Rice (1990), Giroux (1988a, 1988b, 1988c), Lather (1989a, 1989b), McLaren (1988c, 1988d), McLaren and Hammer (1989), Pinar (1988a, 1988c), Whitson (1988, 1991, forthcoming), Stanley and Whitson (1990) and others demonstrates.

Giroux (1988c), for instance, has noted how terms like democracy, justice, and so forth hold no intrinsic meaning but must be struggled for and redefined by each generation. Thus, critical pedagogues like Giroux and McLaren do not argue for transcendental first principles. What they do insist upon is the need to take and justify ethical positions. While it is no longer possible to hold metaphysically grounded knowledge, we can still argue for the continuing need to attempt to conduct critical inquiry and make moral claims.

This recent qualification regarding the role of values in critical pedagogy is important and necessary. First, we should consider the danger of slipping into a neopositivist or neo-Kantian discourse on values. If critical pedagogy must first determine core principles or values as basic criteria for constructing curriculum, how is this different, in essence, from liberal or conservative proposals for educational reform? In most instances, liberals and conservatives would likely support different values, but representatives of both groups generally agree on the need and possibility of identifying an appropriate value position to orient practice and reform. In contrast, one could argue that the history of critical pedagogy points toward the need to move away from such vestiges of positivism. Claims to have identified a set of core values to orient action are not only misguided, they also pose the very real danger of constructing a discourse that will degenerate into a monologue or de facto form of moralizing. This is a point that seems to be understood by critical pedagogues like Cherryholmes, Giroux, McLaren, Pinar, and others who have argued that all value positions are contingent and problematic.

But what of the argument that provisional and contingent value claims should still form the basis for a critical theory of pedagogy? Cherryholmes (1988) notes that our core values, even when their contingent status is acknowledged, are subject to alternative conceptions which are both ambiguous and even contradictory. Therefore, the meaning of values and their application must always be interpreted within specific contexts and any interpretation is subject to further reinterpretation as new conditions and knowledge arise (pp. 172–77). Ultimately, our value decisions "are made in terms of what we find persuasive" (p. 177). McLaren (1988a) seems to make a related point when he notes that it "is not so much whether an ideology is true or false, but whether it is persuasive, coherent, and consistent with particular interests, values, and principles that exist in particular social formations" (p. 177).

If we pursue the implications of such arguments, we must reconsider the argument that contingent value claims are essential to a critical educational theory. I am not suggesting an approach that would deemphasize the importance of values or the need to take ethical positions as critical educators. Quite the contrary, what I am claiming is that the interpretive competence to make contingent value claims is always *prior to* attempts to take ethical positions regarding contingent values. Even the claim that it is necessary to take ethical positions is derived from practical judgment or *phronesis* as described in Chapter 5. The core of a theory for critical pedagogy, therefore, should be the enhancement of teacher and student competence for practical judgment. I recognize that this position will be viewed by some as a form of instrumentalism, or worse, even nihilism. But, I argue that a critical pedagogy rooted in the competence for practical judgment remains an ethical and utopian project for social transformation, and furthermore, that this is not a nihilistic position. Indeed, there is some danger that attempts to ground a critical educational theory in contingent value claims might serve to undermine the very competence required to take ethical positions in specific contexts.

In a critique of positivist influences on the discourse of educational reform, Whitson (1988) presents an argument relevant to the current discussion. According to Whitson, it is a neopositivist discourse which conceives of knowledge in such a way as to create the illusion that we can choose between values such as equality or excellence to guide educational reform. This discourse of positivism rests on certain key assumptions such as 1) "ideas" exist as "conceptual meaning contents, . . . existing prior to and independently of their verbal expression"; 2) " 'instruction' is merely the means chosen for transmitting a fund of positive conceptual entities comprising the 'curriculum' "; and 3) the view that "facts and values do exist as distinct positive entities, in separate 'cognitive' and 'affective' domains. . ." (pp. 292–93). Critical educators have, by and large, criticized and rejected the positivist discourse as explained in Chapter 4. Paulo Freire (1970c) is a case in point. The positivist conceptions of ideas, mind, and knowledge constitute what Freire called "banking" education in which teachers deposit monological conceptions of knowledge in the minds of passive students. In contrast, Freire argues for education as dialogue wherein teaching "cannot be reduced to the act of one person's 'depositing' ideas in another, nor can it become a simple exchange of ideas to be 'consumed' by discussants" (quoted in Whitson 1988, 293). Freire's work emphasizes an important shift away from particular thematic ideas "to the discursive 'thought-language' by which the thematic universe is generated" (p. 293).

However, Freire argues that the shift to a dialogical form of education entails our choosing "liberation" as education's purpose. Whitson contends that this line of argument "implies that other modes of education are still possible for those who do not share Freire's political commitments" (p. 293). Thus, even Freire's approach to educational reform can be accommodated within the hegemonic discourse of the status quo—a discourse that permits "equity" and "excellence" to appear as rival goods. In Chapter 4, we discussed a related point made by James Gee in a commentary on Freire's work. A different example might help clarify Whitson's argument.

Whitson (1988) cites the position taken by Arthur Combs (1972, 23) who has argued that while "we can live with a bad reader; a bigot is a danger to everyone." While Whitson (1988) agrees with Combs' sentiments, he denies the possibility of the choice Combs suggests. Whitson is worth quoting at length on this point.

> Concurring with Freire's stress on dialogue, I want to insist that literacy and mental competence are only attainable through dialogue, and that the "effectiveness" resulting from any reduction of dialogue is necessarily an impairment of intellectual competence tolerated for the sake of reactionary social and political purposes (and not, . . . a deemphasis of social goals in favor of more pressing academic purposes). In other words, I want to argue that we cannot accept bigotry as the price for concentrating on the goal of literacy. Aside from Combs' clear and sound judgment on the foolishness of doing so, and even aside from questions of social justice and morality, I want to make another point, *the point that literacy requires the dialogue that bigotry prevents, so that the bigot is and must be a bad reader.* (p. 294, emphasis added)

Whitson contends that we must move beyond Freire's understanding of dialogue to the insights provided by Bakhtin and Gadamer. Bakhtin used the term *heteroglossia* to refer to the qualitative plurality of language which, in daily use, is composed of numerous and intermixing dialects, jargons, habits, and practices. Thus the term dialogism "is the characteristic epistemological mode of a world, dominated by heteroglossia" (Bakhtin, as quoted in Whitson 1988, 295). This has direct implication for our understanding of literacy.

> Everything means, is understood, as a part of a greater whole—there is constant interaction between meanings, all of which have the potential of conditioning others. Which will affect the other, how it will do so and in what degree is what is actually settled at the moment of utterance. This dialogic imperative. . .insures that there can be no actual monologue. (Bakhtin, ibid.)

Whitson (1988) notes that Bakhtin was working within the same Hegelian tradition as Freire and both stressed reflection and action as "irreducible constitutive dimensions" of dialogue itself, that is, "the *word.*" More recently Gadamer (1982), operating in the same tradition, has emphasized the essentially dialogical nature of linguistic understanding and how language determines both the object and act of interpretation. Even Saussure's structuralism revealed the absence of *positive* terms in language. Rather the meaning of terms is derived as a function of the position of each term within a structure or code of difference. But Bakhtin "through seeing how word-meaning is constituted in the *action* of dialogic utterance. . .was able to surpass the linguistics of Saussure and others who did regard language" as elaborate conventions or pregiven schematization (p. 295). Bakhtin also helped expose the Cartesian dimension of Saussure's linguistics in which language is viewed as a fixed social form external to human subjects who are required to use language "as a material vehicle for outwardly expressing freely conceived internal ideal thoughts" (p. 295). What Saussure failed to acknowledge was that beyond forms of language, humans also employ *forms of combinations* of language forms or what Bakhtin called speech genres.

Heteroglossia is the "natural" human condition, but it is always threatened by a monologism that ultimately denies otherness by pretending to be the last word. Monologue, in Bakhtin's view, was always associated with a type of authority or forms of speech that seek authority (Gunn 1987, 59–60). Monologue closes off discourse by forcing heteroglossia to submit to the artificial and imposed constraints of various systems of understanding. In this regard, human voice functions as the instrument of consciousness, a form of interior resistance to finalization. This competence to use voice to resist monologue is an essential characteristic of our humanness.

The point of this analysis is to call our attention to something essential to our human being-in-the-world. Put another way, while we no longer can claim transcendental human values, we can describe basic human interests (e.g., interpretive competence) that might serve as the basis or ground for a radical theory of educational reform. I refer here to the development of practical social competence (Stanley and Whitson 1990; Whitson and Stanley 1990, 4). Furthermore, I wish to argue that this is both an essential ethical project and one that does not require the concomitant specification of contingent values as a basis for a critical curriculum theory. Drawing on the work of Whitson and Stanley (1990), I am using the term "practical" (or pragmatic) to refer to the character of human *praxis* or action. Practical competence thus refers to "the competence required for praxis, understood as the inherently social and interpretive mode of activity characteristic of human beings" (p. 5). As noted at the end of Chapter 5, the Greek word for such competence is *phronesis* (Random House 1987). *Phronesis* is distinguished from *techne* or the skill required for *poiesis*. The difference between these two terms (*phronesis* and *techne*) can be expressed in English "as the difference between 'action' or 'doing' (*praxis*) and 'production' or 'making' (poiesis)" (Whitson and Stanley 1990, p. 5). Thus, *techne* and *poiesis* involve the skill to produce something that can be defined or conceived in advance so as to provide the specific rules and standards to determine completion of the task.

Phronesis, in contrast, refers to the competence necessary for *praxis*, that is, "human action for the sake of doing what is really good for people" (p. 6). Unlike poiesis, praxis seeks "the realization of human well-being, which, by its nature, must be open to continual reinterpretation" (p. 6). This does not deny that human praxis might be directed toward more immediate goals, but these should not be seen as ends but as intermediate objectives perceived as necessary for the general end of human well-being. As such, intermediate or proximate goals must constantly be reformulated as we constantly reconceptualize our view of human betterment. In other words, *phronesis* simultaneously involves both the competence to reformulate goals as well as the ability to determine goals and the actions necessary to achieve them. This process is antithetical to technical or instrumental action toward predetermined ends. Consequently,

> Practical activity differs from the technical *not* simply because outcomes are unspecified, but because the activity itself is related to the outcomes in more than just an instrumental way, and it is *for this reason* that the objectives cannot be fully specified in advance of the practical activity. . . . Praxis is inherently a mode of activity in which progressive development in understanding the purposes being pursued emerges within the activity itself. (p. 7)

In this way, the possible progressive reconception of human well-being is contained within those practical activities wherein we pursue well-being. As we act, we formulate provisional conceptions of the good pursued, and this activity involves, in turn, a provisional interpretation of ourselves as human beings.

Beyond differentiating *phronesis* from technical competence, we should also understand *phronesis* as both the basic competence for interpretive activity (particularly the pragmatics of language use) and a fundamental ethical capacity. The link between linguistic and ethical competence can be traced to Aristotle's *Politics*. *Phronesis* for Aristotle entailed the ability to participate in the affairs of the polis which required civic and linguistic abilities. Ethics, in the classical Greek sense, included social, moral, and political thought, judgment, and action. Aristotle rejected the Platonic conception of the Good which linked virtue (*arete*) to knowledge (*logos*). Aristotle's theory of ethics understood human virtue as a matter of *ethos* (habit, practice, or custom). In this way, human virtue can be understood as "habituated practical abilities, and hence as matters of ethical competence, rather than the kind of arbitrary 'values' that positivists insist cannot be meaningfully described as right or wrong, competent or incompetent" (Whitson and Stanley 1990, 9).

The recognition of *phronesis* as the basic competence necessary for linguistic interpretation, as well as political and social action, has been stressed in the work of Arendt, Gadamer, and Habermas (Beiner 1983; Bernstein 1983). For these writers, to be human is to exist as an interpreting being. In other words, interpretation (the competence for judgment) is not merely something humans do, rather it is constitutive of our humanness, our being-in-the-world. This human competence for judgment involves all dimensions of human activity including the aesthetic, linguistic, political, and social. While practical judgment is critical in the public sphere, it is no less so in our private activity. Indeed, as we come to understand the centrality of *phronesis*, the boundary between public and private begins to blur. And since *phronesis* involves practices and habits that are intellectual, moral, and aesthetic, we cannot consign practical competence to any distinct domain such as the cognitive or affective categories that pervade mainstream educational discourse (Whitson and Stanley 1990, 9).

Phronesis, therefore, represents a fundamental human interest which encompasses all dimensions of human thought and action, including a basic ethical dimension, a quest for the good or human betterment. It is the case, however, that the good is not to be specified in advance, even by provisional and contingent values. Nevertheless, values are always already at the heart of this basic human project, since one's personal *phronesis* is grounded in a shared culture. We do not develop practical competence in a values vacuum. We always already find ourselves in a multicultural context at a particular historical juncture.

Consequently, a critical pedagogy oriented toward practical competence would involve values analysis in at least three ways. First, the critical examination of the extent to which any society functioned in accordance with its professed aims. This would also involve the interpretation of what those social values really were and how they should be realized. Second is what we might call utopian speculation regarding how we ought to define the "good" or human betterment. Our praxis requires that we do this since it is intrinsic to praxis itself. This activity would include speculation concerning the contingent value claims posed by critical pedagogues. Finally, we need to consider the values and related conditions that might be required for the exercise and expansion of *phronesis*. This involves conceptualizing preferred communities and/or societies. It is true that *phronesis* will always exist in some form wherever humans exist, as it is intrinsic to our human being. It is also true that critical human judgment has a history of survival under the most horrible circumstances (Bernstein 1983). Still, it is obvious that some sociocultural conditions are better suited than others to support and enhance practical judgment.

It should be evident that a critical pedagogy focused on practical competence would necessarily be deeply involved in values analysis, judgment, and social reconstruction. But this does not require (indeed it precludes) the prior grounding of this educational project in any particular value set (however contingent or problematic). An emphasis on practical competence acknowledges the need to take ethical positions since it is structured to help realize a basic human interest and thereby human betterment. Yet the specifics of this human project, including values, can only emerge through our praxis. But this is a praxis that must directly confront the monologue of conservative and mainstream educational (and other) discourses. As Whitson and Stanley (1990) argue, the realization of practical competence requires a dialogic educational project. And we must move beyond the false discourse of positivism which holds that we can choose among or between competing value systems. As Whitson (1988) has explained, a bigot, by definition, is a bad reader. There is no choice involved. The realization of basic human interests requires the practical competence denied by racism, sexism, class discrimination, and so forth. Following this line of argument, the development of practical competence also involves a critical posture, since our praxis must constantly be focused on the extent to which existing sociocultural arrangements do or do not serve basic human interests and betterment. Since this is a process with no final end, critique is intrinsic to praxis.

On the other hand, a critical educational project aimed at practical competence should also address many of the concerns raised by feminists (e.g., Ellsworth 1989), and others influenced by poststructuralist theory. A pedagogy focused on practical competence is focused on an interest shared by individuals and groups. It does *not* specify in advance what shapes the particular project of these individuals and groups should take. This approach to critical pedagogy holds only that such projects cannot be realized without practical competence, and any project must be resisted to the degree it might impair the practical competence of others. A critical pedagogy rooted in practical competence clearly acknowledges the profound limits of reason, the mysteries of alterity, and the inevitability of the unknowable. What this pedagogical project rejects are arguments for a radical incommensurability that would preclude any dialogue across differences. But such an extreme fear of incommensurability does not seem to me what critics of critical pedagogy such as Ellsworth (1989, 1990) have argued. For example, consider Ellsworth's pedagogical invitation

> If you can talk to me in ways that show you understand that your know-ledge of me, the world, and 'Right thing to do' will always be partial, interested and potentially oppressive to others, and if I can do the same, then we can work together on shaping and reshaping alliances for constructing circumstances in which students of difference can thrive. (p. 324)

If I have understood Ellsworth correctly, I agree with this invitation. Furthermore, it is not apparent that her position is in fundamental conflict with the specific approach to the critical theory of education proposed here. Practical competence is a fundamental human interest because meaning is never given but socially constructed. If knowledge was complete and obvious, interpretation would be irrelevant. Partial, socially constructed knowledge is the only kind available to humans. Rationality is never a guarantee of good interpretations; in fact, rationality can function to distort our understanding of what knowledge is possible. This is a point driven home by poststructuralism. Nevertheless, we cannot exercise practical judgment without acting rationally. Partial, contingent knowledge is both the product of our being-in-the-world and the focus of our ongoing praxis. Ellsworth's reference to "students of difference" refers, in practice, to any and all students. Profound difference and the unknowable are characteristics of any educational setting. Practical competence is funda-mental to the praxis of trying to work together across differences and to conducting education in such a way as to enable otherness to thrive. If education for emancipation means anything, it must refer to facili-tating the practical competence (*phronesis*) to realize our basic interest as humans.

CONCLUSIONS

At the start of this inquiry certain questions were posed. What was the nature of social reconstructionism and in what ways was reconstructionism related to more recent efforts to construct a theory of critical pedagogy? To what extent is a reconstructionist curriculum theory still relevant in the current educational context? At this point, certain conclusions, although tentative, seem reasonable.

First there are significant links between reconstructionism and recent efforts to construct a critical pedagogy. This historical debt and linkage is explicit in Giroux's (1988c) recent work, and there are increasing references to reconstructionism on the part of other radical educators. Among the elements of reconstructionist thought reflected in recent radical educational theory are: (a) a focus on the political nature of schooling and how it often serves the interest of dominant groups, (b) the potential of schooling to function as a site of genuine resistance to the dominant order, (c) the role of teachers as transformative intellectuals with the potential to help facilitate sociocultural change toward realizing a better society, (d) a complex view of ideology that cannot be limited to false consciousness but which also is an essential dimension in the construction of knowledge, (e) a central concern with the need to take ethical positions and a rejection of education as either neutral or radically relativistic, and (f) in Brameld's work, an attempt to blend and reconcile elements of American pragmatism and indigenous radicalism with European radicalism (particularly variants of Marxist thought). However, it is also clear that recent developments in critical educational theory present a more complex and useful critique of education theory and practice by way of having incorporated the insights of the new sociology, Critical Theory, neo-Marxism, feminism, cultural studies, neopragmatism, postmodernism, and poststructuralism. Reconstructionist theory remains relevant to educational reform but only in a significantly reconceptualized form. On occasion, reconstructionist theory has verged on becoming an authoritarian form of social engineering (Stanley 1989). The reconstructionists were often too preoccupied with what they perceived to be the relativist dangers inherent in pragmatism and tended to overemphasize the power of rationality, science, and the possibility for objective knowledge.

Second, a reconceptualized reconstructionist approach to critical pedagogy would be focused on realizing the basic human interest in the competence for practical judgment (*phronesis*). Practical judgment is a fundamental human interest not merely because it is something humans can do more or less well but because it is intrinsic to what it means to *be* human. Education may have many purposes, but the realization of *phronesis* must be the most basic and no other purpose should function to inhibit this human interest. The realization of *phronesis* is also a funda-mentally ethical purpose since, by definition, practical judgment involves a praxis to define and obtain the good or human betterment.

Third, radical educational theory must be intrinsically critical. Since no knowledge is given and our conception of the good can only emerge from our praxis, ongoing critique and reinterpretation is a characteristic of practical competence. As explained earlier, the very concepts that have oriented critical educational theory, for example, social transformation and emancipation can be rendered problematic (Cherryholmes 1988). Without an ongoing radical critique we are more vulnerable to the potentially monologic mystification and distortion of discursive regimes of truth, including those we construct as part of our own discourse of educational reform. And this leads us to another related but essential conclusion.

Fourth, a critical educational project should understand human life as textual (Whitson, forthcoming). I do not refer here to textuality as a mere metaphor, methodology, or as an analogue for life as employed by Geertz (1973) or Rorty (1979). Rather our human existence and praxis *is* textual in the sense that, as human subjects, we are largely formed by language, and language is the medium for all praxis. Given the textuality of the human condition, a focus on critical literacy must be a central concern of any critical curriculum theory. This is a primary insight of the poststruc-turalist critique. Consequently, a critical pedagogy must be poststructural if it is to provide us with the competence for effective counterhegemonic praxis.

Fifth, it is clear that the realization of our human interests as interpreting beings requires certain minimum sociocultural conditions. In various ways, scholars as different as Bernstein, Derrida, Dewey, Foucault, Habermas, Popper, Rawls, and Rorty have all recognized how essential certain minimal sociocultural conditions were to enable the realization of human interests. On one level, to make this claim seems no more than trite or obvious. But a careful reading of any of the authors cited above reveals the subtle and complex dimensions of this issue. The recent critique of founda-tionalism (e.g., Bernstein 1983; Gadamer 1975; Rabinow and Sullivan 1987) reveals that the very conditions necessary to realize human interests are themselves a source of debate, interpretation, and struggle. Yet it is clear that certain forms of domination or exclusion (e.g., racism, sexism, homo-phobia, political oppression, censorship, and monological approaches to curriculum, etc.) can and do function to distort and limit human interests.

Although the competence for practical reasoning has survived under the most oppressive environments throughout human history, it will only flourish in communities that provide stability and nurture the growth of *phronesis* or practical judgment and action. In highly pluralistic and modern, industrial societies like the United States, such communities are

most likely to be local phenomena. But education can assist in the
development and expansion of such communities in which *phronesis* might
flourish. Herein lies part of the utopian potential of a critical pedagogy
incorporating the purpose of social reconstruction. Put another way,
education has the potential to provide sites wherein the logic of
communities to realize *phronesis* can be developed and expanded in an
effort to resist domination and contribute to human betterment.

Sixth, the insights of postmodern and poststructural theory have made
clear that we can no longer apply totalizing critiques, metanarratives, or
any other appeals to objective knowledge or transcendental values.[3]
Nevertheless, while radical hermeneutics and poststructuralism have
revealed our knowledge to be more contingent and problematic, it does
not follow that projects aimed at human betterment are either irrational
or impossible (Caputo 1987). Neither despair nor a flight from ethics is
an appropriate response to the poststructuralist critique. Instead, we
should appreciate that this critique gives us a better understanding of the
human condition. While we should not succumb to nihilism, we should
heighten our sense of humility and the importance of keeping our options
open. In other words, while it is absolutely essential that we act to realize
basic human interests, we should do so with caution and restraint—
respecting differences and reluctant to press our schemes "to the last
detail" or to be "willing to draw blood on their behalf" (Caputo 1987, 259).

Seventh, we need to remain sensitive to the very real difficulties posed
by difference (alterity) or otherness. But the absolute otherness of others
should not obscure those aspects of our common sense of fate. The
awareness of difference and its relation to domination is critical to any
educational project, and one of our aims should be the realization of
communities defined by their toleration of dissent and differences. We
must also understand that categories of difference are never given but
culturally constructed—including class, gender, race, and sexual orientation. Since such categories of difference can always be deconstructed (e.g.,
Butler 1990), they are not a stable ground for the construction of
educational theory. A conception of a pedagogy of the unknowable
derived, in part, from the incomprehensible dimension of otherness is
captured in Caputo's (1987) conception of humans as dwelling in
communities "of unknowers who, precisely in virtue of their helplessness,
require. . .one another" (p. 288).

Finally, our awareness of the human condition cannot be limited to
phronesis and our interest in human betterment. As noted above, our praxis
is conducted within the context of rather severe constraints, including the

---

3. We must recall, however, that postmodernism itself has had some tendency toward a
   totalizing critique (see Chapter 5).

limits of rational discourse and the inevitability of difference and the unknowable. But our sense of human suffering is another important consideration. At present, our first impulse seems to be directed toward the elimination of human suffering. But we must reconsider the implication of the poststructuralist and postmodern critique. Suffering might not be a thing that can be eliminated in any total way because it is in human life itself. Neitzche viewed the textuality of human existence as derived in part from human suffering. In accordance with Neitzche's dictum *amor fati*, we must make a compact with life in full. In fact our affirmation of human suffering can inspire our compassion for otherness.

Rorty (1989) makes a related point, arguing that our contingent knowledge does not preclude a more general sense of solidarity. It is reasonable, in Rorty's view, to recommend "that we try to extend our sense of 'we' to people whom we have previously thought of as 'they' " (p. 192). This amounts to moral (albeit historically conditioned) progress, that is, to "see more and more traditional differences...as unimportant when compared with similarities with respect to pain and humiliation—the ability to think of people wildly different from ourselves as included in the range of 'us' " (p. 192). But as Caputo (1987) reminds us, it can never be only compassion and suffering which motivate us. As Neitzche argued, it is laughter that can transform the face of suffering (p. 285). Laughter affirms life, provides the imagination for human possibility, and helps prevent our acceptance of suffering from degenerating into despair (p. 292).

More than sixty years ago, the reconstructionists displayed a remarkable grasp of many of these issues. Their analysis was often too simplistic and, at times, verged dangerously close to a form of social engineering and authoritarianism, as we have seen in Chapters 3 and 4. They were too preoccupied with what they took to be the dangers posed by relativism and they underestimated the limits of critical rationality. Still they understood the need to act in the face of very real concrete human suffering and oppression. The reconstructionists might have been more modest in their assumptions, but they did help clarify the danger of complacency inherent in mainstream educational theory. To stand by, to acquiesce in the domination of others, amounted to complicity in a denial of human potential. Even as we illuminate the limits of rationality unexamined by the reconstructionists, we do so via a rational process.

As I have tried to show, a reconceptualized reconstructionism would aim at the realization of the basic human interest in practical competence and the sociocultural conditions necessary for praxis. This is an ethical conception of pedagogy that strives for human betterment, whose specific shape will emerge from our praxis toward this end. Such praxis involves the simultaneous transmission and transformation of our cultures, while also challenging the value of both processes in a world in which we can never fully grasp the dimensions of otherness. This is a critical pedagogy of neither/nor, oriented by a poststructuralist rejection of false dichotomies, awareness of the unknowable, understanding the limits of rationality, and an awareness of the dangers posed by both nihilism and the terrorism of closure or monologue.[4] It is a pedagogy of hope in the face of the very formidable barriers to critical analysis.

Human hopes and desires might never be grounded in any absolute knowledge, but we can gain a sense of human interests. As we act to realize our human betterment, our critical praxis can lift our thought, as McLaren (1988d) suggests, "beyond the limitations of the present moment in order to be transformed into dreams of possibility. And with dreams we can do wonderful things" (p. 76).

---

4. I wish to thank Jacques Daignault for his insights regarding the terrorist metaphor for monologue as an opposition to the anarchy of nihilism.

BIBLIOGRAPHY

Adler, M. J. 1982. *The padeia proposal: An educational manifesto.* New York: MacMillan.

Alcoff, L. 1988. Cultural feminism vs. poststructuralism: The identity crisis in feminist theory. *Signs* 13(3):405–436.

Althusser, L. 1969. *For Marx.* Trans. B. Brewster. New York: Vintage Books.

———. 1971a. *Lenin and philosophy, and other essays.* Trans. B. Brewster; ed. B. Brewster. London: New Left Books.

———. 1971b. *Lenin and philosophy, and other essays.* New York: Monthly Review Press.

Anderson, P. 1984. *In the tracks of historical materialism.* Chicago: University of Chicago Press.

Apple, M. W. 1979. *Ideology and curriculum.* London: Routledge and Kegan Paul.

———. 1982. *Education and power.* London: Routledge and Kegan Paul.

———. 1986a. National reports and the construction of inequality. *British Journal of Sociology of Education* 7(2):171–190.

———. 1986b. *Teachers and texts: A political economy of class and gender relations in education.* New York: Routledge and Kegan Paul.

———. 1988a. How does ideology become popular? A sympathetic rejoinder to Burbules and Kantor. *Teachers College Record* 90(2):193–195.

———. 1988b. Redefining equality: Authoritarian populism and the conservative restoration. *Teachers College Record* 90(2):167–184.

Apple, M. W., and L. Weis. 1983a. Ideology and practice in schooling: A political and conceptual introduction. In *Ideology and practice in schooling,* ed. M.W. Apple and L. Weis, 3–33. Philadelphia: Temple University Press.

———, eds. 1983b. *Ideology and practice in schooling.* Philadelphia: Temple University Press.

Arac, J, ed. 1986. *Postmodernism and politics.* Minneapolis: University of Minnesota Press.

Arnot, M. 1984. A Feminist perspective on the relationship between family life and school life. *Journal of Education* 166(1):5–24.

Arnot, M. and G. Weiner, eds. 1987. *Gender and the politics of schooling.* London: Open University Press.

Aronowitz, S. and H. A. Giroux. 1985. *Education under siege: The conservative, liberal, and radical debate over schooling.* South Hadley, MA: Bergin and Garvey.

Arons, S. 1983. *Compelling belief: The culture of American schooling.* Amherst, MA: University of Massachusetts Press.

Bakhtin, M. M. 1981. *The dialogic imagination.* Ed. M. Holquist. Austin: University of Texas.

Barnes, D. R. 1971. *The origins and development of Theodore Brameld's philosophy of education.* Unpublished Ph.D. diss. Rutgers University, New Brunswick, N.J.

Barr, R. D., J. L. Barth, and S. S. Shermis. 1977. *Defining the social studies.* Bulletin 51. Arlington, VA: National Council for the Social Studies.

———. 1978. *The nature of the social studies.* Palm Springs, CA: ETC Publications.

Barth, J. L., and S. S. Shermis. 1970. Defining the social studies: An exploration of three traditions. *Social Education* 34(7):743–751.

———. 1980a. Nineteenth century origins of the social studies movement: Understanding the continuity between older and contemporary civic and U.S. history textbooks. *Theory and Research in Social Education* 8(3):29–50.

———. 1980b. Social studies goals: The historical perspective. *Journal of Research and Development in Education* 13:1–11.

———. 1981. Social studies arguments without historical and philosophical foundations are still beside the point or. . . . *Theory and Research in Social Education* 9(2):93–98.

Barthes, R. 1972. *Mythologies.* London: Jonathan Cape.

———. 1974. *S/Z.* Trans. R. Miller. New York: Hill and Wang.

———. 1976. *The pleasure of the text.* New York: Hill and Wang.

Baudrillard, J. 1981. *For a critique of the political economy of the sign.* Trans. C. Levin. St. Louis: Telos Press.

———. 1983a. *In the shadow of the silent majorities.* Trans. P. Foss, P. Patton and J. Johnstone. New York: Semiotext(e).

——. 1983b. *Simulations*. Trans. P. Foss, P. Patton and J. Johnstone. New York: Semiotext(e).

Beiner, R. 1983. *Political judgment*. Chicago: University of Chicago Press.

Bell, D. 1977. *The cultural contradictions of capitalism*. NY: Basic Books.

Bellah, R., R. Madsen, W. M. Sullivan, A. Swidler, and S. M. Tipton. 1985. *Habits of the heart: Individualism and commitment in American life*. Berkeley: University of California Press.

Benhabib, S. 1990. Epistemologies of postmodernism: A rejoinder to Jean-Francois Lyotard. In *Feminism/Postmodernism*, ed. L. J. Nicholson, 107–130. New York: Routledge, Chapman and Hall.

Bennett, W. J. 1984. *To reclaim a legacy: A report on the humanities in higher education*. Washington, D.C.: National Endowment for the Humanities.

——. 1989. *Our children and our country: Improving America's schools and affirming the common culture*. NY: Touchstone.

Berlak, H. 1977. Human consciousness, social criticism, and civic education. In *Building rationales for citizenship education*, ed. J. P. Shaver, 34–47. Arlington, VA: National Council for the Social Studies.

Bernstein, R. J. 1976. *The reconstructing of social and political theory*. New York: Harcourt Brace Jovanovitch.

——. 1983. *Beyond objectivism and relativism: Science, hermeneutics, and praxis*. Philadelphia: University of Pennsylvania Press.

——. ed. 1985. *Habermas and modernity*. Cambridge, MA: The MIT Press.

——. 1986. *Philosophical profiles*. Philadelphia: University of Pennsylvania Press.

Berube, M. 1991. Public image limited: Political correctness and the medias big lie. *Village Voice*, 18 June, 31–37.

Besag, F. P. and J. L. Nelson. 1984. *The foundations of education: stasis and change*. New York: Random House.

Bestor, A. 1969. History in the secondary school. In *The social studies: structure, models and strategies*, ed. M. Feldman and E. Seifman, 183–187. Englewood Cliffs, NJ: Prentice Hall.

Beyer, B. K. 1987. *Practical strategies for the teaching of critical thinking*. Boston: Allyn and Bacon.

Beyer, L. E. and M. W. Apple, eds. 1988. *The curriculum, problems, politics, and possibilities*. Albany: State University of New York Press.

Beyer, L. E. and G. H. Wood. 1986. Critical inquiry and moral action in education. *Educational Theory* 36(1):1–14.

Bloom, A. 1987. *The closing of the American mind: How higher education has failed democracy and impoverished the souls of today's students*. New York: Simon and Schuster.

Bordo, S. 1990. Feminism, postmodernism, and gender-skepticism. In *Feminism/Postmodernism*, ed. L. J. Nicholson, 133–156. NY: Routledge, Chapman and Hall.

Bourdieu, P. 1977a. *Outline of theory and practice*. Cambridge, England: Cambridge University Press.

———. 1977b. The economics of linguistic exchanges. Social *Science Information* 16(6):645–668.

———. 1979. Symbolic power. *Critique of Anthropology* 4(13 & 14):77–85.

———. 1982. The school as a conservative force: Scholastic and cultural inequalities. In *Knowledge and values in social and educational research*, eds. E. Bredo and W. Feinberg, 391–407. Philadelphia: Temple University Press.

Bourdieu, P. and J. C. Passeron. 1977. *Reproduction in education, society and culture*. Beverly Hills, CA: Sage Publishers.

Bowers, C. A. 1969. *The progressive educator and the depression*. New York: Random House.

———. 1970. Social reconstructionism: Views from the left and the right, 1932–1942. *History of Education Quarterly* 10(1):22–52.

———. 1982. Review of Ideology, culture and the process of schooling. *Educational Studies* 13(3/4):420–422.

———. 1987. *Toward a post-liberal theory of education*. New York: Teachers College Press.

Bowles, S. and H. Gintis. 1976. *Schooling in capitalist America*. New York: Basic Books.

Boyer, E. L. 1983. *Higher school: A report on secondary education in America*. New York: Harper and Row.

Brameld, T. 1933. *A philosophic approach to communism*. Chicago: University of Chicago Press.

———. 1935. Karl Marx and the American teacher. *The Social Frontier* 2(2):53–56.

————. 1936a. American education and the social struggle. *Science and Society* 1(1):1–17.

————. 1936b. The role of philosophy in a changing world. *Kadelpian Review* 15(2):128–139.

————. 1938. Metaphysics and Social Attitudes: A concluding perspective. *The Social Frontier* 4(35):256–258.

————. 1940. The need for an American plan. *Frontiers of Democracy* 6(50):111–112,126–127.

————. ed. 1941a. *Workers' education in the United States*. New York: Harper and Brothers.

————. 1941b. The relation of philosophy and science from the perspective of education. *Educational Trends* 9:5–10.

————. 1945. *Design for America*. New York: Hinds, Hayden, Eldridge.

————. 1948. The philosophy of education as philosophy of politics. *School and Society* 68(1768):329–334.

————. 1950. *Patterns of educational philosophy—A democratic interpretation*. New York: World Book.

————. 1956. *Toward a reconstructed philosophy of education*. New York: Holt, Rinehart and Winston.

————. 1965. *The use of explosive ideas in education*. Pittsburgh, PA: University of Pittsburgh Press.

————. 1966–67. Reply to Elizabeth R. Eames. *Studies in Philosophy and Education* 5(1):95–100.

————. 1971. *Patterns of educational philosophy—Divergence and convergence in culturological perspective*. New York: Holt, Rinehart and Winston.

Brameld, T., E. Dale, A. C. Eurich, H. C. Hand, J. P. Leonard, J. E. Mendenhall, and G. Watson. 1942. New essentials for education in a world at war. *Progressive Education* 19(7):360–364.

Brenkman, J. 1979–1980. Mass media: From collective experience to the culture of privatization. *Social Text* 1(1–3):94–109.

Brennan, M. 1989. The political project of pedagogy: Contributions from feminisms. Paper presented at the annual meeting of the American Educational Research Association, San Francisco, April.

Brown, B. F., ed. 1977. *The report of the National Task Force on Citizenship Education*. New York: McGraw-Hill.

Brown, N. O. 1968. *Life Against Death*. London: Sphere Books.

Brown, W. 1987. Where is the sex in political theory? *Women and Politics* 7(1):3–23.

Brubaker, D. L. 1967. *Alternative directions for the social studies*. Scranton, IL: International Textbook Co.

Bruner, J. S. 1960. *The process of education*. Cambridge, MA: Harvard University Press.

———. 1971. "The process of education" revisited. *Phi Delta Kappan* 53(1):18–21.

———. 1982. The language of education. *Social Research* 49(4):835–853.

———. 1986. *Actual minds, possible worlds*. Cambridge, MA: Harvard University Press.

Bunch, C. and S. Pollack, eds. 1983. *Learning our way*. Trumansburg, NY: Crossing Press.

Burbules, N. C. 1986a. Radical educational cynicism and radical education skepticism. In *Philosophy of Education, 1985*, ed. D. Nyberg, 201–205. Urbana, IL: Philosophy of Education Society.

———. 1986b. Review of *Education under siege*, by S. Aronowitz and H. Giroux. *Educational Theory* 36(3):301–313.

———. 1988. The neglect of politics in critical educational studies. Paper presented at the annual meeting of the American Educational Research Association, New Orleans, LA, April.

Burbules, N. C. and H. Kantor. 1988. Redefining equality reconsidered. *Teachers College Record* 90(2):185–191.

Burbules, N. and S. Rice. 1990. Dialogue across differences: Continuing the conversation. Paper presented at the annual Conference on Curriculum Theory and Classroom Practice, Bergamo Center, Dayton, OH, October.

Butler, J. 1990. Gender trouble, feminist theory, and psychoanalytic discourse. In *Feminism/Postmodernism*, ed. L. J. Nicholson, 324–340. NY: Routledge, Chapman and Hall.

Butts, R. F. 1979. The revival of civic learning: A rationale for the education of citizens. *Social Education* 43(5):359–364.

———. 1980. *The revival of civic learning: A rationale for the education of citizens in American schools*. Bloomington, IN: Phi Delta Kappa.

Caputo, J. D. 1987. *Radical hermeneutics: Repetition, deconstruction, and the hermeneutic project*. Bloomington, IN: Indiana University Press.

Cazden, C. 1987. *Classroom discourse: The language of teaching and learning*. Portsmouth, NH: Heinemann.

Chapman, C. J. and G. S. Counts. 1924. *Principles of education*. Chicago: Houghton Mifflin.

Cherryholmes, C. H. 1988. *Power and criticism: Poststructural investigations in education*. New York: Teachers College Press.

Childs, J. L. 1936. Democracy, education, and the class struggle. The Social Frontier 2(9):274–278.

Chodorow, N. J. 1978. *The reproduction of mothering: Psychoanalysis and the sociology of gender*. Berkeley: University of California Press.

―――. 1985. Gender, relation, and difference in psychoanalytic perspective. In *The future of difference*, ed. H. Eisenstein and A. Jardine, 3–19. New Brunswick, NJ: Rutgers University Press.

Christian, B. 1987. The race for theory. *Cultural Critique* 6:51–63.

―――. 1988. The race for theory. *Feminist Studies* 14(1):67–69.

Clark, K. 1968. *Civilization*. London: Sphere Books.

―――. 1969. *Civilization*. New York: Harper and Row.

Clecak, P. 1983. *America's quest for the ideal self: Dissent and fulfillment in the 60s and 70s*. New York: Oxford University Press.

Combs, A. W. 1972. *Educational accountability: Beyond behavioral objectives*. Washington, D. C.: Association for Supervision and Curriculum Development.

―――. 1981. What the future demands of education. *Phi Delta Kappan* 62(5):369–372.

Cook-Gumperz, J. 1986. *The social construction of literacy*. Cambridge: Cambridge University Press.

Coombs, J. R. 1971. Objectives of value analysis. In *Values education*, Forty-first Yearbook, ed. L. E Metcalf, 1–28. Washington, D.C.: National Council for the Social Studies.

Counts, G. S. 1926. The place of the school in the social order. *National Education Association: Addresses and Proceedings* 64:308–315.

―――. 1927. *The social composition of boards of education*. Chicago: University of Chicago Press.

———. 1930. *The American road to culture: A social interpretation of education in the United States*. New York: John Day.

✳ ———. 1932. *Dare the schools build a new social order*. New York: John Day.

———. 1934a. Educating for tomorrow. *The Social Frontier* 1(1):5–7.

———. 1934b. *The social foundation of education*. New York: Charles Scribner's Sons.

———. 1938. *The prospects of American democracy*. New York: John Day.

———. 1969. *Dare the schools build a new social order*. 1932. New York: Arno Press and New York Times.

Cremin, L. 1961. *The transformation of the school*. New York: Alfred Knopf.

Cuban, L. 1984. *How teachers taught: Constancy and change in American classrooms, 1890–1980*. New York: Longman.

Culler, J. D. 1982. *On deconstruction: Theory and criticism after structuralism*. Ithaca, NY: Cornell University Press.

Culley, M. and C. Portuges, eds. 1985. *Gendered subjects: The dynamics of feminist teaching*. Boston: Routledge and Kegan Paul.

Dale, M. 1986. Stalking a conceptual chameleon: Ideology in marxist studies of education. *Educational Theory* 36(3):241–257.

Deleuze, G. 1986. *Foucault*. Minneapolis: University of Minnesota Press.

Dennis, L. J. 1989. Beyond Dewey: The social reconstructionism of G. S. Counts and J. L. Childs. Paper presented at the annual meeting of the American Educational Research Association. San Francisco, March.

Derrida, J. 1976. *Of grammatology*. Baltimore: Johns Hopkins University Press.

———. 1978a. Violence and metaphysics. In *Writing and difference*. Trans. A. Bass. Chicago: University of Chicago Press.

———. 1978b. *Writing and difference*. Trans. A Bass. London: Routledge and Kegan Paul.

———. 1979. *Spurs: Nietzsche's styles*. Trans. B. Harlow. Chicago: Chicago University Press.

———. 1980. *Archeology of the frivilous: Reading condillac*. Trans. J. P. Leavey, Jr. Pittsburgh: Duquesne University Press.

———. 1982. The conflict of faculties. In *Languages of knowledge and of inquiry*, ed. M. Riffaterre. New York: Columbia University Press.

———. 1983. The principle of reason: The university in the eyes of its pupils. *Diacritics* 19(3):20.

———. 1984a. No apocalypse, not now (full speed ahead, seven missiles, seven missives). *Diacritics* 14(2):20–31.

———. 1984b. Of an apocalyptic tone recently adopted in philosophy. Trans. J. P. Leavey. *Oxford Literary Review* 6(2):3–37.

———. 1984c. *Otobiographies: Nietzsche's teaching and the politics of the proper names.* Paris: Galiee.

———. 1988. Afterward: Toward an ethic of discussion. In *Limited Inc,* 111–160. Evanston, IL: Northwestern University Press.

Descombs, V. 1980. *Modern French philosophy.* Cambridge, MA: Cambridge University Press.

Dewey, J. 1916. *Democracy and education: An introduction to the philosophy of education.* New York: MacMillan.

———. 1928. Progressive education and the science of education. *Progressive Education* 5(3):197–204.

———. 1934. Can education share in social reconstruction? *The Social Frontier* 1(1):11–12.

———. 1935a. The crucial role of intelligence. *The Social Frontier* 1(5):9–10.

———. 1935b. The need for orientation. *Forum* 93(6):333–335.

———. 1936. Class struggle and the democratic way. *The Social Frontier* 2(8):241–242.

———. 1937. Education and social change. *The Social Frontier* 3(26):235–238.

———. 1962. *The school and society.* Chicago: The University of Chicago Press.

Dewey, J. and J. L. Childs. 1933a. The social-economic situation and education. In *Educational Frontier,* ed. W. H. Kilpatrick, 32–72. New York: D. Appleton-Century.

———. 1933b. The underlying philosophy of education. In *Educational Frontier,* ed. W. H. Kilpatrick, 287–320. New York: D. Appleton-Century.

Dews, P. 1986. *From poststructuralism to postmodernity: Habermas's counter-perspective.* ICA Documents 4, 12–16. London: Institute for Contemporary Arts.

————. 1987. *Logics of disintegration: Post-structuralist thought and the claims of critical theory.* New York: Verso Books.

Dinnerstein, D. 1976. *The mermaid and the minotaur: Sexual arrangements and the human malise.* NY: Harper and Row.

DiStefano, C. 1990. Dilemmas of difference: Feminism, modernity, and postmodernism. In *Feminism/Postmodernism,* ed. L. J. Nicholson, 63–82. NY: Routledge, Chapman and Hall.

Donald, J. and S. Hall, eds. 1986. Introduction. In *Politics and ideology,* ix–xx. Milton Keynes: Philadelphia: Open University Press.

Dougan, A. M. *The historical search for a definition of the social studies.* unpublished manuscript. Indiana University.

Dreyfus, H. L. and P. Rabinow. 1983. *Michel Foucault: Beyond structuralism and hermeneutics.* Chicago: The University of Chicago Press.

D'Souza, D. 1990. *Illiberal education: The politics of race and sex on campus.* New York: Free Press.

Eagleton, T. 1983. *Literacy theory: An introduction.* Minneapolis: University of Minnesota Press.

————. 1986. Marxism, structuralism, and post-structuralism. In *Against the grain,* ed. T. Eagleton, 89–98. London: Verso Books.

Eames, E. R. 1966–1967. Review of *The use of explosive ideas in education* and *Education as power,* by Theodore Brameld. *Studies in Philosophy and Education* 5(1):87–95.

Ellsworth, E. 1988. Why doesn't this feel empowering? Working through the repressive myths of critical pedagogy. Paper presented at the Tenth Conference on Curriculum Theory and Classroom Practice. Dayton, OH, October.

————. 1989. Why doesn't this feel empowering? Working through the repressive myths of critical pedagogy. *Harvard Educational Review* 59(3):297–324.

————. 1990. Steps toward classroom practices grounded in context and difference. Paper presented at the Annual Bergamo Conference on Curriculum Theorizing. Dayton, OH, October.

Engle, S. H. 1960. Decision Making: The heart of social studies instruction. *Social Education* 24(7):301–304, 306.

————. 1964. Decision-making: The heart of social studies instruction. In *Crucial issues in the teaching of social studies: a book of readings,* eds. B. G. Massialas and A. M. Kazamias, 28–35. Englewood Cliffs, NJ: Prentice-Hall.

Fetsko, W. 1979. Textbooks and the new social studies. *Social Studies* 70(2):51–55.

Feyerabend, P. 1978. *Science in a free society*. London: NLB.

Fielding, R. 1981. Social education and social change: Constraints of the hidden curricula. In *Social/Political education in three countries: Britain, West Germany, and the United States*, eds. I. Morrissett and A. M. Williams. Boulder, CO: Social Science Education Consortium, and ERIC Clearinghouse for Social Science Education.

Fine, M. 1989. Silencing and nurturing voice in an improbable context: Urban adolescents in public school. In *Critical pedagogy, the state and cultural struggle*, eds. H. A. Giroux and P. McLaren, 152–173. New York: State University of New York Press.

———. forthcoming. *Framing dropouts*. Albany, NY: State University of New York Press.

Finn, C. E., D. Ravitch, and R. T. Fancher, eds. 1984. *Against mediocrity: The humanities in America's high schools*. New York: Holmes and Meier.

Fish, S. 1980. *Is there a text in this class? The authority of interpretive communities*. Cambridge, MA: Harvard University Press.

———. 1982. Working on the chain gang: Interpretation in the law and in literary criticism. *Critical Inquiry* 9(1):201–216.

Flax, J. 1990. Postmodernism and gender relations in feminist theory. In *Feminism/Postmodernism*, ed. L. J. Nicholson, 39–62. New York: Routledge, Chapman and Hall.

Foucault, M. 1972. *The archaeology of knowledge*. New York: Harper Colophon Books.

———. 1973a. *Madness and civilization: A history of insanity in the age of reason*. New York: Vintage Books.

———. 1973b. *The order of things*. New York: Vintage Books.

———. 1975. *The birth of the clinic: An archaeology of medical perception*. New York: Vintage Books.

———. 1979. *Discipline and punish*. New York: Vintage Books.

———. 1980a. *Language, counter-memory, practice*. Ithaca, NY: Cornell University Press.

———. 1980b. *Power/Knowledge: Selected interviews and other writings, 1972–1977*. Trans. C. Gordon; ed. C. Gordon. New York: Pantheon Books.

———. 1980c. *The history of sexuality*. Vol. 1. New York: Pantheon.

Fowler, B. P. 1930. President's message. *Progressive Education* 7(4):159.

Fraenkel, J. R. 1977. *How to teach about values: An analytical approach.* Englewood Cliffs, NJ: Prentice-Hall.

———. 1980. Goals for teaching values and value analysis. *Journal of Research and Development in Education* 13(2):93–102.

Fraser, N. and L. J. Nicholson. 1990. Social criticism without philosophy: An encounter between feminism and postmodernism. In *Feminism/ Postmodernism*, ed. L. J. Nicholson, 19–38. New York: Routledge, Chapman and Hall.

Freire, P. 1970a. Cultural action and conscientization. *Harvard Educational Review* 40(3):452–477.

———. 1970b. *Pedagogy of the oppressed.* Trans. M. B. Rames. New York: Seabury Press.

———. 1970c. *Pedagogy of the oppressed.* Trans. M. B. Rames. New York: Herder and Herder.

———. 1970d. The adult literacy process in cultural action for freedom. *Harvard Educational Review* 40(3):205–225.

———. 1973. *Education for critical consciousness.* New York: Seabury Press.

———. 1985. *The politics of education.* South Hadley, MA: Bergin and Garvey.

Freire, P. and D. Macedo. 1987. *Literacy: Reading the word and the world.* South Hadley, MA: Bergin and Garvey.

Gadamer, H. 1975. *Truth and method.* Trans. G. Borden and J. Cumming; eds. G. Borden and J. Cumming. New York: Seabury Press.

———. 1982. *Truth and method.* Eds. G. Borden and J. Cumming. New York: Crossroads.

Gandal, K. 1986. Michel Foucault: Intellectual work and politics. *Telos* 67(Spring):121–134.

Gee, J. P. 1988. The legacies of literacy: From Plato to Freire through Harvey Graff. *Harvard Educational Review* 58(2):195–212.

Geertz, C. 1973. *The interpretation of cultures.* New York: Basic Books.

———. 1983. *Local knowledge: Further essays in interpretive anthropology.* NY: Basic Books.

Genovese, E. D. 1991. Heresy yes—sensitivity, no. *New Republic* 204(15, April 15):30–35.

Gilligan, C. 1982. *In a different voice.* Cambridge, MA: Harvard University Press.

Giroux, H. A. 1981. *Ideology, culture, and the process of schooling.* Philadelphia: Temple University Press.

———. 1983a. *Theories and resistance in education.* South Hadley, MA: Bergin and Garvey.

———. 1983b. Theories of reproduction and resistance in the new sociology of education: A critical analysis. *Harvard Educational Review* 53(3):257–293.

———. 1984. Public philosophy and the crisis in education. *Harvard Educational Review* 54(2):186–194.

———. 1985. Critical pedagogy, cultural politics and the discourse of experience. *Journal of Education* 167(2):22–41.

———. 1986. Authority, intellectuals, and the politics of practical learning. *Teachers College Record* 88(1):22–40.

———. 1988a. Border pedagogy in the age of postmodernism. *Journal of Education* 170(3):162–181.

———. 1988b. Postmodernism and the discourse of educational criticism. *Journal of Education* 170(3):5–30.

———. 1988c. *Schooling and the struggle for public life: Critical pedagogy in the modern age.* Minneapolis: University of Minnesota Press.

———. 1990. Rethinking the boundaries of educational discourse: Modernism, postmodernism, and feminism. *College Literature* 17(2,3):1–50.

———. forthcoming. Postmodernism as border pedagogy: Redefining the boundaries of race and ethnicity. *Education and Society.*

Giroux, H. A. and P. McLaren. 1986. Teacher education and the politics of engagement. *Harvard Educational Review* 56(3):213–238.

———. eds. 1989. *Critical pedagogy, the state and cultural struggle.* Albany: State University of New York Press.

Giroux, H. A. and A. P. Penna. 1979. Social education in the classroom: The dynamics of the hidden curriculum. *Theory and Research in Social Education* 7(1):21–42.

Giroux, H. A. and R. I. Simon. 1988. Schooling, popular culture, and a pedagogy of possibility. *Journal of Education* 170(1):9–26.

———. eds. 1989. *Popular culture, schooling and everyday life.* South Hadley, MA: Bergin and Garvey.

Gitlin, T. 1987. *The sixties: Years of hope, days of rage.* New York: Bantam Books.

Goldmark, B. 1968. *Social studies: A method of inquiry.* Belmont, CA: Wadsworth Publishing Co.

Goodlad, J. J. 1984. *A place called school: Prospects for the future.* New York: McGraw-Hill Book Company.

Graff, H. J. 1979. *The literacy myth: Literacy and social structure in the 19th century city.* New York: Academic Press.

———. 1981. *Literacy and social development in the west: A reader.* Cambridge: Cambridge University Press.

———. 1987a. *The labyrinths of literacy: Reflections on literacy past and present.* New York: The Falmer Press.

———. 1987b. *The legacies of literacy: Continuities and contradictions in western culture and society.* Bloomington, IN: University of Indiana Press.

Gramsci, A. 1971. *Selections from the prison notebook.* Trans. Q. Hoare and G.N. Smith; eds. Q. Hoare and G. N. Smith. New York: International Publishers.

Grossberg, L. 1986. Teaching the popular. In *Theory in the classroom*, ed. C. Nelson, 177–200. Chicago: University of Illinois Press.

Grumet, M. R. 1988. *Bitter milk: Women and teaching.* Amherst, MA: University of Massachusetts Press.

———. 1989. Generations: Reconceptualist curriculum theory and teacher education. *Journal of Teacher Education* 40(1):13–17.

Gunn, G. 1987. *The culture of criticism and the criticism of culture.* Oxford: Oxford University Press.

Haas, J. D. 1979. Social studies: Where have we been? Where are we now? *Social Studies* 70(4):147–154.

———. 1981. The uses of rationales, goals and objectives in the social studies. *Social Studies* 72(6):249–253.

Habermas, J. 1971. *Knowledge and human interests.* Trans. J. J. Shapiro. Boston: Beacon Press.

———. 1973a. A postscript to knowledge and human interests. *Philosophy of the Social Sciences* 3:157–189.

———. 1973b. *Theory and practice.* Trans. J. Viertel. Boston: Beacon Press.

——. 1976. The analytical theory of science and dialetics. In *The positivist dispute in German sociology*, ed. T. W. Adorno, 131–162. London: Heinemann Educational Books Ltd.

——. 1979. *Communication and the evolution of society*. Trans. T. McCarthy. Boston: Beacon Press.

——. 1987. *The philosophical discourse of modernity*. Trans. F. G. Lawrence. Cambridge, MA: MIT Press.

Haraway, D. 1990. A manifesto for cyborgs: Science, technology, and socialist feminism in the 1980s . In *Feminism/Postmodernism*, ed. L. J. Nicholson, 190–233. New York: Routledge, Chapman and Hall, Inc.

Harding, S. 1986. The instability of the analytical categories of feminist theory. *Signs* 11(4):645–665.

——. 1990. Feminism, science, and the anti-enlightenment critiques. In *Feminism/Postmodernism*, ed. L. J. Nicholson, 83–106. New York: Routledge, Chapman and Hall.

Harding, S. and M. Hintikka, eds. 1983. *Discovering reality: Feminist perspectives on epistemology metaphysics, methodology, and philosophy of science*. Dordrecht, Holland: Reidel Press.

Hartsock, N. 1987a. Re-thinking modernism: Minority vs. majority theories. *Cultural Critique* 7:187–206.

——. 1987b. The feminist standpoint: Developing the ground for a specifically feminist historical materialism. In *Feminism and methodology*, ed. S. Harding, 157–180. Bloomington, IN: University of Indiana Press.

——. 1990. Foucault on power: A theory for women? In *Feminism/Postmodernism*, ed. L. J. Nicholson, 157–175. New York: Routledge, Chapman and Hall.

Haskell, T. L. 1984a. Professionalism versus capitalism: R. H. Tawney, E. Durkheim and C. S. Peirce on the disinterestedness of professional communities. In *The authority of experts*, ed. T.L. Haskell, 180–225. Bloomington, IN: University of Indiana Press.

——. ed. 1984b. *The authority of experts: Studies in history and theory*. Bloomington, IN: University of Indiana Press.

Heath, S. B. 1983. *Ways with words: Language, life and work in communities and classrooms*. Cambridge, MA: Cambridge University Press.

Hebdige, D. 1979. *Subculture: The meaning of style*. New York: Methuen.

Hertzberg, H. W. 1981. *Social studies reform: 1880–1980*. Report of Project Span. Boulder, CO: Social Science Education Consortium.

Hirsch, E. D. 1987. *Cultural literacy: What every American needs to know.* Boston: Houghton Mifflin.

Hooks, B. 1984. *Feminist Theory: From margin to center.* Boston: South Ed. Press.

Hunt, M. P. and L. E. Metcalf. 1955. *Teaching high school social studies.* 1st edition. New York: Harper and Row.

————. 1968. *Teaching high school social studies.* 2nd edition. New York: Harper and Row.

Huyssen, A. 1984. Mapping the postmodern. *New German Critique* 33:5–52.

Jaggar, A. 1983. *Feminist politics and human nature.* Totawa, NJ: Rowman and Allanheld.

Jameson, F. 1979–1980. Reification and utopia in mass culture. *Social Text* 1(1–3, Winter):130–148.

————. 1983. Postmodernism and consumer society. In *The anti-aesthetic: Essays on postmodern culture,* ed. Hal Foster, 111–125. Port Townsend, WA: Bay Press.

————. 1984a. Postmodernism or the cultural logic of late capitalism. *New Left Review* (146):53–92.

————. 1984b. The politics of theory: Ideological positions in the postmodernism debate. *New German Critique* 33:53–65.

Jenness, D. 1990. *Making sense of the social studies.* New York: MacMillan Publishing Company.

Johnson, M. 1926. The educational principles of the school of organic education, Fairhope, Alabama. In *The foundations and technique of curriculum-construction, part I. Curriculum-making: past and present. The twenty-sixth yearbook of the National Society for the Study of Education,* ed. G. M. Whipple, 349–351. Bloomington, IL: Public School Publishing.

Kaplan, E. A. 1987. *Rocking around the clock: Music, television, postmodernism and consumer culture.* New York: Methuen Books.

————. ed. 1988. *Postmodernism and its discontents, theories, practices.* New York: Verso.

Kellner, D. 1978. Ideology, Marxism, and advanced capitalism. *Socialist Review* 8(6):37–65.

————. 1988. Postmodernism as social theory: Some challenges and problems. *Theory, Culture and Society* 5:239–269.

Kenway, J. and H. Modra. 1989. Feminist pedagogy and emancipatory possibilities. *Critical Pedagogy Networker* 2(2 & 3):1–17.

Kilpatrick, W. H., ed. 1933. *Educational Frontier.* New York: D. Appleton-Century.

———. 1936. High Marxism defined and rejected. *The Social Frontier* 2(9):272–274.

Kimball, R. 1990. *Tenured radicals: How politics has corrupted our higher education.* New York: Harper Row.

King-Hele, D. 1970. *The end of the twentieth century?* New York: McMillan.

Kliebard, H. M. 1986. *The struggle for the American curriculum, 1893–1958.* Boston: Routledge and Kegan Paul.

Kneller, G. F. 1965. *Educational anthropology: An introduction.* New York: John Wiley and Sons.

———. 1971. *Introduction to the philosophy of education.* New York: John Wiley and Sons.

Kohl, H. 1980. Can the schools build a new social order? *Journal of Education* 162(3):57–66.

Kohlberg, L. 1975. The cognitive-developmental approach to moral education. *Phi Delta Kappan* 56(10):670–677.

Kristeva, J. 1980. *Desire in language: A semiotic approach to literature and art.* Ed. L. S. Roudiez. New York: Columbia University Press.

———. 1982. Women's time. In *Feminist theory: A critique of ideology,* eds. N. O. Keohane, M. Z. Rosaldo and B. C. Gelpi, 31–53. Chicago: University of Chicago Press.

———. 1984. *Revolution in poetic language.* Trans. M. Waller. New York: Columbia University Press.

Krug, M. 1967. *History and the social sciences: New approaches to the teaching of the social studies.* Waltham, MA: Blaisdell Publishing.

Kuhn, T. 1970. *The structure of scientific revolutions.* 2d ed., enl. Chicago: University of Chicago Press.

Lacan, J. 1977. *Ecrits: A selection.* Trans. A. Sheridan. New York: W. W. Norton & Co., Inc.

———. 1978. *The four fundamental concepts of psychoanalysis.* Trans. A. Sheridan; ed. J. Miller. New York: W. W. Norton & Co. Ltd.

Laclau, E. 1983. The impossibility of society. *Canadian Journal of Political and Social Theory* 7(1–2):21–23.

———. 1988. Politics and the limits of modernity. In *Universal abandon? The politics of postmodernism*, ed. A. Ross, 63–82. Minneapolis: University of Minnesota Press.

Laclau, E. and C. Mouffe. 1985. *Hegemony and socialist strategy*. London: Verso Books.

Lasch, C. 1979. *The culture of narcissism*. New York: Warner Books.

———. 1984. *The minimal self: Psychic survival in troubled times*. New York: Norton and Company.

Lather, P. 1989a. Deconstructing/Deconstructive inquiry: The politics of knowing and being known. Paper presented at the annual meeting of the American Educational Research Association. San Francisco, CA, March.

———. 1989b. Reinscribing otherwise: The play of values in the practices of the human sciences. Paper presented at the Alternative Paradigms for Inquiry Conference sponsored by Phi Delta Kappa International and Indiana University. San Francisco, CA, March.

Lehman, D. 1990. *Signs of the times: Deconstruction and the fall of Paul de Man*. New York: Poseidon Press.

Leming, J. L. 1981. On the limits of rational moral education. *Theory and Research in Social Education* 9(1):7–34.

———. 1989. The two cultures of social studies education. *Social Education* 53(6):404–408, October.

Lens, S. 1976. The doomsday strategy. *The Progressive* 40:12–35, February.

Lentricchia, F. 1984. *Criticism and social change*. Chicago: University of Chicago Press.

———. 1988. *Ariel and the police*. Madison: University of Wisconsin Press.

Levi-Strauss, C. 1979. *Myth and Meaning*. New York: Schoeken.

Lewis, M. and R. Simon. 1986. A discourse not intended for her: Learning and teaching within patriarchy. *Harvard Educational Review* 56(4):457–472.

Lilge, F. 1952. Reason and ideology in education. *Harvard Educational Review* 22(4):247–256.

Liston, D. P. 1985. Marxism and schooling: A failed or limited tradition. *Educational Theory* 35(3):307–312.

————. 1986. On facts and values: An analysis of radical curriculum studies. *Educational Theory* 36(2):449–464.

————. 1988. *Capitalist schools: Explanations and ethics in radical studies of schooling.* New York: Routledge, Chapman and Hall.

Liston, D. P. and K. M. Zeichner. 1987. Critical pedagogy and teacher education. *Journal of Education* 169(3):117–137.

Lorde, A. 1984. *Sister outsider.* New York: The Crossing Press.

Lowe, W. T. 1969. *Structure and the social studies.* Ithaca, NY: Cornell University Press.

Lucas, C. J. 1984. *Foundations of education, schooling and the social order.* Englewood Cliffs, NJ: Prentice-Hall.

Lugones, M. C. and E. V. Spelman. 1983. Have we got a theory for you! Feminist theory, cultural imperialism, and the demand for "The Woman's Voice". *Women's Studies International Forum* 6(6):573–581.

Luke, C. Feminist politics in radical pedagogy. unpublished manuscript. Townsville, Australia: James Cook University, Department of Social and Cultural Studies.

Lyotard, J. F. 1984. *The postmodern condition: A report on knowledge.* Manchester University Press.

Margolis, J. Z. 1986. *Pragmatism without foundations: Reconciling realism and relativism.* New York: Blackwell.

Mascia-Lees, F., P. Sharpe, and C. B. Cohen. 1989. The postmodernist turn in anthropology: Cautions from a feminist perspective. *Signs* 15(1):7–33.

Massialas, B. G. and B. Cox. 1966. *Inquiry in the social studies.* New York: McGraw-Hill.

McCarthy, C. 1988. Rethinking liberal and radical perspectives on racial inequality in schooling: Making the case for nonsynchrony. *Harvard Educational Review* 58(3):265–279.

McCarthy, T. 1989–1990. The politics of the ineffable: Derridas deconstructionism. *The Philosophical Forum* 22(1 & 2):146–168.

McClellan, J. E. 1968. Theodore Brameld and the architecture of confusion. In *Toward an effective critique of American education*, 129–190. Philadelphia: J. B. Lippincott.

McLaren, P. 1986. Review article—Postmodernity and the death of politics: A Brazilian reprieve. *Educational Theory* 36(4):389–401.

———. 1988a. Broken dreams, false promises, and the decline of public schooling. *Journal of Education* 170(1):41–65.

———. 1988b. Culture or cannon? Critical pedagogy and the politics of literacy. *Harvard Educational Review* 58(2):213–234.

———. 1988c. On ideology and education: Critical pedagogy and the politics of education. *Social Text* 19 & 20 (1–2):153–185.

———. 1988d. Schooling the postmodern body: Critical pedagogy and the politics of enfleshment. *Journal of Education* 170(3):53–83.

———. 1989. *Life in schools: An introduction to critical pedagogy in the foundations of education.* New York: Longman Inc.

———. Forthcoming a. Post-colonial pedagogy: Post-colonial desire and decolonized community. *Education and Society.*

———. Forthcoming b. Postmodernism/Post-colonialism pedagogy. *Education and Society.*

———. Forthcoming c. Review of *Capitalist schools: Explanations and ethics in radical studies of schooling*, by D. P. Liston. *Teachers College Record.*

McLaren, P. and R. Hammer. 1989. Critical pedagogy and the postmodern challenge: Toward a critical postmodernist pedagogy of liberation. *Educational Foundations* 3(3):29–62.

McNeil, L. M. 1983. Defensive teaching and classroom control. In *Ideology and curriculum*, eds. M. W. Apple and L. Weis, 114–142. Philadelphia: Temple University Press.

McRobbie, A. 1978. Working class girls and the culture of feminity. In *Women take issue: Aspects of women's subordination*, ed. Women's Studies Group Center for Contemporary Cultural Studies, 96–108. London: Hutchinson.

Meadows, D. H., D. L. Meadows, J. Randers, and W. W. Behrens. 1972. *The limits of growth.* Report of the Club of Rome. New York: Universe Books.

Megill, A. 1985. *Prophets of extremity: Nietzsche, Heidegger, Foucault, Derrida.* Berkeley: University of California Press.

Mehlinger, H. 1981. Social studies: Some gulfs and priorities. In *The social studies.* Eightieth yearbook of the National Society for the Study of Education, eds. H. D. Mehlinger and O. L. Davis, Jr. Chicago: University of Chicago Press.

Mertz, E. and R. A. Parmentier, eds. 1985. *Semiotic mediation: Sociocultural and psychological perspectives*. New York: Academic Press.

Metcalf, L. E., ed. 1971. *Values education: Rationale, strategies, and procedures*. Forty-first Yearbook. Washington, D.C.: National Council for the Social Studies.

Minh-ha, T. T. 1986–87. Introduction. In *Discourse*, vol. 8, 6–9.

Montag, W. 1988. What is at stake in the debate on postmodernism? In *Postmodernism and its discontents: Theories and practices*, ed. E. A. Kaplan, 88–103. New York: Verso Books.

Morrissett, I., ed. 1967. *Concepts and structure in the new social science curriculum*. New York: Holt, Rinehart and Winston.

———. 1979. Citizenship, social studies, and the academician. *Social Education* 43(1):12–17.

Morrissett, I. and J. D. Haas. 1982. Rationales, goals, and objectives in social studies. In *The current state of the social studies: A report of Project SPAN*, ed. Project SPAN Staff and Consultants. Boulder, CO: Social Science Education Consortium.

Morrissett, I. and W. W. Stevens, Jr., eds. 1971. *Social Science in the schools: A search for rationale*. New York: Holt, Rinehart and Winston.

Mouffe, C. 1988. Radical democracy: Modern or postmodernism? In *Universal abandon: The politics of postmodernism*, ed. A. Ross, 31–45. Minneapolis: University of Minnesota Press.

Myrdal, G. 1944. *An American dilemma*. New York: Harper and Row.

National Commission on Excellence in Education. 1983. *A nation at risk: The imperative for educational reform*. Washington, D.C.: U.S. Government Printing Office.

National Commission on Social Studies in the Schools. 1989. *Charting a Course: Social studies for the twenty-first century*. Washington, D.C.: National Commission on Social Studies in the Schools.

Naylor, D. T. 1974. An in-depth study of the perceptions of public school educators and other significant school related groups concerning aspects of nationalistic instruction. Ph.D. diss. Rutgers University, New Brunswick, NJ.

Nelson, J. L. 1974. *Introduction to value inquiry: A student process book*. Rochelle Park, NJ: Hayden Press.

———. 1977. Perceptions of censorship and controversy: Censorship policy in a school district. Paper presented at the annual meeting of the American Educational Studies Association. Colorado Springs, November.

———. 1980a. Social criticism and the basis for education. Paper presented at the annual meeting of the American Educational Studies Association. Colorado Springs, November.

———. 1980b. The uncomfortable relationship between moral education and citizenship instruction. In *Moral development and politics*, eds. R. Wilson and G. Schochet. New York: Praeger Publishers.

———. 1982. Ideological dimensions of political restraint and censorship. Paper presented at the annual meeting of the College and University Faculty Assembly of the National Council for the Social Studies. Boston, November.

Nelson, J. L., K. Carlson, and T. Linton. 1972. *Radical ideas and the schools.* Englewood Cliffs, NJ: Prentice-Hall.

Nelson, J. L. and J. U. Michaelis. 1980. *Secondary social studies.* Englewood Cliffs, NJ: Prentice-Hall.

Newmann, F. M. 1967. Questioning the place of the social science disciplines in education. *Social Education* 31(7):593–596.

———. 1970. Consent of the governed and citizenship education in modern America. In *Social studies in the secondary schools: A book of readings*, eds. W. F. Gardner and F. A. Johnson, 25–35. Boston: Allyn and Bacon Inc.

———. 1975. *Education for citizen action: Challenge for secondary curriculum.* Berkeley, CA: McCutchen.

———. 1981a. Collective identity: A critical problem for social education and adolescent psychology. Paper presented at the Conference on Moral Motivation and Social Commitment, Association for Moral Education. New York, November.

———. 1981b. Teacher's prospectives on ideological issues: Research agenda for social studies in the 1980's. Paper presented at the annual meeting of the National Council for the Social Studies. Detroit, MI, November.

———. 1984. Social studies in the U.S. schools: Mainstream practice and radical potential. Paper presented at the annual meeting of the Social Science Education Consortium. Irsee, Federal Republic of Germany, June.

Newmann, F. M. and D. W. Oliver. 1970. *Clarifying public controversy: An approach to teaching social studies.* Boston: Little, Brown and Company.

Nicholson, C. 1989. Postmodernism, feminism, and education: The need for solidarity. *Educational Theory* 39(3):197–205.

Nicholson, L. J., ed. 1990. *Feminism/Postmodernism.* New York: Routledge, Chapman and Hall.

Nielsen, K. 1977. Religiosity and powerlessness. *The Humanist* 37(3):46–48.

Noddings, N. 1984. *Caring: A feminist approach to ethics and moral education.* Berkeley: University of California Press.

Norris, C. 1985. *Contest of faculties: Philosophy and theory after deconstruction.* New York: Methuen.

————. 1987. *Derrida.* Cambridge, MA: Harvard University Press.

Oliner, P. 1983. Putting 'community' into citizenship education: The need for prosociality. *Theory and Research in Social Education* 11(2):65–81.

Oliver, D. W. and J. P. Shaver. 1966. *Teaching public issues in the high school.* Boston: Houghton Mifflin.

Ophuls, W. 1980. Citizenship and ecological education. *Teachers College Record* 82(2):217–242.

Pagano, J. A. 1987. The schools we deserve. *Curriculum Inquiry* 17(1):107–122.

————. 1988. The claim of philia. In *Contemporary curriculum discourses,* ed. W. F. Pinar, 514–530. Scottsdale, AZ: Gorsuch Scarisbrick Publishers.

————. 1990. *Exiles and communities: Teaching in the patriarchal wilderness.* Albany, NY: State University of New York Press.

Paglia, C. 1991. Ninnies, pedants, tyrants, and other academics. Section 7. *New York Times Book Review,* 5 May, 1, 29, 33.

Palonsky, S. and J. L. Nelson. 1980. Political restraint in the socialization of student teacher. *Theory and Research in Social Education* 7(4):19–34.

Parmentier, R. J. 1985. Signs' place in "media res": Peirce's concept of semiotic mediation. In *Semiotic mediation: Sociocultural and psychological perspectives,* eds. E. Mertz and R. J. Parmentier, 23–48. New York: Academic Press Inc.

Pinar, W. F., ed. 1988a. *Contemporary curriculum discourses*. Scottsdale, AZ: Gorsuch Scarisbrick Publishers.

————. 1988b. Introduction. In *Contemporary curriculum discourses*, ed. W. F. Pinar, 1–13. Scottsdale, AZ: Gorsuch Scarisbrick Publishers.

————. 1988c. Time, place, and voice: Curriculum theory and the historical movement. In *Contemporary curriculum discourses*, ed. W. F. Pinar, 264–277. Scottsdale, AZ: Gorsuch Scarisbrick Publishers.

————. 1989. A reconceptualization of teacher education. *Journal of Teacher Education* 40(1):9–12.

Pinar, W. F., W. M. Reynolds, and W. Hsu. forthcoming. *Understanding curriculum: A comprehensive introduction to the study of curriculum*. New York: Longman.

Platt, J. R. 1966. *The steps to man*. New York: John Wiley.

Popper, K. R. 1968. *Conjectures and refutations*. New York: Harper Torchbooks.

————. 1976. The logic of the social sciences. In *The positivist dispute in German sociology*, ed. T. W. Adorno, 87–104. London: Heinemann Educational Books Ltd.

Poster, M., ed. 1988. *Baudrillard: Selected writings*. Trans. J. Mourrain. Stanford, CA: Stanford University Press.

————. 1989. *Critical theory and poststructuralism: In search of a context*. Ithaca, NY: Cornell University Press.

Poulantzas, N. 1975. *Classes in contemporary society*. London: New Left Books.

Presseisen, B. A. 1985. *Unlearned lessons: Current and past reforms for school improvement*. Philadelphia: The Falmer Press.

Putnam, H. 1983. *Realism and reason*. Cambridge, England: Cambridge University Press.

Rabinow, P., ed. 1984. *The Foucault reader*. New York: Pantheon.

Rabinow, P. and W. M. Sullivan, eds. 1987. *Interpretive social science: A second look*. Berkeley: University of California Press.

Rajchman, J. 1983–84. Foucault's dilemma. *Social Text* 8(Winter/Spring):24.

————. 1986. Ethics after Foucault. *Social Text* 13/14(Winter/Spring):165–183.

————. 1988. Habermas's complaint. *New German Critique* 45:163–191.

Random House Dictionary of the English Language. 1987. 2nd unabridged edition. New York: Random House.

Raths, L. E., M. Harmin, and S. B. Simon. 1978. *Values and teaching: Working with values in the classroom.* 2nd edition. Columbus, OH: Charles E. Merrill.

Raup, R. B. 1936. Shall we use the class dynamic? *The Social Frontier* 2(4):106–109.

Ravitch, D. and C. E. Finn. 1987. *What do our 17-year-olds know?* New York: Harper and Row.

Raywid, M. A., C. A. Tesconi, Jr., and D. R. Warren. 1984. *Pride and promise: Schools of excellence for all the people.* Washington, D.C.: American Educational Studies Association.

Reischauer, E. O. 1973. *Toward the 21st Century: Education for a changing world.* New York: Vintage Books.

Reitz, C. and D. T. Martin. 1984. Review of *Theory and resistance in education: A pedagogy for the opposition* by H. A. Giroux. *Educational Studies* 15(2):163–174.

Rippa, S. A. 1971. Education in a free society. New York: David McKay.

Robbins, B. 1991 a. Othering the academy: Professionalism and multi-culturalism. *Social Research* 58(2):355–372.

———. 1991 b. Tenured radicals,the new McCarthyism, and 'PC'. *New Left Review* 188(3):151–156.

Rochberg-Halton, E. 1986. *Meaning and modernity: Social theory in the pragmatic attitude.* Chicago: University of Chicago Press.

Roman, L., L. K. Christian-Smith, and E. Ellsworth, eds. 1988. *Becoming feminine: The politics of popular culture.* New York: Falmer Press.

Rorty, R. 1979. *Philosophy and the mirror of nature.* Princeton, NJ: Princeton University Press.

———. 1980. Pragmatism, relativism, and irrationalism. *Proceedings and Addresses of the American Philosophical Association* 53(6):719–738.

———. 1982. *Consequences of pragmatism.* Minneapolis: University of Minnesota Press.

———. 1985. Solidarity or objectivity? In *Post-analytic philosophy*, eds. J. Rajchman and C. West, 3–19. New York: Columbia University Press.

————. 1986. Introduction. In *John Dewey: Later Works, 1925–1953*, xi. Carbondale, IL: Southern Illinois University Press.

————. 1987. Posties. *London Review of Books* 9(15, 3 September):11–12.

————. 1989. *Contingency, irony, and solidarity.* New York: Cambridge University Press.

Rugg, H. 1921. How shall we reconstruct the social studies? *The Historical Outlook* 3(5):184–189.

————. 1923a. Do social studies prepare pupils adequately for life activities? In *The social studies in the elementary and secondary school.* Twenty-second yearbook of the National Society for the Study of Education, Part II, 1–27. Bloomington, IL: Public School Publishing Company.

————. Chairman. 1923b. *The social studies in the elementary and secondary school.* Twenty-second yearbook of the National Society for the Study of Education, Part II. Bloomington, IL: Public School Publishing Company.

————. Chairman. 1926. Curriculum-making: Past and present. The foundations and technique of curriculum-construction, Part I. Twenty-sixth yearbook of the National Society for the Study of Education. Bloomington, IL: Public School Publishing Company.

————. 1931. *An introduction to problems of American culture.* Boston: Ginn.

————. 1932–1933. Social reconstruction through education. *Progressive Education* 9 & 10(8 & 1, December/January):11–18.

————. 1933. *The great technology: Social chaos and the public mind.* New York: John Day.

————. 1935. The American scholar faces a social crisis. *The Social Frontier* 1(6):10–13.

————. 1936a. *American life and school curriculum.* Boston: Ginn.

————. 1936b. The American mind and the "class" problem. *The Social Frontier* 2(5):138–142.

————. 1940. *Citizenship and civic affairs.* Boston: Ginn.

————. 1941. *That men may understand: An American in the long armistice.* New York: Doubleday, Doran.

Ryan, K. 1986. The new moral education. *Phi Delta Kappan* 68(4):228–233.

Sarup, M. 1984. *Marxism/Structionalism/Education.* London: Falmer Press.

———. 1989. *An introductory guide to: Post-structuralism and postmodernism.* Athens, GA: University of Georgia Press.

Schell, J. 1982. *The fate of the earth.* New York: Borzoi Books, Knopf.

Schlesinger, A. M., Jr. 1991. *The disuniting of America: Reflections on a multicultural society.* Knoxville, TN: Whittle Direct Books.

Scholes, R. 1985. *Textual power.* New Haven, CT: Yale University Press.

———. 1988. Deconstruction and communication. *Critical Inquiry* 14(2):278–295.

———. 1989. *The protocols of reading.* New Haven: Yale University Press.

Schwab, J. J. 1968. Structure of the disciplines: Meanings and significances. In *Democracy, pluralism and the social studies,* eds. J. P. Shaver and H. Berlak, 289–305. Boston: Houghton Mifflin.

Schwartz, J. 1979. The work of Harold Rugg and the question of objectivity. *Journal of Curriculum Theorizing* 1(2):100–228.

Scollon, R., and S. B. K. Scollon. 1981. *Narrative, literacy and face in interethnic communication.* Norwood, NJ: Ablex.

Scribner, S., and M. Cole. 1981. *The psychology of literacy.* Cambridge, MA: Harvard University Press.

Searle, J. 1990. The battle over the university. *The New York Review of Books* 37(19):34–42.

Sears, J. T. 1988. The glass bead game of curriculum theorizing: Reconceptualism and the new orthodoxy. Paper presented at the Annual Conference on Curriculum Theorizing and Practice, Bergamo Center. Dayton, OH, October.

Senesh, L. 1971. Orchestration of social sciences in the curriculum. In *Social science in the schools: A search for rationale,* eds. I. Morrissett and W. W. Stevens, Jr., 125–135. New York: Holt, Rinehart and Winston.

Shaver, J. P. 1967. Social studies: The need for redefinition. *Social Education* 31(7):588–592, 596.

———. ed. 1977. *Building rationales for citizenship education.* Arlington, VA: National Council for the Social Studies.

———. 1979. Political and economic socialization in elementary school social studies textbooks: A reaction. *Theory and Research in Social Studies* 7(1):43–48.

Shaver, J. P., and H, Berlak, eds. 1968. *Democracy, pluralism and the social studies.* Boston: Houghton Mifflin.

Shaver, J. P., O. L. Davis, Jr., and S. W. Helburn. 1979. *An interpretive report on the status of pre-collegiate social studies education based on three NSF-funded studies.* Washington, DC: National Science Foundation.

Shaver, J. P. and W. Strong. 1976. *Facing value decisions: Rationale-building for teachers.* 1st edition. Belmont, CA: Wadsworth.

———. 1982. *Facing value decisions: Rationale-building for teachers.* 2nd edition. New York: Teachers College Press.

Shaw, P. 1987. The dark ages of humanities. *The Intercollegiate Review* 23(1):5-14.

Shermis, S. S. 1982. A response to our critics: Reflective inquiry is not the same as social science. *Theory and Research in Social Education* 10(2):45-50.

Shermis, S. S. and J. L. Barth. 1980. The functions of problems and problem-solving in the history of the social studies movement. Paper presented at the annual meeting of the National Council for the Social Studies. New Orleans, November.

———. 1982. Teaching for passive citizenship: A critique of philosophical assumptions. *Theory and Research in Social Education* 10(4):17-37.

———. 1983. Problem definition, problem-solving and social problems: Reconceptualizing the thought process in education. *Journal of Thought* 18:73-93.

Shor, I. 1979. *Critical teaching and everyday life.* Boston: South End Press.

———. 1986. *Culture wars.* Boston: Routledge and Kegan Paul.

Shrewsbury, C. M. 1987a. Feminist pedagogy: A bibliography. *Women's Studies Quarterly* 15(3 & 4):116-124.

———. 1987b. What is feminist pedagogy? *Women's Studies Quarterly* 15(3 & 4):6-14.

Silberman, C. E. 1970. *Crisis in the classroom: The remaking of American education.* New York: Random House.

Simon, R. I. 1987. Empowerment as a pedagogy of possibility. *Language Arts* 64(4):370-382.

Sirotnik, K. A. 1989. What goes on in classrooms? Is this the way we want it? In *The Curriculum: Problems, politics and possibilities,* eds. L. E. Beyer and M. W. Apple, 56-74. Albany, NY: State University of New York Press.

Sizer, T. 1984. *Horace's compromise: The dilemma of the American high school.* Boston: Houghton Mifflin.

Small, A. W. 1896. Demands of sociology upon pedagogy. Addresses and Proceedings of the National Educational Association. Illinois: The University of Chicago Press.

Smith, A. 1981. Education and the future. An interview with Alvin Toffler. *Social Education* 45(6):422–426.

Snow, C. P. 1959. *The two cultures and the scientific revolution.* New York: Cambridge University Press.

Stake, R. E. and J. A. Easley, Jr. 1978. *Case studies in science education.* Washington, D.C.: National Science Foundation.

Stanley, W. B. 1979. The philosophy of social reconstruction and contemporary curriculum rationales in social education. Ph.D. diss. Rutgers University, New Brunswick, NJ.

———. 1981a. Indoctrination and social education: A critical analysis. *Social Education* 45(3):200, 202–204.

———. 1981b. The radical reconstructionist rationale for social education. *Theory and Research in Social Education* 8(4):55–79.

———. 1981c. Toward a reconstruction of social education. *Theory and Research in Social Education* 9(1):67–89.

———. 1985a. Recent research in the foundations of social education: 1976–1983. In *Review of research in social studies education: 1976–1983,* ed. W. B. Stanley, 309–399. Washington, D.C.: National Council for the Social Studies.

———. 1985b. Reconstructionism for today's social education. *Social Education* 49(5):384–389.

———. 1987. Christopher Lasch as social educator. *Educational Theory* 37(3):229–250.

———. 1989. Beyond pragmatic inquiry: A critical analysis of Lawrence Metcalf's approach to social education. *The International Journal of Social Studies Education* 3(3):63–83.

Stanley, W. B. and J. L. Nelson. 1986. Social education for social transformation. *Social Education* 50(7):528–530, 532–534.

Stanley, W. B., and J. A. Whitson. 1990. Practical competence, human interest, and schooling. Paper presented at the annual meeting of the Conference on Curriculum Theory and Classroom Practice. Dayton, OH, October.

Stott, L. 1990. A response to Professors Lather, McLaren, Hammer, and Shapiro. *Educational Foundations* 4(3):84–85.

Strike, K. A. 1989. *Liberal justice and the Marxist critique of education*. New York: Routledge and Kegan Paul.

Sultan, M. A. 1989. A Habermasian evaluation of the Neo-Marxian contributions to curriculum theory. Paper presented at the annual meeting of the American Educational Research Association. San Francisco, CA, March.

Toffler, A. 1971. *Future shock*. New York: Bantam Books.

———. ed. 1974. *Learning for tomorrow, the role of the future in education*. New York: Vintage Books.

———. 1980. *The third wave*. New York: Random House.

Vonk, H. G. 1973. Education and the 27-year countdown. *Phi Delta Kappan* 54(8):514–517.

Weiler, K. 1988. *Women teaching for change: Gender, class, and power*. South Hadley, MA: Bergin and Garvey.

Wesley, E. and S. Wronski. 1958. *Teaching social studies in high schools*. Boston: D.C. Heath.

West, C. 1988. Postmodernism and black America. *Zeta Magazine* 1(6):27–29.

———. 1989. *The American evasion of philosophy: A genealogy of pragmatism*. Madison, WI: The University of Wisconsin Press.

Wexler, P. 1987. *Social analysis of education*. London: Routledge and Kegan Paul.

Wexler, P. and J. A. Whitson. 1982. Hegemony and education. *Psychology and Social Theory* 3:31–42.

White, C. S. 1982. A validation study of the Barth-Shermis social studies preference scale. *Theory and Research in Social Education* 10(2):1–20.

Whitson, J. A. 1988. The politics of "non-political" curriculum: Heteroglossia and the discourse of "choice" and "effectiveness". In *Contemporary curriculum discourses*, ed. W. F. Pinar, 279–330. Scottsdale, AZ: Gorsuch Scarisbrick.

———. 1991. *Constitution and curriculum: Semiotic analysis of cases and controversies in education, law, and social science*. London and Philadelphia: Falmer Press.

———. Forthcoming. Post-structuralist pedagogy as counter-hegemonic praxis (Can we find the baby in the bathwater?). *Education and society* 9(1).

Whitson, J. A. and W. B. Stanley. 1988. Practical competence: A rationale for social education. Paper presented at the annual meeting of the National Council for the Social Studies. Orlando, FL, November.

———. 1990. Developing practical competence in social studies education. Paper presented at the annual meeting of the National Council for the Social Studies. Orlando, FL, November.

Wiggins, S. 1971. Economics in the curriculum. In *Social science in the schools: A search for rationale*, eds. I. Morrisett and W. W. Stevens, Jr., 93–107. New York: Holt, Rinehart and Winston.

Wiley, K. B. 1977. The status of pre-college science, mathematics, and social science education, 1955–1975. Washington, DC: National Science Foundation.

Williams, R. 1977. *Marxism and literature*. London: Oxford University Press.

———. 1979. *Politics and letters: Interviews with New Left Review*. London: New Left Books.

Willis, P. 1977. *Learning to labour*. Westmead, England: Saxon House.

Winter, G, 1981. *Liberating creation: Foundation of religious social ethnics*. New York: Crossroad Press.

Wood, D. 1987. Beyond deconstruction? In *Contemporary French philosophy*, ed. A. P. Griffiths, 175–194. New York: Cambridge University Press.

Woodward, C. V. 1991. Freedom and the universities. *The New York Review of Books*, 38(13):32–37.

Yeatman, A. 1990. A feminist theory of social differentiation. In *Feminism/Postmodernism*, ed. L. J. Nicholson, 281–289. New York: Routledge, Chapman and Hall.

Young, I. M. 1990. The ideal of community and the politics of difference. In *Feminism/Postmodernism*, ed. L. J. Nicholson, 300–323. New York: Routledge, Chapman and Hall.

Young, R. V. 1987. Constitutional interpretation and literary theory. *The Intercollegiate Review* 23(1):49–60.

Yudice, G. 1989. Marginality and the ethics of survival. In *Universal Abandon?*, ed. A. Ross, 214–236. Minneapolis: University of Minneapolis Press.

NAME INDEX

SUBJECT INDEX